Keys to BIBLE PROPHECY

JAMES C. MORRIS

DISPENSATIONAL PUBLISHING HOUSE, INC.

Copyright © 2019 James C. Morris All rights reserved.

No part of this publication may be reproduced, stored in a retrieval system, or transmitted in any way by any means, electronic, mechanical, photocopy, recording, or otherwise, without the prior permission of the copyright owner, except as provided by USA copyright law.

"Scripture taken from the New King James Version.
Copyright © 1979, 1980, 1982 by Thomas Nelson, Inc.
Used by permission. All rights reserved."

Printed in the United States of America

First Edition, First Printing, 2019

ISBN: 978-1-945774-33-1

Dispensational Publishing House, Inc.
PO Box 3181 Taos, NM 87571

www.dispensationalpublishing.com

DISPENSATIONAL
QuickPRINT

This is a DPH Quick Print book. Our QuickPrint process allows us to get books to the market at a much quicker pace and lower cost than the full book publishing process. If you discover errors in this book, please contact the publisher so that these errors may be fully removed in future editions.

Ordering Information:
Quantity sales. Special discounts are available on quantity purchases by churches, associations, and others. For details, contact the publisher at the address above.

Orders by U.S. trade bookstores and wholesalers. Please contact the publisher:
Tel: (844) 321-4202

1 2 3 4 5 6 7 8 9 10

This book is dedicated to the Lord Jesus Christ, the only Son of the only God, without whose sacrifice at Calvary this book would be both pointless and impossible. It is also dedicated, in a lessor sense, to those that backed the writer with prayer during the years of research and writing that went into it, and to his beloved wife Fina, who lovingly cared for him during this time.

Table of Contents

Preface 1

Key Time Periods in Bible Prophecy 7
Daniel's seventy weeks 7
The seventieth week 10
The first half of the week 12
The last half of the week 16
Gog's attack 22
The millennium 23

Key Individuals in Bible Prophecy 25
The First Key Individual 25
The Second Key Individual 42
The Third Key Individual 50
The Fourth Key Individual 68
The Fifth Key Individual 68

Key Events in Bible Prophecy 81
Early Events – Setting the Stage 81
The First Half of the Week 96
The Middle of the Week 104
The Last Half of the Week 124
Rescue – The LORD's Campaigns 132
Restoration – The Ancient Promises Fulfilled 148
The Millennium 160
After the Millennium 170

Appendix 179
Key Concepts for Interpreting Bible Prophecy 179
Key Principles of Prophetic Interpretation 181
Common Errors in Prophetic Interpretation 182

Maps 225
The Lands of Gomer and the Roman Empire 228
The Land of Magog and Gog's Northern Allies 229
The Lands of the Kings of the North and South With
the Assyrian Empire 230
The Path of the Assyrian 231
Future Israel and the Lord's Campaigns 232

Indexes 235
Scriptures Cited 235
Authorities Cited 247
Ancient Words Discussed 248
Ancient Individuals Mentioned 249
Peoples and Nations Mentioned 251
Places Mentioned 254
Key Time Periods 256
Key Individuals 257
Key Events 258
Prophetic Symbols Discussed 261
Inspired Explanations of Symbols 261

List of Illustrations

Prophetic Time Chart *6*

The Temple Treasure Panel on the Arch of Titus *27*

The Roma Sestertius of Vespasian *32*

*Third Asian Map From Ziletti's 1574 Reproduction
of Ptolemy's Second Century Atlas Titled "Geographia"* *73*

The Oriental Institute Prism *115*

PREFACE

It seems of late there are hundreds of new books on Bible prophecy. These books present such a wide variety of interpretations that many conclude it is impossible to ever really understand the subject. Why does this babble of competing voices exist? It is the natural result of a basic error. Many Bible students are simply not aware of many prophecies that are expressly stated in plain words. Not being aware these prophecies exist, they have never felt a need to study them. They are attempting to interpret the deep, mysterious parts of Biblical prophecy, but do not know about many simple parts. Since **"no prophecy of Scripture is of any private interpretation,"** (2 Peter 1:19) this has left them without important scriptural reference points for evaluating their interpretations. So they are unable to distinguish between reasonable and unreasonable conclusions.

This book is an attempt to address this problem. It reviews many prophecies that are stated so clearly they need no interpretation. The deep, mysterious parts are simply left out. The point of this book is to minimize interpretation by concentrating on expressly stated prophecies. But it is not possible to completely eliminate interpretation from such a study. Even simple statements sometimes require interpretation. It has therefore been used where the true meaning seems both obvious and important. It has also been used where it seemed unusually helpful. But such interpretation has been reduced as far as seemed practical.

The first section of this book is devoted to specific time periods in which events are prophesied to take place. Each of these periods is expressly defined, both as to its starting point and length. The meaning of many prophecies becomes clear when we understand these time periods.

It is impossible to understand such a complex account without first understanding the individuals involved. The second section is therefore devoted to various individuals specifically discussed in Bible prophecy.

Finally, the third section traces through the prophetic scriptures, examining many details that are expressly stated in plain words. In some cases scripture clearly gives the order in which these events will take place. In other cases the order is obvious. In many cases the approximate time is defined by the time periods discussed in the first section. In a few cases I have simply inserted events in places that seemed reasonable. But although some of these events may not be presented in the correct order, every one of them will most certainly happen exactly as prophesied.

Once the simple prophecies discussed in this book have been thoroughly understood, a Bible student will have a foundation for interpreting more difficult prophecies. Such interpretation is outside of the subject matter of this book. But a few helpful sections have been included in an appendix. The first of these presents key concepts for interpreting Bible prophecy. The second is a list of key principles of prophetic interpretation. The last is a review of common errors in prophetic interpretation, with an explanation of why each of these is incorrect.

Most important of all, we must remember that the Bible is the word of God. **"All Scripture *is* given by inspiration of God, and *is* profitable for**

doctrine, for reproof, for correction, for instruction in righteousness." (2 Timothy 3:16) Because it comes from God, it must be treated with reverence. We are not free to interpret the Bible as we please. Instead, we are responsible to learn what it teaches. The fact that it comes from God means that it is completely accurate in all of its details. It is important to pay careful attention to the fine details in each prophecy. For it is in these details that we learn where and how they apply. This book is largely a study of these details, and of what they teach us about the various prophecies involved.

Some may imagine that it is a new idea to take notice of numerous prophetic details pointed out in this book. But in actual fact, I am far from the first to do so. Instead, at least the essence of most of these details was pointed out by nineteenth century dispensational commentators,[1] among whom the most notable were J. N. Darby and his associate William Kelly, whom I consider "the Dean of prophetic expositors." But in the twentieth century many of these details began to be neglected.

Again, some will doubtless complain that I have skipped around all over the Bible to put this outline together. But God says that **"precept *must be* upon precept, precept upon precept, Line upon line, line upon line, Here a little, there a little."** (Isaiah 28:10) The prophetic scriptures were not simply written out in a continuous story. Coming events were scattered about in an apparently haphazard fashion. This was done for a reason. Jesus told His own that **"it has been given to you to know the mysteries of the kingdom of heaven, but to them it has not been given."** (Matthew 13:11) Those who really want to know God's prophetic message can find it. But this is possible only through diligent study.

Before we begin, some may find it interesting to note how this book came to be. In or about 1966, I read four commentaries on the book of Ezekiel. When the writers of these four books came to chapters 38 and 39,

---

[1] The works of many of these nineteenth century writers are available online at http://www.stempublishing.com.

each of them stated the modern identities of all the nations listed in that prophecy as joining together to attack Israel in the last days.

And all four lists were different!

I snorted, and said to myself, "Enough of this nonsense. I'm going to find out for myself who they are." At first, I was muttering to himself, "where am I ever going to find this information?" But within a few months, this had changed to "where am I ever going to find time to read all these books?" For I had discovered that the Kent State University Library, in Kent, Ohio, which was only about sixty miles from where I lived at that time, was the fifth largest library in the world. And it had literally hundreds of volumes actually written in ancient times. Each of these very many volumes had the original language and an English translation on facing pages. So it was possible to actually study the works of ancient writers from many nations, without having to learn all the languages involved. Although I was not a student at that university, the library kindly allowed me to purchase a "courtesy card" which granted me full usage of this marvelous collection. Most of the ancient geographical and historical sources cited in this book were found in that library, although some of them came from other libraries.

This led to a study that stretched over approximately 35 years, during which time, in addition to my studies of the scriptures themselves, I studied the most ancient available records of many nations, from Israel, Egypt, Babylonia, Persia, Assyria, Armenia, Greece, and Rome, to as far afield as Scandinavia and even China, until I had hard proof from multiple ancient sources of the modern identities of most of the nations mentioned in Bible prophecy. Unfortunately, The Russian language was never reduced to writing until the ninth century. So the oldest available Russian records are medieval, rather than ancient. But I also studied these at length, along with medieval Armenian records.

Around the turn of the century I began to teach Bible prophecy online, but as I did so, I was met with the inappropriate claim that dispensationalism could not even possibly be correct, because it was never taught before around 1830 or so.

From my previous studies, I already knew that this was incorrect. But this led me to embark again upon the sea of ancient literature for well over five more years, this time studying what many ancient Christian writers had actually taught about Bible prophecy. My main resource for this study was the widely circulated nineteenth century collection commonly called "The Early Church Fathers." This is a 38 volume set, divided into three series, titled "Ante-Nicene Fathers," (10 volumes) "Nicene & Post-Nicene Fathers, first series" (14 volumes) and "Nicene & Post-Nicene Fathers, second series." (also 14 volumes) This collection has been reproduced by several modern publishers, and is easily available online at various web addresses. Most of the ancient Christian writings cited in this book are from that set. But some are from other sources.

So this book is the product of well over 40 years of research, plus three years of map drawing, to say nothing of the many years spent writing, editing and, revising the text. It is now sent forth with the prayer that the saints of God will be benefitted in proportion to the effort invested in its production.

James C. Morris

Prophetic Time Chart

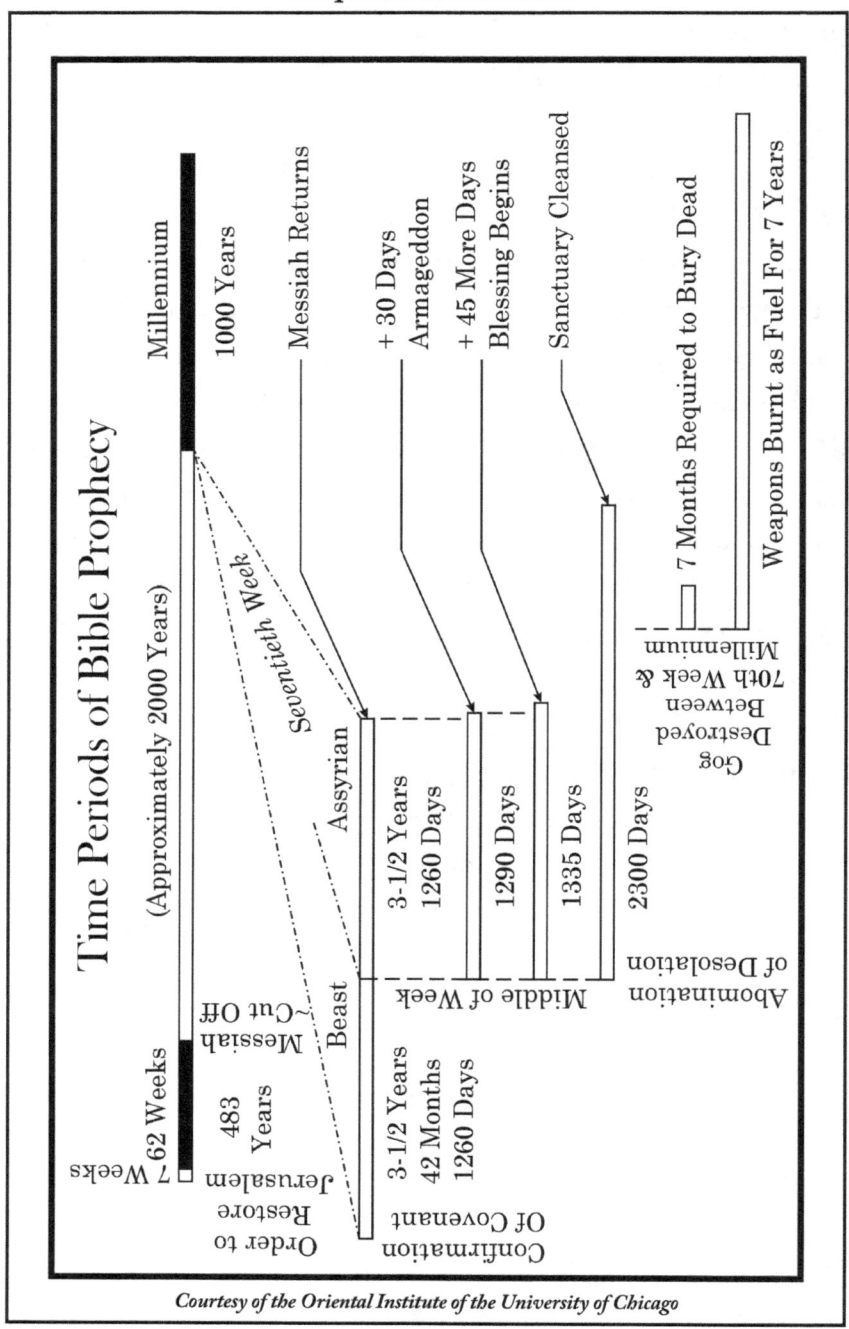

Courtesy of the Oriental Institute of the University of Chicago

KEY TIME PERIODS IN BIBLE PROPHECY

Some Bible prophecies are stated in broad generalizations, but many coming events are clearly stated in high detail. In like manner, the time periods in which these events will take place are often precisely stated. End time prophecy cannot be properly understood without a knowledge of these expressly stated time periods.

Daniel's seventy weeks

This understanding begins with the seventy weeks revealed to Daniel. These include the basic reference points from which most of the other time periods are measured. Daniel was told:

> **"Seventy weeks are determined For your people and for your holy city, To finish the transgression, To make an end of sins, To make reconciliation for iniquity, To bring in everlasting righteousness, To seal up vision and prophecy, And to anoint**

the Most Holy. Know therefore and understand, That from the going forth of the command To restore and build Jerusalem Until Messiah the Prince, There shall be seven weeks and sixty-two weeks; The street shall be built again, and the wall, Even in troublesome times. And after the sixty-two weeks Messiah shall be cut off, but not for Himself;

And the people of the prince who is to come Shall destroy the city and the sanctuary. The end of it *shall be* with a flood, And till the end of the war desolations are determined. Then he shall confirm a covenant with many for one week; But in the middle of the week He shall bring an end to sacrifice and offering. And on the wing of abominations shall be one who makes desolate, Even until the consummation, which is determined, Is poured out on the desolate." (Daniel 9:24-27)

To understand this prophecy, we must first notice to whom it refers. **"Seventy weeks are determined For your people and for your holy city."** These seventy weeks are determined for Daniel's people and for Daniel's holy city. Daniel was a Jew, so his people are the Jews. As a Jew, Daniel's holy city was Jerusalem. So from this first sentence we realize these seventy weeks are for the Jews and for Jerusalem. This is about the Jewish people and their holy city Jerusalem. Indeed, this is the case with most of Bible prophecy. Other nations are usually mentioned only in their relationship to Judah and Israel.

These seventy weeks are determined **"To finish the transgression, To make an end of sins, To make reconciliation for iniquity, To bring in everlasting righteousness, To seal up vision and prophecy, And to anoint the Most Holy."** While **"reconciliation for iniquity"** was made on the cross nearly two thousand years ago, many of the events in this list have still not taken place. We thus understand that whatever these seventy weeks represent, they span thousands of years. (See the chart on page 6.)

Daniel was told **"*That* from the going forth of the command To restore and build Jerusalem Until Messiah the Prince, *There shall be* seven weeks and** sixty-two weeks." There were to be sixty-nine weeks divided into two smaller periods, the first one **"seven weeks"** long and the second lasting **"sixty-two weeks."** This sixty-nine week period would last **"from the going forth of the command To restore and build Jerusalem Until Messiah the Prince."**

The command **"To restore and build Jerusalem"** went forth in Nehemiah 2:5-6. Some say there is proof that this went forth four hundred and eighty-three ancient Jewish years *to the day* before our Lord's triumphal entry into Jerusalem. The proof they offer indeed shows this is correct, as closely as it is possible to determine. But saying that it was exactly that long *to the day* requires making assumptions that, while very likely correct, cannot be proved.

What is the significance of four hundred and eighty-three years? This is seven times sixty-nine. Sixty-nine weeks of years after **"the going forth of the command To restore and build Jerusalem"** our Lord Jesus presented Himself to Jerusalem as its Messiah. (See the chart on page 6.) Some, of course, will have a problem with taking a week to mean seven years. They will condemn this as gross and unwarranted interpretation of the kind we are supposedly not using. But this is not the case. Each occurrence of the English word *week* in this prophecy is a translation of the Hebrew word *shabuwa*.[2] (word number 7620 in Strong's Hebrew Dictionary) This Hebrew word literally meant *sevened*. It was used for a period of seven days, and thus had the same meaning as our English word *week*, but it also meant seven years.

This can be seen in the sabbath year of rest the LORD decreed for the land. He told Moses **"When you come into the land which I give you, then the land shall keep a sabbath to the LORD. Six years you shall sow your field, and six years you shall prune your vineyard, and gather its fruit; but in the seventh year there shall be a sabbath of solemn rest for the land, a sabbath to the LORD. You shall neither sow your field nor prune your vineyard."** (Leviticus 25:2-4) Compare this with the LORD'S command to **"Remember the Sabbath day, to keep it holy. Six days you shall labor and do**

---

2 For ease of reference, this book uses only Strong's transliterations.

all your work, but the seventh day *is* the Sabbath of the LORD your God. *In it* you shall do no work: you, nor your son, nor your daughter, nor your male servant, nor your female servant, nor your cattle, nor your stranger who *is* within your gates. For *in* six days the LORD made the heavens and the earth, the sea, and all that *is* in them, and rested the seventh day. Therefore the LORD blessed the Sabbath day and hallowed it." (Exodus 20:8-11) The same word, sabbath, was used to describe both the seventh day and the seventh year.

This shows that in the Old Testament the concept of a *week* applied equally to periods of seven days and seven years. This is not just an interpretation, but a fully legitimate Hebrew meaning of the word.

The seventieth week (See the chart on page 6)

We remember that **"seventy weeks are determined."** (Daniel 9:24) It is important to notice the order in which this prophecy said the events would take place. Of the seventy weeks, there would first be **"seven weeks and sixty-two weeks."** (Daniel 9:25) Then two events were to take place **"after the sixty-two weeks."** These were **"Messiah shall be cut off, but not for Himself; And the people of the prince who is to come Shall destroy the city and the sanctuary."** (Daniel 9:26) The first of these plainly refers to our Lord's death on the cross. The second was done by the ancient Romans under the leadership of Titus. (see page 26) Since Daniel was told this would be done by **"the people of the prince who is to come,"** this **"prince who is to come"** has to be a Roman. He cannot come from any other nation, for then he would not be a **"prince"** of **"the people"** who destroyed **"the city and the sanctuary."**

After the destruction of **"the city and the sanctuary,"** (Daniel 9:26) we read; **"Then he shall confirm a covenant with many for one week."** (Daniel 9:27) We need to notice that in this prophecy, the confirmation of the covenant comes after **"the city and the sanctuary"** are destroyed. Failure to notice this detail has caused many errors in prophetic interpretation. No Roman ruler has made such a covenant with Jewish people since Jerusalem was destroyed, so we know this speaks of the future. (Remember that we saw on page 8 that this prophecy is about the Jewish people.)

The covenant confirmed by the **"prince who is to come"** was to be **"for one week."** (verse 27) This has to be the seventieth week of the prophecy, for no other single week is mentioned. This seventieth week is the great subject of most of Bible prophecy. Many have advanced various theories as to when it will begin, but we find it defined here. It begins when this covenant is confirmed.

There will be a major disturbance in the middle of this week. (See the chart on page 6.) We read that **"in the middle of the week He[3] shall bring an end to sacrifice and offering."** This event divides the week into two half weeks. We see each of these half weeks in numerous other prophecies. Depending on the circumstances, they are referred to as **"a time, times, and half a time"** (three and a half years), **"forty-two months"** (again three and a half years - this term is used only of the first half week), and **"one thousand two hundred and sixty days"** (exactly three and a half ancient ancient Jewish years, which were 360 days long). (See the chart on page 6.)

Here we need to notice the extreme precision of Biblical terms. We now know that a year is actually 365-1/4 days, or 5-1/4 days longer than the ancient Jewish year of 360 days. Our God, of course, knew this when He gave the scriptures. How could the Holy Spirit state these periods in varying terms the people would understand, and still use terms that are precisely accurate? He did it by avoiding the word *year*, calling it a *time* instead of a *year*.

The original texts where the word **"time"** was used to mean a year were written in three different languages, so three different ancient words were

---

3 In the New King James translation, which we are using, scriptures that were originally given in the form of poetry are arranged in poetical format, with the first word of each line capitalized. This was done in many of the Old Testament prophecies we will examine. The word **"He"** in this passage is capitalized because it is the first word in a line of poetry, not to imply that it refers to God. **"He"** has to mean the Roman prince because that is the last person mentioned.

used for **"time."** The first place is **in Daniel 7:25, where we read "a time and times and half a time"** This was written in Chaldean, the language of ancient Babylon, where Daniel lived. The Chaldean word translated time was *'iddan*. (word number 5732 in Strong's Hebrew Dictionary) This word was also used for the seven **"times"** during which Nebuchadnezzar was punished in Daniel 4:16, 23, 25, and 32. The second ancient word used is found in the expression **"a time, times, and half a time"** in Daniel 12:7. This part of Daniel was written in Hebrew, so the Hebrew word *mow'ed* was used. (word number 4150 in Strong's Hebrew Dictionary) And the third ancient word was used in Revelation 12:14, where we again read **"a time, times and half a time."** The Revelation was written in Greek, so the Greek word *kairos* was used. (word number 2540 in Strong's Greek Dictionary)

Each of these three ancient words meant a precisely determined time. They were sometimes used of an event that took place at a particular time, like a festival. They were also used of a precisely determined length of time. In this sense, they were commonly used to represent a year. But none of these words actually meant a *year*. The Holy Spirit used these words, each of which would be understood to mean a year, because He was not speaking of actual years, but of the years of the ancient Jews.

The first half of the week

In Daniel seven, the prophet saw a vision of four great beasts which **"came up from the sea, each different from the other."** (verse 3) His interpreter told him that **"Those great beasts, which are four, *are* four kings which arise out of the earth."** (Daniel 7:17) The last of these beasts drew particular attention:

> **"After this I saw in the night visions, and behold, a fourth beast, dreadful and terrible, exceedingly strong. It had huge**

iron teeth; it was devouring, breaking in pieces, and trampling the residue with its feet. It *was* different from all the beasts that *were* before it, and it had ten horns. I was considering the horns, and there was another horn, a little one, coming up among them, before whom three of the first horns were plucked out by the roots. And there, in this horn, *were* eyes like the eyes of a man, and a mouth speaking pompous words." (Daniel 7:7-8)

In answer to his inquiry, Daniel was told that:

> "The fourth beast shall be A fourth kingdom on earth, Which shall be different from all *other* kingdoms, And shall devour the whole earth, Trample it and break it in pieces. The ten horns *are* ten kings *Who* shall arise from this kingdom. And another shall rise after them; He shall be different from the first *ones*, And shall subdue three kings.[4] He shall speak *pompous* words against the Most High, Shall persecute the saints of the Most High, And shall intend to change times and law. Then *the saints* shall be given into his hand For a time and times and half a time." (Daniel 7:23-25)

Here we have the first mention of a half week. **"*The saints* shall be given into his hand For a time and times and half a time."** Page 28 explains in detail how we know this king is the future Roman ruler we have already noticed. But why are they given into his hand **"for a time and times and half a time"**?

We also see this beast in Revelation 13. **"Then I stood on the sand of the sea. And I saw a beast rising up out of the sea, having seven heads and ten horns, and on his horns ten crowns, and on his heads a blasphemous name."** (verse 1) As in Daniel 7, this beast **"opened his mouth in blasphemy**

---

4 Notice that this fourth beast is interpreted as a king in verse 17 and as a kingdom in verses 23 and 24. This application of the word *king* to a *kingdom* is common in Bible prophecy. Thus the various parts of the image in Daniel 2 are interpreted as kingdoms in verse 39 and as kings in verse 44. Again, in Daniel 11:5-34 the terms **"king of the South"** and **"king of the North"** are applied over a number of generations spanning about 130 years.

against God, to blaspheme His name, His tabernacle, and those who dwell in heaven."** (verse 6) And **"It was granted to him to make war with the saints and to overcome them."** (verse 7) And **"he was given authority to continue for forty-two months."** (verse 5) This **"forty-two months"** is three and a half years, the same period as the **"time and times and half a time"** during which **"*The saints* shall be given into"** his hand in Daniel 7:24-25.

But after this **"forty-two months,"** or **"a time and times and half a time"** his control breaks down. He will not be allowed to persecute the saints any longer than this. The shortness of this period is figuratively represented in the words, **"The ten horns which you saw are ten kings who have received no kingdom as yet, but they receive authority for one hour as kings with the beast."** (Revelation 17:12)

In the last part of Revelation 13 a second beast arises:

> **"And he exercises all the authority of the first beast in his presence, and causes the earth and those who dwell in it to worship the first beast, whose deadly wound was healed. He performs great signs, so that he even makes fire come down from heaven on the earth in the sight of men. And he deceives those who dwell on the earth by those signs which he was granted to do in the sight of the beast, telling those who dwell on the earth to make an image to the beast who was wounded by the sword and lived. He was granted *power* to give breath to the image of the beast, that the image of the beast should both speak and cause as many as would not worship the image of the beast to be killed."** (Revelation 13:12-15)

The result of this is that **"All who dwell on the earth will worship him, whose names have not been written in the Book of Life of the Lamb slain from the foundation of the world."** (verse 8) But God warns mankind against this through two powerful witnesses **"and they will prophesy one thousand two hundred and sixty days, clothed in sackcloth."** (Revelation 11:3) This **"one thousand two hundred and sixty days"** is exactly three and a half ancient Jewish years, the same period as the **"forty-two months"** (Revelation 13:5) and the **"time and times and half a time"** (Daniel 7:25) of the beast's unchallenged control.

We see this same period of **"forty-two months"** again in Revelation 11:1-2, where John **"was given a reed like a measuring rod. And the angel stood, saying, 'Rise and measure the temple of God, the altar, and those who worship there. But leave out the court which is outside the temple, and do not measure it, for it has been given to the Gentiles. And they will tread the holy city underfoot *for* forty-two months.'"** True worship is taking place in the temple, so both it and the worshipers are measured, but not anything **"outside the temple,"** because **"it has been given to the Gentiles. And they will tread the holy city underfoot *for* forty-two months."**

During the last half of the week, Jerusalem will be under siege (see page 131) after having been fortified. (see page 130) So during that time, although the gentiles will occupy the land, they will not be able to **"tread the holy city underfoot."** But now, during this first half week, the fourth beast of Daniel 7:23 controls the city, oppressing the saints. As we saw on page 13, this is also the **"beast"** that rises up **"out of the sea"** in Revelation 13:1. For more detail on this, see pages 98 to 99.

Again, we know this takes place in the first half of the week because in the last half the righteous will not be in the temple. (see page 108) They will be forced to flee at the middle of the week, (see page 105) and in the second half they will be in the wilderness. For more detail on this see pages 107 to 108.

Finally, we read that when the two witnesses **"finish their testimony, the beast that ascends out of the bottomless pit will make war against them, overcome them, and kill them. And their dead bodies *will lie* in the street of the great city which spiritually is called Sodom and Egypt, where also our Lord was crucified."** (Revelation 11:7-8) This last detail once again shows that all this takes place in the first half of the week.

This is because the city **"where also our Lord was crucified"** is unquestionably Jerusalem. So the beast will kill these two witnesses in Jerusalem. But we just noticed that during the last half of the week, Jerusalem will be under siege (again, see page 131) after having been fortified. (and once more, see page 130) So in the last half of the week the beast could not be in the city to kill them.

The last half of the week

We remember that in the middle of the week the Roman prince **"shall bring an end to sacrifice and offering."** (Daniel 9:27, page 11) This verse continues with the words that **"on the wing of abominations shall be one who makes desolate, Even until the consummation, which is determined, Is poured out on the desolate."**

Our Lord spoke of this, saying:

> **"Therefore when you see the *'abomination of desolation,'* spoken of by Daniel the prophet, standing in the holy place (whoever reads, let him understand), then let those who are in Judea flee to the mountains. Let him who is on the housetop not go down to take anything out of his house. And let him who is in the field not go back to get his clothes. But woe to those who are pregnant and to those who are nursing babies in those days! And pray that your flight may not be in winter or on the Sabbath. For then there will be great tribulation, such as has not been since the beginning of the world until this time, no, nor ever shall be." (Matthew 24:15-21)**

How long will this **"great tribulation"** last? In Daniel 12, after being told in verse 1 that **"there shall be a time of trouble, Such as never was since there was a nation, *Even* to that time."** Daniel **"heard the man clothed in linen, who *was* above the waters of the river, when he held up his right hand**

and his left hand to heaven, and swore by Him who lives forever, that *it shall be* for a time, times, and half *a time;* and when the power of the holy people has been completely shattered, all these *things* shall be finished." (verse 7)

When will this happen? The first words of Daniel 12:1, which we just noticed, are **"At that time."** Thus we see that Daniel 12 is a continuation of what Daniel had been told in chapter 11. The last six verses of that chapter (Daniel 11:40-45) had just described the campaign of an evil attacker it called **"the king of the North."** So the **"time of trouble"** of Daniel 12:1 begins when the **"the king of the North"** comes down upon **"the glorious land."** (Daniel 11:40-41) It seems obvious that **"the glorious land"** means Judea, Daniel's homeland.

Again, as we just noticed, our Lord said **"then let those who are in Judea flee to the mountains… For then there will be great tribulation."** Thus we see that the **"time of trouble, Such as never was since there was a nation,** *Even* **to that time"** will begin when **"the king of the North"** invades the land of Judea. It will last **"a time, times, and half** *a time"* and it shall be finished **"when the power of the holy people has been completely shattered."** This **"time, times, and half** *a time"* is the first mention of the last half of the seventieth week.

We find this second **"time and times and half a time"** again in Revelation 12, where the prophet saw **"a great sign."** The sign was **"a woman clothed with the sun, with the moon under her feet, and on her head a garland of twelve stars. Then being with child, she cried out in labor and in pain to give birth."** (Revelation 12:1-2) **"And another sign appeared in heaven: behold, a great, fiery red dragon having seven heads and ten horns, and seven diadems on his heads. His tail drew a third of the stars of heaven and threw them to the earth. And the dragon stood before the woman who was ready to give birth, to devour her Child as soon as it was born."** (Revelation 12:3-4)

The fact that these are called "signs" clearly shows they are symbols. This is not about a woman and a dragon. It is about things represented by a woman and a dragon. To understand these symbols we must make a short exception to the main point of this book, which is to concentrate on expressly stated prophecies that need no interpretation. This exception is made because of the importance of this point to the last half of the seventieth week, and because the meaning seems quite clear when this prophecy is compared with others. We read that the woman **"bore a male Child who was to rule all nations with a rod of iron. And her Child was caught up to God and His throne."** (Revelation 12:5) This is plainly our Lord Jesus, who will **"rule all nations with a rod of iron."** (See Psalm 2:7-9) We are expressly told that the dragon is **"that serpent of old, called the Devil and Satan."** (Revelation 12:9) But why is he seen with seven heads and ten horns?

We noticed on page 13 that the ten horns represent ten kings who will arise from the ancient Roman empire. But what do the seven heads represent? We see such a beast again in Revelation 17, where we are told that **"The seven heads are seven mountains on which the woman sits."** (verse 9) This is not the same woman as the one we are considering in chapter 12. In chapter 17 the prophet was told that **"the woman whom you saw is that great city which reigns over the kings of the earth."** (verse 18) Rome was unquestionably the city that was reigning **"over the kings of the earth"** at the time this was written. It is widely known that from ancient times, Rome has long been called "the city of seven hills."[5] So the seven heads, like the ten horns, represent the Roman empire. We thus see this dragon as Satan acting through Roman power. This becomes more clear when we notice that **"the dragon stood before the woman who was ready to give birth, to devour her Child as soon as it was born."** We remember that when our Lord was born, the Roman governor tried to kill him. (Matthew 2:12-16)

But who is the woman? If she represented Mary, the mother of Jesus, she would not be **"a great sign."** This would simply be an account of the birth of Jesus. Besides, **"the woman was given two wings of a great eagle, that she might fly into the wilderness to her place, where she is nourished**

---

[5] For more detail on this, with physical proof, see page 32.

for a time and times and half a time, from the presence of the serpent." (Revelation 12:14) Scripture contains no account of such a flight of Mary into the wilderness.

Her flight (with Joseph) was into Egypt, not into the wilderness, and it lasted until Herod died (Matthew 2:19), not for three and a half years. Again, we read that **"her child was caught up to God and His throne. Then the woman fled into the wilderness."** (Revelation 12:5-6) Mary's flight into Egypt was long before Jesus ascended into heaven. But this woman fled into the wilderness after **"her Child was caught up to God and to His throne."**

Alternately, if the woman spoke of mankind as having given birth to Jesus, she would represent the entire human race. If that were the case, who would she be fleeing from, and who would be left to persecute her as we read in Revelation 12:13. Further, no other scripture speaks of such a flight of all mankind.

If the woman represents neither Mary nor mankind, she must represent Israel, the nation that bore our Lord. Many scriptures speak of such a flight of the righteous remnant of Israel. This is further suggested by the **"garland of twelve stars"** that was on her head. Taken by itself, this might speak either of the twelve tribes of Israel or of the twelve apostles. But if it were the twelve apostles, the woman would be the church. This would not fit the rest of the sign, for the church did not give birth to Jesus. Thus we see it is unreasonable to think the woman represents anything but Israel.

But in this respect it is important to understand that in God's sight **"they *are* not all Israel, who *are* of Israel, nor *are they* all children because they are the seed of Abraham; but *'In Isaac your seed shall be called'* That is, those who *are* the children of the flesh, these are not the children of God; but the children of the promise are counted as the seed."** (Romans 9:6-8) Thus in the vision of the woman, as in many other scriptures, the righteous remnant of Israel is looked upon as the entire nation. That is, the wicked among them are not recognized as true Israelites. The Lord says of these that **"I will purge the rebels from among you, and those who transgress against Me; I will bring them out of the country where they dwell, but they shall not enter the land of Israel."** (Ezekiel 20:38)

The period when the woman is nourished, which is **"a time and times and half a time,"** (Revelation 12:14) speaks again of the half week of trouble for Daniel's people, the half week we previously saw in Daniel 12. (see page 16)

Many think this is the same period as the **"time and times and half a time"** when **"*the saints* shall be given into"** the hand of the little horn in Daniel 7:25. But at this time the woman **"is nourished for a time and times and half a time, from the presence of the serpent."** (Revelation 12:14) In the first time period **"*the saints* are given into"** the Roman's hand. In the second they are **"nourished... from the presence"** of the Roman. Thus we see that these two periods are not the same, even though they have the same length. (See the chart on page 6.) We remember that a great disturbance will take place **"in the middle of the week."** (Daniel 9:27, page 11)

This is the time of the **"one who makes desolate"** (Daniel 9:27) when **"The city shall be taken, The houses rifled, And the women ravished. Half of the city shall go into captivity, But the remnant of the people shall not be cut off from the city."** (Zechariah 14:2) **"And it shall come to pass in all the land,' Says the LORD, '*That* two-thirds in it shall be cut off *and* die, But *one*-third shall be left in it:'"** (Zechariah 13:8) This is **"the time of Jacob's trouble"** found in Jeremiah 30:7.

Like the first half week, the last half is also mentioned in days. The woman of Revelation 12 **"fled into the wilderness, where she has a place prepared by God, that they should feed her there one thousand two hundred and sixty days."** (Revelation 12:6) Again like the first half of the week, this period is exactly the **"time and times and half a time"** (three and a half ancient Jewish years of 360 days each) that the woman is nourished **"from the presence of the serpent."** (Revelation 12:14)

In Daniel 12, after he was told in verse seven of the **"time, times, and half *a time*,"** Daniel asked **"what *shall be* the end of these *things*?"** (Daniel 12:8) He was told that **"from the time *that* the daily *sacrifice* is taken away, and the abomination of desolation is set up, *there shall be* one thousand two hundred and ninety days. Blessed *is* he who waits, and comes to the one thousand three hundred and thirty-five days."** (Daniel 12:11-12) The first of these periods is just thirty days more than the 1260 day second half of the week. The second is forty-five days more than that. (See the chart on page 6.) The first delay appears to be the time during which the Lord destroys the nations that had gathered together against Jerusalem. The events of this period are traced in detail in the chapter titled "Rescue - The LORD's Campaigns," beginning on page 132.

Since **"he who waits"** through the second delay is blessed, its end evidently marks the beginning of Israel's blessing as described in the chapter titled "Restoration - The Ancient Promises Fulfilled," beginning on page 148.

There is one more time period expressed in days:

> **"Then I heard a holy one speaking; and *another* holy one said to that certain *one* who was speaking, 'How long *will* the vision *be, concerning* the daily *sacrifices* and the transgression of desolation, the giving of both the sanctuary and the host to be trampled under foot?' And he said to me, 'For two thousand three hundred days; then the sanctuary shall be cleansed.'"** (Daniel 8:13-14)

Some have thought this must refer to something that happened in ancient times, because it is almost three years more that the last half week. (See the chart on page 6.) But this scripture clearly states otherwise. Gabriel told Daniel, **"Look, I am making known to you what shall happen in the latter time of the indignation; for at the appointed time the end shall be."** (Daniel 8:19) Then he added that **"the vision of the evenings and mornings Which was told is true; Therefore seal up the vision, For it refers to**

many days in the future." (verse 26) The word *days* in **"two thousand three hundred days"** was translated from the Hebrew word *'ereb* (word number 6153 in Strong's Hebrew Dictionary) followed by the Hebrew word *boqer*. (word number 1242 in Strong's Hebrew Dictionary) These words literally mean *evenings* and *mornings*, as the translation renders verse 26. So we see that the Hebrew wording clearly implies a meaning of two thousand three hundred literal, twenty-four hour, days. And Gabriel expressly stated that this **"shall happen in the latter time of the indignation,"** and that the vision of the **"two thousand three hundred days"** **"refers to many days in the future."**

The difficulty with the additional three years disappears when we remember the great temple described in Ezekiel 40-43. Unless the Lord raised it miraculously, such a temple could hardly be built in less than three years. Indeed, the construction of such a temple in only three years would in itself be almost a miracle. The **"two thousand three hundred days"** in Daniel 8:14 will be until **"the sanctuary shall be cleansed."** It would not seem that this would happen until the new temple was complete. Thus the problem disappears, with the sanctuary of the new temple being cleansed **"two thousand three hundred days"** after **"the transgression of desolation."**

Gog's attack

Bible prophecy contains three other time periods not directly referenced to Daniel's seventieth week. Two of these are connected with the invasion and defeat of Gog. (See the chart on page 6.)

In Ezekiel 38 and 39, Israel is attacked by a great coalition led by Gog. The Lord Himself will destroy this army. (Ezekiel 38:19-39:6) **"Then those who dwell in the cities of Israel will go out and set on fire and burn the weapons, both the shields and bucklers, the bows and arrows, the javelins and spears; and they will make fires with them for seven years."** (Ezekiel 39:9)

Gog's army will have to be buried, so **"'For seven months the house of Israel will be burying them, in order to cleanse the land. Indeed all the people of the land will be burying, and they will gain renown for it on the day that I am glorified,' says the Lord GOD. 'They will set apart men regularly employed, with the help of a search party, to pass through the land and bury those bodies remaining on the ground, in order to cleanse it. At the end of seven months they will make a search.'"** (Ezekiel 39:12-14)

The millennium (See the chart on page 6)

While there are many that deny that there will be such a time, it is stated in such clear words that it is simple unbelief to deny it. This period is defined so clearly as to require no explanation at all. The exact words of scripture are:

> **"Then I saw an angel coming down from heaven, having the key to the bottomless pit and a great chain in his hand. He laid hold of the dragon, that serpent of old, who is *the* Devil and Satan, and bound him for a thousand years; and he cast him into the bottomless pit, and shut him up, and set a seal on him, so that he should deceive the nations no more till the thousand years were finished. But after these things he must be released for a little while. And I saw thrones, and they sat on them, and judgment was committed to them. Then *I saw* the souls of those who had been beheaded for their witness to Jesus and for the word of God, who had not worshiped the beast or his image, and had not received *his* mark on their foreheads or on their hands. And they lived and reigned with Christ for a thousand years. But the rest of the dead did not live again until the thousand years were finished. This *is* the first resurrection. Blessed and holy *is* he who has part in the first resurrection. Over such the second death has no power, but they shall be priests of God and of Christ, and shall reign**

with Him a thousand years. Now when the thousand years have expired, Satan will be released from his prison and will go out to deceive the nations which are in the four corners of the earth, Gog and Magog, to gather them together to battle, whose number *is* as the sand of the sea." (Revelation 20:1-8)

In these eight verses, our God stated six times that this period would last a thousand years. Could He have made it more plain? While events which take place after this are mentioned in Bible prophecy, this is the last time period that is expressly defined.

KEY INDIVIDUALS IN BIBLE PROPHECY

The First Key Individual

The prince who is to come

This is the ruler[6] of the revived Roman empire. In the prophecy of the seventy weeks, this coming ruler is identified by the words: **"And**

---

6 The word ***prince*** in this passage is a translation of the Hebrew word ***nagiyd***. This word does not signify the son of a king, as our English word ***prince*** does, but rather means a leader or commander. This Hebrew word (number 5057 in Strong's Hebrew Dictionary) is used forty-four other times in the Old Testament. Of these forty-four times, it is used only once in reference to a son of a king before he himself became king. In this place it was used of Abijah, but not to say that he was the king's son, but that the king appointed him **"as chief, to be leader among his brothers."** (2 Chronicles 11:22)

This word was used seventeen times in reference to currently reigning kings of Israel or Judah. It was used of Saul in 1 Samuel 9:16, 10:1; of David in 1 Samuel 13:14, 25:30, 2 Samuel 5:2, 6:21, 7:8, 1 Chronicles 11:2, 17:7, 28:4, and Isaiah 55:4; of Solomon in 1 Kings 1:35 and 1 Chronicles 29:22; of Jeroboam in 1 Kings 14:7; of Baasha in 1 Kings 16:2; and of Hezekiah in 1 Kings 20:5; and of Messiah in Daniel 9:25.

after the sixty-two weeks Messiah shall be cut off, but not for Himself; And the people of the prince who is to come Shall destroy the city and the sanctuary." (Daniel 9:26)

We need to notice that two events were to occur **"after the sixty-two weeks." "Messiah shall be cut off, but not for Himself."** And **"the people of the prince who is to come Shall destroy the city and the sanctuary."**

In Luke 21:5-6 our Lord warned the people of Judea that this would happen. **"As some spoke of the temple, how it was adorned with beautiful stones and donations, He said, 'These things which you see; the days will come in which not *one* stone shall be left upon another that shall not be thrown down.'"** Then, in verses 20-24 of the same chapter He added: **"But when you see Jerusalem surrounded by armies, then know that its desolation is near. Then let those who are in Judea flee to the mountains, let those who are in the midst of her depart, and let not those who are in the country enter her. For these are the days of vengeance, that all things which are written may be fulfilled. But woe to those who are pregnant and to those who are nursing babies in those days! For there will be great distress in the land and wrath upon this people. And they will fall by the edge of the sword, and be led away captive into all nations. And Jerusalem will be trampled by Gentiles until the times of the Gentiles are fulfilled."**[7] This sounds very like the final words of Daniel 9:26: **"The end of it *shall be* with a flood, And till the end of the war desolations are determined."** A conquering army flows over everything like a flood, destroying everything in its path.[8]

According to history, these prophecies were fulfilled in 70 A.D., about forty years after our Lord was crucified. Under the command of Titus, the armies of Rome destroyed Jerusalem and burned the temple. The heat from

---

[7] We know this cannot refer to the destruction of Jerusalem at the middle of Daniel's seventieth week because after that destruction the remnants of Jerusalem will be fortified (see page 130) and the city will be besieged. (see page 131) So at that time the gentiles will not be able to **"trample"** Jerusalem, because they will be held outside the walls.

[8] This figure of speech is used again in Isaiah 59:19, where we read, **"When the enemy comes in like a flood, The Spirit of the LORD will lift up a standard against him."**

the fire melted the temple's gold, and it ran down between the stones of the foundation. To recover the gold, the Romans had to remove every last stone. The Romans commemorated this victory with the Arch of Titus, which still stands in Rome. As can be seen in the photo below, this arch shows the victory parade when Titus returned. Soldiers are shown carrying items from the temple in Jerusalem, including silver trumpets, the table of showbread, and a menorah, a distinctively Jewish lamp from the Holy Place. It had a central column and three branches out of each side, making a total of seven. (see Exodus 25:23-39)

The Temple Treasure Panel on the Arch of Titus

Photo Copyright © 1997 Leo C. Curran. Used by permission.

In Daniel 9:26, the prophet was *not* told that **"the city and the sanctuary"** would be destroyed by **"the prince who is to come."** He was rather told this would be done by **"the people of the prince who is to come."** That is, this **"prince who is to come"** would rule over **"the people"** who destroyed "the city and the sanctuary." We thus understand that this **"prince who is to come"** will be a ruler of Rome.

Daniel's informer continued, **"Then he shall confirm a covenant with many for one week; But in the middle of the week He shall bring an end to sacrifice and offering."** (Daniel 9:27) 2 Thessalonians 2:4 tells us there will be a time when **"the man of sin... the son of perdition"** **"sits as God in the temple of God, showing himself that he is God."** Such an outrage could not take place in **"the temple of God"** while true worship continued. So this prince must first **"bring an end to sacrifice and offering."** There can be little doubt that this is the abomination mentioned at the end of Daniel 9:27: **"And on the wing of abominations shall be one who makes desolate."**

The fourth beast's little horn

In Daniel 7; the prophet saw a vision by night, **"and behold, the four winds of heaven were stirring up the Great Sea. And four great beasts came up from the sea, each different from the other."**(verses 2-3) This vision's meaning is not left to our imagination, for in verses 15 to 17 of this chapter we read that Daniel was grieved in his spirit, and the visions of his head troubled him.

So he **"came near to one of those who stood by, and asked him the truth of all this."** He was told that **"Those great beasts, which are four, *are* four kings *which* arise out of the earth."**

These four kings founded four kingdoms repeatedly seen in the prophecies of Daniel. They are first seen in chapter two, where in verses 38-40 Nebuchadnezzar was told that he was the first of these, and three more would come after him. In chapter five Nebuchadnezzar's kingdom was conquered by Darius the Mede. (verses 30-31) In chapter eight we are told this second kingdom, which was shared by the Medes and the Persians, would fall to Greece. (verses 20-21, compare verse 7) This is repeated in the first two verses of chapter eleven. The fourth kingdom is not named, but it is described.

In Daniel 2:40 we read that **"the fourth kingdom shall be as strong as iron, inasmuch as iron breaks in pieces and shatters everything; and like iron that crushes, *that kingdom* will break in pieces and crush all the others."** Then Daniel said, **"After this I saw in the night visions, and behold, a fourth beast, dreadful and terrible, exceedingly strong. It had huge iron teeth; it was devouring, breaking in pieces, and trampling the residue with its feet. It *was* different from all the beasts that *were* before it."** (Daniel 7:7-8) This beast was **"different from"** all the others. This is so important the Holy Spirit repeated it three times. The second time is in verse 19, where Daniel **"wished to know the truth about the fourth beast, which was different from all the others, exceedingly dreadful, *with* its teeth of iron and its nails of bronze, *which* devoured, broke in pieces, and trampled the residue with its feet."**

Then in verse 23 Daniel was told, **"The fourth beast shall be A fourth kingdom on earth, Which shall be different from all *other* kingdoms, And shall devour the whole earth, Trample it and break it in pieces."** The next great empire after Greece was Rome, the fourth of these ancient empires, whose irresistible power crushed all other kingdoms of the known world. Rome differed from the rest of these ancient kingdoms in that in addition to having a king (the emperor) it had an elected Senate.

This fourth beast had ten horns, and as Daniel was considering them **"there was another horn, a little one, coming up among them, before whom three of the first horns were plucked out by the roots."** (Daniel 7:8) In verse 20 Daniel asked about **"the ten horns that *were* on its head, and the other *horn* which came up, before which three fell."** He was told that **"The ten horns *are* ten kings Who shall arise from this kingdom. And another shall rise after them; He shall be different from the first *ones*, And shall subdue three kings."** (verse 7:24) Thus we understand that ten kings were to arise from the ancient Roman empire. These ten kings would be followed by one more, an eleventh, who would subdue three of the first ten.[9]

It is interesting to notice that as this horn came up, it was **"little."** (Remember Daniel 7:8 says that **"there was another horn, a little one, coming up among them."**) From this detail we realize that, although he will eventually **"subdue three kings,"** (verse 24) he first appears on the scene as a **"little"** king. We also need to notice that Daniel was specifically told that this king shall **"rise after"** the first ten kings, and that **"He shall be different from the first** *ones*.**"** These details should help in recognizing this wicked ruler when he appears. For more detail on this see page 91.

"And there, in this horn, *were* **eyes like the eyes of a man, and a mouth speaking pompous words."** (Daniel 7:8) In verse 20 Daniel asked about **"that horn which had eyes and a mouth which spoke pompous words, whose appearance** *was* **greater than his fellows."** In verse 25 he was told this king **"shall speak** *pompous* **words against the Most High."** but in addition to his pompous words, this king **"Shall persecute the saints of the Most High, And shall intend to change times and law."** (verse 25) And Daniel **"was watching; and the same horn was making war against the saints, and prevailing against them."** (verse 21)

Daniel **"watched till thrones were put in place, And the Ancient of Days was seated; His garment** *was* **white as snow, And the hair of His head** *was* **like pure wool. His throne** *was* **a fiery flame, Its wheels a burning fire; A fiery stream issued And came forth from before Him. A thousand thousands ministered to Him; Ten thousand times ten**

---

[9] In light of this clear prophecy, it is remarkable that many think this future Roman ruler will come into power by peaceful means. This idea evidently comes from Daniel 11:21-24. But that is part of a long account in Daniel 11:5-32. This passage does not speak of the future, but deals with ancient empires to identify the kings of the South and of the North, whose future actions are detailed in Daniel 11:40-45. Some defend this idea by pointing to Revelation 6:2, where we see a rider on a white horse. They identify this rider with the coming Roman prince, and point out that he has a bow, but no arrows are mentioned. They reason that arrows are not mentioned because he comes in peacefully. But they fail to notice that this prophecy expressly says **"he went out conquering and to conquer."**

thousand stood before Him. The court was seated, And the books were opened."** (Daniel 7:9-10)

In the next verse (11) he continued: **"I watched then because of the sound of the pompous words which the horn was speaking; I watched till the beast was slain, and its body destroyed and given to the burning flame."** In verse 22 he described this as **"until the Ancient of Days came, and a judgment was made *in favor* of the saints of the Most High, and the time came for the saints to possess the kingdom."** Daniel was told **"But the court shall be seated, And they shall take away his dominion, To consume and destroy *it* forever."** (verse 26) For **"the saints of the Most High shall receive the kingdom, and possess the kingdom forever, even forever and ever."** (verse 18) It should be clear to even the most casual reader that all this has not yet happened. We therefore realize that this prophecy speaks of events that will take place in the future.

The eighth king of "the beast that was, and is not, and yet is."

"The beast that was, and is not, and yet is," (Revelation 17:8) is identified by its seven heads, which represent **"seven mountains, on which the woman sits."** (verse 9) It is well known that from ancient to modern times, Rome has long been called "the city of seven hills."[10] But it is not so well known how strongly Revelation 17:9 fits ancient Roman thought.

---

10 Some might complain that a hill is not the same as a mountain. But the Greek word translated ***mountain*** in Revelation 17:9 is ***oros***. (word number 3735 in Strong's Greek Dictionary) This Greek word can also be translated ***hill***, as can be seen in Matthew 5:14, Luke 4:29, and Luke 9:37.

The photograph below shows a Roman coin called a sestertius (a fourth of a denarius). It was minted by the emperor Vespasian about twenty years before the Revelation was written, and depicts Rome as a woman (the goddess Roma) seated on seven hills.

The Roma Sestertius of Vespasian

Retouched from photo in "The Goddess Roma In the Art of the Roman Empire" by Cornelius C. Vermeule III, Cambridge (Massachusetts) and London, 1959, Plate III, figure 24. Used by permission of the Museum of Fine Arts, Boston.

The woman is also **"that great city which reigns over the kings of the earth."** (verse 18) Rome unquestionably ruled the world at the time this was written. There can be no reasonable doubt that these two passages were intended to identify Rome as the subject of this prophecy. This beast has the ten horns of Daniel's fourth beast. (verse 17:3) Remember that **"The ten horns *are* ten kings *Who* shall** arise from this kingdom." (Daniel 7:24, pages 13, 29) This is very specific. These ten kings will arise from within the ancient Roman Empire, not from other places. Thus we realize that this does not mean that the ten kings represent ten divisions of the entire world, as many think today, but only ten kingdoms from within the area occupied by the ancient Roman Empire. And they **"are ten kings who have received no kingdom as yet, but they receive authority for one hour as kings with the beast. These are of one mind, and they will give their power and authority to the beast."** (Revelation 17:12-13)

No voluntary union of ten kings with a Roman ruler has occurred at any time since this statement was made. It is therefore something that will happen in the future.

From all this we understand four things. First, the Roman Empire will be revived. Second, this will take place through a voluntary union of ten kings. Third, these kings will arise from within the ancient Roman empire. And fourth, these ten kings had not yet come into power when the Revelation was given.

This will take place in two stages. **"There are also seven kings. Five have fallen, one is,** *and* **the other has not yet come. And the beast that was, and is not, is himself also the eighth, and is of the seven, and is going to perdition."** (Revelation 17:10-11) At the time this was said, five previous governments of Rome had already fallen,[11] and she now had a sixth.

John was told that Rome would have another government after this one, followed by **"the beast that was, and is not."** This last ruler, the eighth, is not one of the ten kings, but another to whom the ten **"will give their power and authority."** This parallels the little horn of Daniel's fourth beast, who first overthrows three of the first ten and then assumes power over them all. (Daniel 7:24) The statement that he **"is of the seven"** again shows that this eighth king rules over the revived Roman Empire.

---

11 Rome was first ruled by kings, then by consuls; followed by decemvirs and then by consular tribunes. (See "The History of Rome," by Livy, book 5, chapter 2. And "the Annals of Imperial Rome," by Tacitus, book 1, chapter 1.) During these governments, the Roman Senate had occasionally appointed dictators in extreme emergencies. These had always been given power for only six months or until the emergency was over. But Rome's fifth form of government was different. One after another, military commanders began to violently seize dictatorial power by force of arms, as recorded by the ancient historian Appian in a book called "The Civil Wars." This continued for a period of about a hundred years, finally ending when the Senate granted absolute power to Augustus Caesar, thus establishing Rome's sixth government, the line of emperors called Caesars. This government was in power when the Revelation was given and lasted until the fall of the Roman empire. So the one which **"has not yet come"** has to be future. Calling each of these governments a king is in keeping with the principle described in footnote 4 on page 13.

The **"beast that was, and is not, and yet is"** was scarlet in color and **"full of names of blasphemy."** (Revelation 17:3) Verse 8 tells us that it **"will ascend out of the bottomless pit and go to perdition."** Under the eighth king, this beast, along with the ten kings, **"will make war with the Lamb,"** but **"the Lamb will overcome them, for He is Lord of lords and King of kings; and those *who are* with Him *are* called, chosen, and faithful."** (verse 14) This parallels the end of the little horn of Daniel's fourth beast: **"I watched then because of the sound of the pompous words which the horn was speaking; I watched till the beast was slain, and its body destroyed and given to the burning flame."** (Daniel 7:11)

The healed head of the beast that rises up out of the sea

In Revelation 13:1, the prophet **"stood on the sand of the sea."** And saw a beast **"rising up out of the sea."** This beast is identified by having **"seven heads and ten horns, and on his horns ten crowns, and on his heads a blasphemous name."** The seven heads and ten horns clearly identify this beast as yet another symbol of Rome. John saw one of the beast's heads **"as if it had been mortally wounded, and his deadly wound was healed."** (verse 13:3) Many think this means the coming Roman ruler will be wounded in the head, and will miraculously recover. But we have already seen in Revelation 17 (see page 33) that these seven heads represent seven successive governments of Rome. (verse 10) Verse 12 tells us the ten kings are represented by its ten horns, not by its seven heads. Also, the mortal wound was in one of the beast's seven heads. But verse 11 says this final **"beast"** is not one of these seven, but **"the eighth."**

From all this we understand that the mortal wound is not in the head of the final ruler, but in one of the governments of Rome. And indeed, this is what history tells us. After ruling the world for hundreds of years, the Roman Empire was finally destroyed, becoming **"the beast that was, and is not."** But although the beast **"was, and is not;"** it **"yet is."** (Revelation 17:8) So the beast does not die, but its deadly wound is healed. The government of Rome that was destroyed was the line of emperors called Caesars. From the healing of the deadly wound we understand that Rome will be revived. But it will not only be revived as a power. It will again have an emperor, a king, the strong leader we have been discussing.

The Beast

The prophetic scriptures often describe kingdoms as beasts, but only one individual is called **"the beast."** This is the last king of the revived Roman empire. Mentioned many times in the Revelation, he is most completely described in chapter 13. This name should not be confused with the term **"the beast that ascends out of the bottomless pit,"** which refers, not to the king, but to the empire. This last term occurs twice. The first of these is Revelation 11:7; **"When they finish their testimony, the beast that ascends out of the bottomless pit will make war against them, overcome them, and kill them."** The second time is Revelation 17:8; **"The beast that you saw was, and is not, and will ascend out of the bottomless pit and go to perdition. And those who dwell on the earth will marvel, whose names are not written in the Book of Life from the foundation of the world, when they see the beast that was, and is not, and yet is."**

There are two problems in the common translation of a key statement about **"the beast."** Most translations render the last part of Revelation 13:7 to read that he was given **"authority over every tribe, tongue, and nation."** If this were the only possible translation of this sentence, there could be no question as to its meaning. But the Greek word translated *authority* here (and in verses 2, 4, 5, and 12) is *exousia*. (word number 1849 in Strong's Greek Dictionary) This word is often used of *official authority*, but that is not its only meaning. It also means *power*, as in the ability to control. For this use of *exousia* see Romans 9:21 and 1 Corinthians 7:37.

We note this to understand that this word does not *necessarily* mean the Beast's power will be official. Footnote 13 on page 38 shows one way he could exercise nearly universal power without needing any official authority outside of his own territory.

But that is not the only problem in the translation of Revelation 13:7. The Greek word translated **"every"** in this passage is *pas*. (word number 3956 in Strong's Greek Dictionary) This Greek word literally means *all*. But like our English word *all*, it does not necessarily mean *absolutely* all. *Pas* is the Greek word used in Matthew 27:1, where we read that **"all the chief priests and elders of the people plotted against Jesus to put Him to death."** But Luke 23:50-51 says that Joseph of Arimathea was a member of the council and **"had not consented to their decision and deed."** Also, Nicodemus opposed the council in John 7:50-51 and came with Joseph to bury Jesus in John 19:39. In English, we add the word *absolutely* to the word *all* to make it absolute. In Greek, this was done by adding a syllable to *pas*, making it *hapas*. (word number 537 in Strong's Greek Dictionary) This is the word used in Luke 17:27, where we read that **"Noah entered the ark, and the flood came and destroyed them all."** If the Holy Spirit had meant that **"the beast"** would be given authority over *absolutely* all tribes, tongues, and nations, it would seem that He would have used the word *hapas*. But He said *pas*, not *hapas*.[12]

Thus we understand that the Greek words used in this scripture do not *necessarily* mean that **"the beast"** will become the ruler of the entire world. That is a possible interpretation of this passage, if it is taken by itself. But other scriptures show that this is an error. In this regard the first thing we need to notice is that in *every* other reference to this power, it is presented only as a revival of the ancient Roman empire.

---

[12] The same consideration applies to the Beast's following in verse 3 of this chapter, where we read that **"all the world marveled and followed the beast"** and to his worship in verse 8, where we read that **"All who dwell on the earth will worship him…"** The Greek word translated *all* in both of these places is *pas*, not *hapas*.

The next thing we need to notice is that other kings will continue to exist throughout the time of this evil ruler's reign. We see this in Revelation 16. While **"the beast"** is gathering his last great army, we read of **"the kings of the East"** in verse 12 and **"the kings of the earth and of the whole world."** in verse 14. These references are only general, but scripture specifically speaks of two great powers that will continue to exist during that time.

The first of these is **"the Assyrian."** Isaiah 10:12 says that this evil invader will be punished **"when the Lord has performed all His work on mount Zion and on Jerusalem."** Verse 20 of the same chapter says **"And it shall come to pass in that day *That* the remnant of Israel, And such as have escaped of the house of Jacob, Will never again depend on him who defeated them, But will depend on the Lord, the Holy One of Israel, in truth."** It should be clear to even the most casual student of prophecy that the Lord's **"work on mount Zion and on Jerusalem"** will not be completed until He returns in power, nor will Israel learn to **"depend on the Lord, the Holy One of Israel, in truth"** until that time. For more information on this see pages 50 to 54.

The second of these powers is Gog. Ezekiel 39:7 says that after Gog is destroyed the Lord **"will not *let them* profane"** His holy name **"anymore."** Again, Ezekiel 39:22 says that **"the house of Israel shall know that I *am* the LORD their God from that day forward."**

Neither of these could possibly apply until after the time when they allow **"the man of sin"** to sit **"as God in the temple of God, showing himself that he is God."** (2 Thessalonians 2:3-4) For more information on Gog, see pages 78 to 80. For more information on why **"the beast"** will not rule the entire world, see pages 205 to 207.

"The beast" demands worship as God, helped on in this by a second beast that John saw **"coming up out of the earth."** This second beast is also called **"the false prophet,"** and is the king of revived Judah. (see page 46) The second beast **"causes all, both small and great, rich and poor, free and**

slave, to receive a mark on their right hand or on their foreheads, and that no one may buy or sell except one who has the mark or the name of the beast, or the number of his name." (Revelation 13:16-17)[13]

Accepting the Beast's mark involves some kind of recognition of his claim to be God, for Revelation 14:9-11 says, **"Then a third angel followed them, saying with a loud voice, 'If anyone worships the beast and his image, and receives *his* mark on his forehead or on his hand, he himself shall also drink of the wine of the wrath of God, which is poured out full strength into the cup of His indignation. He shall be tormented with fire and brimstone in the presence of the holy angels and in the presence of the Lamb. And the smoke of their torment ascends forever and ever; and they have no rest day or night, who worship the beast and his image, and whoever receives the mark of his name.'"** Whether the angel is literal or figurative, this plainly indicates a warning of sufficient clarity that no one can mistake the message.

Even before this final judgment, there will be severe punishment on all who accept the mark of the beast. In Revelation 16 John saw seven angels

---

13 When I was young I thought this meant the Beast would make a law that no one would be allowed to buy or sell without this mark. But in recent years the banking community has advanced a plan to completely eliminate cash by reducing all money to nothing but credits in banks. They say this would reduce crime, as it would become impossible to steal money. But the bankers point out that the credit, debit, and ATM cards commonly used today could still be stolen. So they propose to replace them with tattoos that can be read by scanners. Their proposed location for this tattoo is the right hand, or if that has been maimed, the forehead. Under this system, instead of only being illegal, it would be impossible to buy or sell anything except through the system. But the plan has a dark side, for whoever controlled the system would be able to control everyone.

It is a serious mistake to interpret Bible prophecy from current events. But this sounds remarkably like Revelation 13:16-17. If the Beast could persuade the world to let him implement such a plan, he would literally have power over ***essentially*** * **"every tribe, tongue, and nation,"** even if he never became the official ruler of the world. (see Revelation 13:7) This is not unthinkable; for many nations, including the United States, have already declared an intention to adopt such a system. The technology to do this is already in place. We see it everyday in the scanners used to check out merchandise in supermarkets and other places of business.

Some have made much of a more frightening version of this concept, involving microchips implanted under the skin. The technology to do this has been developed, but is not yet in place. This would even make it possible to monitor an individual's movements, but no Biblical prophecy speaks of any government having such a system.

*For my reasons for adding the word *"essentially,"* see pages 36, 205-206.

with seven bowls. **"So the first went and poured out his bowl upon the earth, and a foul and loathsome sore came upon the men who had the mark of the beast and those who worshiped his image."** (verse 2) **"Then the fifth angel poured out his bowl on the throne of the beast, and his kingdom became full of darkness; and they gnawed their tongues because of the pain."** (verse 10)

Even as there will be terrible punishment on those who worship the beast, there will be a rich reward for those who refuse to do so, even though the punishment for their refusal is death. For in heaven the prophet **"saw *something* like a sea of glass mingled with fire, and those who have the victory over the beast, over his image and over his mark *and* over the number of his name, standing on the sea of glass, having harps of God."** (Revelation 15:2)

In Revelation 13:18 we read, **"Here is wisdom. Let him who has understanding calculate the number of the beast, for it is the number of a man: His number *is* 666."** This is commonly interpreted to mean that the numerical values of the letters in the name of **"the beast"** will add up to 666. Various schemes of applying values to the letters of the alphabet have been used to find this sum in current names ranging all the way from a title claimed by the Pope to various American political figures. All this is error.

The time discussed in Bible prophecy has not yet begun. The beast is not yet revealed. But when he comes, **"him who has understanding"** will recognize him from the many descriptions in Scripture. The correct way to calculate his number will then be apparent, and will confirm his identity.

The beast's authority will only last for a short time, for **"he was given authority to continue for forty-two months."** (Revelation 13:5) This time is figuratively called **"one hour"** in Revelation 17:12. But while his world-wide power will be broken at this time, he will retain a position of leadership. For in the madness of his rebellion, he will join with the **dragon** and the **false prophet** in leading an army in open revolt against the Almighty God. But this will be futile. **"And I saw three unclean spirits like frogs *coming* out of the mouth of the dragon, out of the mouth of the beast, and out of the mouth of the false prophet. For they are spirits of demons, performing signs, *which go out to the kings of the earth and of the whole world, to gather them to the battle of that great day of God Almighty.*" (Revelation 16:13-14) "**And I saw the beast, the kings of the earth, and their armies, gathered together to make war against Him who sat on the horse and against His army.**" (Revelation 19:19) "**Then the beast was captured, and with him the false prophet who worked signs in his presence, by which he deceived those who received the mark of the beast and those who worshiped his image. These two were cast alive into the lake of fire burning with brimstone.**" (Revelation 19:20)

This awful punishment is not temporary, for John "**saw thrones, and they sat on them, and judgment was committed to them. Then *I saw* the souls of those who had been beheaded for their witness to Jesus and for the word of God, who had not worshiped the beast or his image, and had not received *his* mark on their foreheads or on their hands. And they lived and reigned with Christ for a thousand years.**" (Revelation 20:4) After the thousand years have passed, the **beast** and the **false prophet** will still be in the lake of fire. And even then their punishment continues, for in Revelation 20:10 we read that "**The devil, who deceived them, was cast into the lake of fire and brimstone where the beast and the false prophet *are*. And they will be tormented day and night forever and ever.**" The word "**they**" in this passage specifically includes not only "**the devil,**" but also "**the beast and the false prophet.**" All three of these wicked individuals "**will be tormented day and night forever and ever.**"

There are many that do not believe that God will punish sinners in an eternal hell. But this prophecy plainly says he will. This particular statement applies only to three individuals, two men and the devil. But beginning in the very next verse this same judgement is expanded to include all the wicked dead.

> "Then I saw a great white throne and Him who sat on it, from whose face the earth and the heaven fled away. And there was found no place for them. And I saw the dead, small and great, standing before God, and books were opened. And another book was opened, which is *the Book* of Life. And the dead were judged according to their works, by the things which were written in the books. The sea gave up the dead who were in it, and Death and Hades delivered up the dead who were in them. And they were judged, each one according to his works. Then Death and Hades were cast into the lake of fire. This is the second death. And anyone not found written in the Book of Life was cast into the lake of fire." (Revelation 20:11-15)

Jesus warned of this by repeatedly calling **"hell," "the fire that shall never be quenched—where *'Their worm does not die And the fire is not quenched.'"*** He stressed this by repeating it three times over in Mark 9:43-48.

On another occasion Jesus told about a rich man and a beggar named Lazarus. This is often called the parable of the rich man and Lazarus. But it was not a parable. A parable is a fictional story told to illustrate a point. This was an anecdote, a short factual account told to illustrate a point. Jesus said that the rich man **"died and was buried. And being in torments in Hades,"** he begged for relief, saying **"I am tormented in this flame."** (Luke 16:22-24)

We have examined these passages to understand that the holy scriptures plainly state that the wicked dead will be **"tormented."** This will take place both in **"Hades,"** their temporary holding place, and in their final prison, **"the lake of fire."** And will continue **"forever and ever."** Could any warning be more solemn?

Who will receive such punishment? Many think **"hell"** is an unusual punishment reserved for only the most extreme of sinners. But the Bible plainly says otherwise. It says that **"He who believes in Him is not condemned; but he who does not believe is condemned already, because he has not believed in the name of the only begotten Son of God. And this is the** condemnation, that the light has come into the world, and men loved darkness rather than light, because their deeds were evil." (John 3:18-19) The deciding factor will not be how relatively good or evil a person's life was, but whether or not that person chose to believe in Jesus.

> "For God so loved the world that He gave His only begotten Son, that whoever believes in Him should not perish but have everlasting life."(John 3:16)

If we choose to believe this, we will be pardoned. But everyone who refuses to believe will be condemned. For more information on this, see pages 173 to 174.

The Second Key Individual

The king

The king of revived Judah, which is now called Israel. (Daniel 11:36-40) Many think this blasphemous "**king**" is the Roman **"prince"** of Daniel 9:26. But the language of Bible prophecy is very precise. Every detail has meaning. The Hebrew word translated **"prince"** in Daniel 9:26 is *nagiyd*. (word number 5057 in Strong's Hebrew Dictionary) We saw in footnote 6 (page 25) that this word means *leader* or *commander*. But the Hebrew word translated "**king**" in this passage is *melek*. (word number 4428 in Strong's Hebrew Dictionary) This word literally means a *king*. Even such an apparently small difference as whether someone is called a *melek* or a *nagiyd* is important. This "**king**" is not the same person as **"the prince."**

We notice that **"the king"** shall not regard **"the God of his fathers,"** (Daniel 11:37) but shall instead honor "a god which his fathers did not know." (verse 38) The term, **"the God of his fathers,"** is not just a generic reference to some god worshiped in past generations. Some form of this term is used of the God of Israel fifty-eight times in the Old Testament. When the Lord sent Moses to the children of Israel He told him **"Thus you shall say to the children of Israel: 'The LORD God of your fathers, the God of Abraham, the God of Isaac, and the God of Jacob , has sent me to you. This *is* My name forever, and this *is* My memorial to all generations."** (Exodus 3:15) Thus we see that the God this **king** shall ignore is none other than the God of Israel; and that in calling Himself **"the God of his fathers,"** the Lord was identifying this **" king"** as an Israelite.

Most modern translations render this clause *"the gods of his fathers."* This is a possible translation because the Hebrew word for *God* (*'elohiym*, word number 430 in Strong's Hebrew Dictionary) is plural. But the Hebrew scriptures use *'elohiym* for the one true *God* of Israel about two thousand four hundred times. (Including Deuteronomy 6:4, **"Hear, O Israel: The LORD our God, the LORD *is* one!"**) While it was used of the *gods* of the heathen only about two hundred times. Whether *'elohiym* should be translated *God* or *gods* can only be determined from the context. Nothing in Daniel 11:37 implies a plural sense for this word. But if *"the gods of his fathers"* were correct, this would be the only place the Holy Spirit used this formula in speaking of false gods. Translators did not begin to use the plural word *gods* in this verse until the notion that **"the king"** is **"the prince"** became popular. So we realize this idea is the basis of the plural translation. Thus we understand that using the plural translation to prove this idea is only reasoning in a circle.

'Elohiym has a singular form, *'elowahh.* (word number 433 in Strong's Hebrew Dictionary) But the fact that it is not used never justifies translating *'elohiym* as *gods*. *'Elowahh* is used only sixteen times outside of the book of Job.[14] But it is used in every reference to false gods in the passage we are considering (the word rendered **"any god"** in verse 37 and the **"god"** worshiped by **"the king,"** mentioned twice in verse 38 and once in verse 39).

---

14 Although unusual in the rest of scripture, *'elowahh* is used more than forty times in the book of Job.

This adds strength to the conclusion that the term **"the God of his fathers"** in this passage refers to the one true God of Israel, for a different word is used of all gods that are unquestionably false.

In Daniel 11:40 **"the king"** is attacked by **"the king of the South"** and **"the king of the North."** The result is that **"the king of the North"** overruns many nations, including Judah, **"the glorious land."** (verses 41-45) But **"the king"** continues to prosper **"till the wrath has been accomplished."** (verse 36) How does he escape? We learn this detail in Zechariah 11:17, where, as **"the worthless shepherd,"** he **"leaves the flock!"**[15] We see this again in the missing **shepherd** of Zechariah 10:2, in the missing **king** of Micah 4:9, and the fainthearted **king** of Jeremiah 4:9. For this crime **"A sword *shall be* against his arm And against his right eye; His arm shall completely wither, And his right eye shall be totally blinded."** (Zechariah 11:17)

Our Lord contrasted himself to this **"worthless shepherd"** by saying **"I am the good shepherd. The good shepherd gives His life for the sheep. But a hireling, *he who is* not the shepherd, one who does not own the sheep, sees the wolf coming and leaves the sheep and flees; and the wolf catches the sheep and scatters them. The hireling flees because he is a hireling and does not care about the sheep. I am the good shepherd; and I know My *sheep*, and am known by My own. As the Father knows Me, even so I know the Father; and I lay down My life for the sheep."** (John 10:11-15) In so contrasting Himself to this evil individual, our Lord was pointing him out as:

The Antichrist

The great false messiah who rises in imitation of the true Messiah, our Lord Jesus Christ. He is mentioned by this title only in 1 John 2:18; **"you have heard that the Antichrist is coming."** Many, if not most, seem to have

---

15 We recognize this shepherd as a king of Judah because he will be raised up "in the land." (Zechariah 11:16)

completely missed the significance of this title. The Greek word transliterated ***Christ*** is ***Christos***, (word number 5547 in Strong's Greek Dictionary) meaning ***the anointed one***. It is the Greek equivalent of the Hebrew word ***mashiyach***, (word number 4899 in Strong's Hebrew Dictionary) which is transliterated ***Messiah***. This title, though it applies to our Lord Jesus, does not mean ***God***. Its literal meaning, ***the anointed one***, means He is ***God's chosen one***. Jesus said **"I proceeded forth and came from God; nor have I come of Myself, but He sent Me."** (John 8:42) Even so, the Antichrist will claim to be the chosen representative of God.

But, like the true Messiah, the Antichrist will claim to be more than just a messenger of God. In John 1:1 we read that **"In the beginning was the Word, and the Word was with God, and the Word was God."**[16] So in imitating Jesus, the Antichrist makes a similar dual claim. As the **king** of Judah, he will exalt himself above all gods, yet he will honor another as God.

> **"He shall regard neither the God of his fathers nor the desire of women, nor regard any god; for he shall exalt himself above *them* all. But in their place he shall honor a god of fortresses; and a god which his fathers did not know he shall honor with gold and silver, with precious stones and pleasant things. Thus he shall act against the strongest fortresses with a foreign god, which he shall acknowledge, *and* advance *its* glory."** (Daniel 11:37-39)

The Antichrist is the one who will come **"in his own name,"** whom the Jews **"will receive."** (John 5:43) He has to be a Jew, for many scriptures show that Messiah is a Jew. Though blinded to many prophecies, the Jews know that their Messiah will be one of themselves. It would therefore be impossible to convince them that a gentile was their Messiah.

---

16 **"The Word"** is none other than Jesus, for **"the Word became flesh and dwelt among us, and we beheld His glory, the glory as of the only begotten of the Father, full of grace and truth."** (John 1:14)

The beast that comes up out of the earth

In Revelation 13:11 John saw **"another beast coming up out of the earth, and he had two horns like a lamb and spake like a dragon."** This beast looked like a lamb; (**"the Lamb of God,"** John 1:29, 36) but he could be recognized when he spoke, for he **"spake like a dragon."** (**"the great dragon… that serpent of old, called the Devil and Satan,"** Revelation 12:9) On page 44 we noticed our Lord's clearly stated contrast between Himself and **"the worthless shepherd."** Now we see a beast who looks like the Lord, but can be recognized when he speaks, for he speaks like the Devil.

We know that in Biblical prophecy a beast represents a king, for as we noticed on page 28, Daniel was told that **"Those great beasts, which are four, *are* four kings *which* arise out of the earth."**(Daniel 7:17) But this beast can not be the king of the revived Roman Empire, for that is the beast that John had seen **"rising up out of the sea"** (Revelation 13:1) This is **"another beast."** (verse 11) The next verse stresses this by twice referring to **"the first beast."** (Revelation 13:12) We should remember that God does not waste words. Every detail in a prophecy is significant. If God says something, it is important. If He says it twice, how much more so. The Holy Spirit considered this so important He repeated it three times in just two verses! This beast is not the same as the previous one.

This second beast **"deceives those who dwell on the earth by those signs which he was granted to do in the sight of the beast, telling those who dwell on the earth to make an image to the beast who was wounded by the sword and lived.**[17] **He was granted *power* to give breath to the**

---

[17] This does not refer to the worthless shepherd's sword wound in Zechariah 11:17, but to the beast's deadly wound in Revelation 13:3. Although a sword is mentioned in Zechariah 11:17 but not Revelation 13:3, the worthless shepherd's wounds will not be healed. We are specifically told that **"His arm shall completely wither, And his right eye shall be totally blinded."** (Zechariah 11:17) Further, the worthless shepherd's wounds, though serious, will not be life threatening. There would be nothing remarkable about such wounds being healed. But the beast's wound in Revelation 13:3 was mortal. It will seem unreasonable that the beast could have survived. The

image of the beast, that the image of the beast should both speak and cause as many as would not worship the image of the beast to be killed." (Revelation 13:14-15)

Many think this proves the first beast is the Antichrist, but they forget that Jesus taught men to worship the Father. (see John 4:21-24) The Antichrist will imitate the true Christ. Even as the true Christ taught us to worship the Father, the Antichrist will teach men to worship the Beast. Even as the true Christ did signs and wonders to make men believe, (see John 4:48) the Antichrist will perform **"great signs, so that he even makes fire come down from heaven on the earth in the sight of men."** (Revelation 13:13)

The false prophet

This **"false prophet"** will work signs in the presence of the beast. He will use these signs to deceive **"those who received the mark of the beast and those who worshiped his image."** (Revelation 19:20) From these details we recognize him as the beast that John saw **"coming up out of the earth,"** for that was the work of this beast in Revelation 13:13-15. But here we see the one who does this job called **"the false prophet."**

We have been noticing that the Antichrist imitates the true Christ. But the Satanic imitation goes beyond this to an unholy trinity. We see this in Revelation 16:13, where John **"saw three unclean spirits like frogs *coming* out of the mouth of the dragon, out of the mouth of the beast, and out of the mouth of the false prophet."** These three will act together in their crimes and will be together in their punishment.

> **"Then the beast was captured, and with him the false prophet who worked signs in his presence, by which he deceived those who received the mark of the beast and those who worshiped**

---

world will therefore marvel that the beast's **"deadly wound was healed."** (Revelation 13:3)

> his image. These two were cast alive into the lake of fire burning with brimstone."[18] (Revelation 19:20)

> "The devil, who deceived them, was cast into the lake of fire and brimstone where the beast and the false prophet *are*. And they will be tormented day and night forever and ever." (Revelation 20:10)

In this unholy trinity, **"the dragon,"** or the devil, takes the place of the Holy Spirit. In like manner **"the beast,"** that is, the Roman ruler, takes the place of the Father, and **"the false prophet"** takes the place of the Son.

The man of sin

Also called **"the son of perdition."** He **"opposes and exalts himself above all that is called God or that is worshiped, so that he sits as God in the temple of God, showing himself that he is God."** (2 Thessalonians 2:3-4) Those who take part in this evil worship are charged with adultery.

> **"On a lofty and high mountain You have set your bed; Even there you went up To offer sacrifice. Also behind the doors and their posts You have set up your remembrance; For you have uncovered yourself *to those other* than Me, And have gone up to them; You have enlarged your bed And made *a covenant* with them; You have loved their bed, Where you saw *their* nudity. You went to the king with ointment, And increased your perfumes; You sent your messengers far off, And *even* descended to Sheol."** (Isaiah 57:7-9)

This passage graphically shows Jehovah's jealousy at this false worship. But it also names the evil seducer. The object of this adulterous worship is none other than **"the king."** On pages 42 to 44 we saw that this is one of

---

[18] Two men (Enoch, in Genesis 5:22-24, and Elijah, in 2 Kings 2:11-12) were so holy that they were taken to heaven without tasting death. These two will be so evil that they will be cast alive into the lake of fire, only to be joined later by the devil himself.

the prophetic titles of the wicked **king** of revived Judah. This again shows him to be the Antichrist.

The lawless one

> "**The coming of the *lawless one* is according to the working of Satan, with all power, signs, and lying wonders, and with all unrighteous deception among those who perish, because they did not receive the love of the truth, that they might be saved. And for this reason God will send them strong delusion, that they should believe the lie, that they all may be condemned who did not believe the truth but had pleasure in unrighteousness.**" (2 Thessalonians 2:9-12)

This is one of the most frightening of all prophecies. God **"will send them strong delusion, that they should believe the lie."** This will be **"because they did not receive the love of the truth, that they might be saved,"** and because they **"did not believe the truth but had pleasure in unrighteousness."** This prophecy tells us that mankind will believe the Antichrist's lie.[19] But more than that, it expressly states that this belief will not just be a result of the hardness of their hearts. It will be the direct result of a sovereign act of God, as we also see in Isaiah 66:3-4, where the Lord says, **"Just as they have chosen their own ways, And their soul delights in their abominations, So will I choose their delusions, And bring their fears on them; Because, when I called, no one answered, When I spoke they did not hear; But they did evil before My eyes, And chose that in which I do not delight."** This seems unfair to many, and quite unlike our God to many others, but it is plainly declared in the scriptures.

Thus we see that **"the king," "the Antichrist,"** the beast that John saw **"coming up out of the earth," "the false prophet," "the man of sin,"** and

---

19 That is, that **"the beast"** is God, and he is the messiah, God's anointed messenger.

"the lawless one" are all the same person. We also see this in his punishment. **"Tophet" "is prepared"** for **"the king,"** and **"the breath of the LORD, like a stream of brimstone, Kindles it."** (Isaiah 30:33) **"The man of sin, the son of perdition,"** who is **"the lawless one,"** will be consumed by the Lord **"with the breath of His mouth"** and destroyed **"with the brightness of His coming."** (2 Thessalonians 2:8) And with **"the beast," "the false prophet"** will be **"cast alive into the lake of fire burning with brimstone."** (Revelation 19:20)

The Third Key Individual

The Assyrian

The king of revived Assyria.[20] (Isaiah 10) He is missed by many students because they assume these prophecies deal only with the ancient Sennacherib, king of Assyria. (Isaiah 36-37) There can be no doubt that Sennacherib was the occasion of these prophecies; but they are filled with details that go far beyond him to the last days.

1 Peter 1:10-11 says that **"the prophets... who prophesied of the grace *that would come* to you,"** **"inquired and searched carefully... searching what, or what manner of time, the Spirit of Christ who was in them was indicating when He testified beforehand the sufferings of Christ and the glories that would follow."** Both suffering and glory were prophesied for the Messiah. But how could both be true? Since the time of the New Testament, we now know these prophecies applied to two different times, separated by thousands of years. This mixture of prophecies concerning widely separated times is very common in scripture, as becomes evident when we study the Assyrian.

Sennacherib attacked Judah during the righteous reign of king Hezekiah, who **"trusted in the LORD God of Israel, so that after him was none like him**

---

20 It may surprise some to learn that an ethnic group in northern Iraq still calls themselves "Assyrians."

among all the kings of Judah, nor who were before him. For he held fast to the LORD; he did not depart from following Him, but kept His commandments, which the LORD had commanded Moses." (2 Kings 18:5-6)

"Also the hand of God was on Judah to give them singleness of heart to obey the command of the king and the leaders, at the word of the LORD." (2 Chronicles 30:12) But "after these deeds of faithfulness, Sennacherib king of Assyria came and entered Judah; he encamped against the fortified cities, thinking to win them over to himself." (2 Chronicles 32:1) Hezekiah cried out to the Lord, who answered him, "I will defend this city, to save it For My own sake and for My servant David's sake." (Isaiah 37:35)

But in Isaiah 10:6, the Lord says of the king of Assyria that "I will send him against an ungodly nation, And against the people of My wrath I will give him charge, To seize the spoil, to take the prey, And to tread them down like the mire of the streets."[21] Both Hezekiah and his people had been righteous and the Lord promised to save them from Sennacherib. But in the day described in Isaiah 10 the nation will have been ungodly and He will send Assyria to punish them. The first Assyrian was an enemy of God, while the second will actually be His agent.

But this latter day Assyrian does not intend to serve God, "nor does his heart think so." (Isaiah 10:7) He will therefore be punished "when the LORD has performed all His work on Mount Zion and on Jerusalem." (verse 12) "And it shall come to pass in that day that the remnant of Israel, And such as have escaped of the house of Jacob, Will never again depend on him who defeated them, But will depend on the LORD, the Holy One of Israel, in truth." (verse 20)

These details clearly apply to the last days. The Lord's "work on Mount Zion and on Jerusalem" will not be finished until all prophecy concerning

---

21 Some might think this refers to Assyria's successful attack on Israel, but in this prophecy that attack has already taken place, (verse 11) while the attack referred to is still future.

them has been fulfilled, and even to this day Israel has not learned to **"depend on the Lord, the Holy One of Israel, in truth."**

In Micah 5:5-6 we read that **"When the Assyrian comes into our land, And when he treads in our palaces, Then we will raise against him Seven shepherds and eight princely men. They shall waste with the sword the land of Assyria, And the land of Nimrod at its entrances; Thus He shall deliver *us* from the Assyrian, When he comes into our land And when he treads within our borders."** This prophecy, which was given at about the same time as that of Isaiah, was never fulfilled in ancient times.[22] When Sennacherib invaded Judea, no one rose to oppose him, much less **"Seven shepherds and eight princely men."** And neither Israel nor Judah has never wasted **"the land of Assyria" "with the sword."**

In Isaiah 14, immediately after saying the Assyrian would be destroyed, (verses 24-27) the Lord added, **"do not rejoice, all you of Philistia, Because the rod that struck you is broken; For out of the serpent's roots will come forth a viper, And its offspring *will be* a fiery flying serpent...**

Wail, O gate! Cry, O city! All you of Philistia *are* dissolved; For smoke will come from the north, And no one *will be* alone in his appointed times." (verses 29-31) In stating that **"out of the serpent's roots will come forth a viper"** and that **"its offspring *will be* a fiery flying serpent,"** this passage clearly sets forth two separate attacks, one in the past (relative to the time referred to) and one in the future. These two attacks are separated in time by an unspecified number of generations, as the second attacker is the **" offspring"** of the first.

Shortly after this prophecy was given, Sennacherib attacked the land of the Philistines. Some might think this was the second attack mentioned

---

22 A few translations render the word ***when*** in each place it occurs in this passage as ***if*** or ***should***, from an alternate meaning of the Hebrew word ***kiy***. (word number 3588 in Strong's Hebrew Dictionary) But the overwhelming majority of all translations render Micah 5:5-6 essentially as given in our version. If this passage were merely a boast, as such a translation makes it, this would be the only such boast in scripture. But if the majority rendering is correct, this is only one of a number of prophecies foretelling a future Assyrian invasion.

in this prophecy. But this would require that the first attack be one that had been made by either Tiglath-Pileser III or Sargon II. Each of these previous Assyrian kings had been an ancestor of Sennacherib. Each of them had conquered Philistia. And both of them were dead. But the words **"the rod that struck you is broken"** could not realistically be applied to either of them. The power of Assyria had not been **"broken"** when either of these kings had died. On the other hand, both Isaiah 37:35 and 2 Kings 19:35 tell of a most remarkable destruction of Sennacherib's army by **"the angel of the Lord."** The words **"the rod that struck you is broken"** clearly fit this defeat. These facts make it clear that Sennacherib is the first attacker in this prophecy, not the second one.

The future attack **"will come from the north."** For the significance of this, see the section below on **"the king of the North."** (pages 54 to 55)

In the first chapter of Nahum **"*one* Who plots evil against the LORD, A wicked counselor,"** (verse 11) comes forth from Nineveh, (Nahum 2:8 and 3:7) the ancient capitol of Assyria.[23] In the next to the last verse of the prophecy, this **"wicked counselor"** is expressly called the **"king of Assyria."** (Nahum 3:18) The Lord declares that He will make **"an utter end"** of this invasion, adding that **"affliction will not rise up a second time."** (Nahum 1:9) He then tells His people that **"though I have afflicted you, I will afflict you no more."** (verse 12) The Divine history and many prophecies clearly show that Judah's affliction did not end at the destruction of Sennacherib. The Assyrian invasion was only the beginning of her great and long affliction, which has not yet ended. Indeed, their greatest affliction is still future.

Both the severity and the long duration of this affliction are stressed in the fifth through the tenth chapters of Isaiah. The twenty-fifth verse of the fifth chapter tells us, **"Therefore the anger of the LORD is aroused against His people; He has stretched out His hand against them And stricken**

---

23 In the news, we often hear about the neighborhood of ancient Nineveh by its modern name of Mosul. This center of fighting in Iraq is the home of the world's largest surviving community of Assyrians.

them." Then follow the words; **"For all this His anger is not turned away, But His hand *is* stretched out still."** These last words are repeated over and over in the following chapters. (Isaiah 9:12, 9:17, 9:21, and 10:4) The significance of this doleful refrain finally appears in Isaiah 10:24-25: **"Therefore thus says the Lord GOD of hosts: 'O My people, who dwell in Zion, do not be afraid of the Assyrian. He shall strike you with a rod and lift up his staff against you, in the manner of Egypt. For yet a very little while and the indignation will cease, as will My anger in their destruction.'"**

The Lord's indignation against His people who dwell **"in Zion,"** that is, **"Jerusalem,"** (verse 32) will continue until **"the Assyrian"** is destroyed. When this takes place, however, the indignation will cease and His anger will finally be **"turned away."** How fitting it is that the first of the gentile conquerors of God's people should also be the last; that Judah's thousands of years of suffering should finally be ended in the destruction of their first great oppressor.

The king of the North

The king of the revived northern splinter of the empire of Alexander the Great, that is, the Seleucid empire, in Daniel 11:40-45. The third verse of this chapter said that **"a mighty king"** would arise. We then read that **"when he has arisen, his kingdom shall be broken up and divided toward the four winds of heaven, but not among his posterity nor according to his dominion with which he ruled; for his kingdom shall be uprooted, even for others besides these."** (Daniel 11:4) The next twenty-seven verses (Daniel 11:5-32) describe a long series of wars between **"the king of the North"** and **"the king of the South."** This account covers a number of generations, mentioning events which took place over a period of approximately 130 years. Every act of **"the king of the North"** in this account was actually committed by one of the Seleucids, a dynasty that ruled out of Antioch in Syria. Every act of **"the king of the South"** was actually committed by one of the Ptolemies, a dynasty that ruled out of Alexandria in Egypt.

The Ptolemies ruled only over Egypt, but the Seleucids ruled over an empire that included almost all of the area of the previous Assyrian empire.[24] As can be seen in the map on page 230, the area which was held by both the Assyrian and Seleucid empires covers most of today's Syria and Iraq.

It is remarkable that many otherwise competent students of prophecy miss the plain testimony of this passage. They recognize that in the first twenty-seven verses **"the king of the North"** in each generation is the current ruler of the Seleucid empire. But then they say that in the last part of the chapter (the part that remains to be fulfilled) the meaning of this term changes. In the future portion of this prophecy (verses 40-45) they interpret this term to mean Gog, the king of Russia. Why would the Holy Spirit use a full twenty-seven verses to identify **"the king of the North,"** only to have the meaning change when He came to the application? This idea rebels against reason. But it is not only unreasonable, it twists the entire fabric of prophecy into a hopeless muddle. **"The king of the North"** is not Gog, but **"the Assyrian"** we examined in the last section of this book. (pages 50 to 54)

It is important to remember that when Alexander the Great died, his four generals divided his kingdom **"toward the four winds of heaven,"** as we read in Daniel 11:4. Two of these generals were Seleucus and Ptolemy, the first kings of these warring dynasties. At the time of the division, Ptolemy took the southern portion of the kingdom and Seleucus got the eastern portion.

But soon after, Seleucus also took over the northern portion and moved his throne there. When we remember this, we realize that **"the king of the North"** is not just the king of some northern land. He is the king of a particular northern land, that is, the northern splinter of Alexander's kingdom. This becomes important when we consider:

---

24 Since the Seleucids ruled out of Antioch in Syria, they are sometimes called the kings of Syria. While this is technically correct, referring to them in this way masks the true identity of **"the Assyrian."**

The male goat's little horn

In Daniel 8, the prophet saw a male goat, which **"*had* a notable horn between his eyes."** (verse 5) But **"the large horn was broken, and in place of it four notable ones came up toward the four winds of heaven."** (verse 8) Daniel was then told that **"the male goat *is* the kingdom of Greece. The large horn that *is* between its eyes *is* the first king. As for the broken *horn* and the four that stood up in its place, four kingdoms shall arise out of that nation, but not with its power."** (verses 21-22) As we have just noticed, four kingdoms arose out of the empire of Alexander the Great, the first of the great Grecian kings. **"And out of one of them came a little horn which grew exceedingly great toward the south, toward the east, and toward the Glorious *Land*."** (verse 9) The detail that this little horn came **"out of one of"** the four kingdoms shows that it can not represent either the Roman leader or the Russian one; for Alexander's empire did not include Rome or any part of Russia.

We are specifically told these things will happen **"in the latter time of their kingdom, When the transgressors have reached their fullness."** (verse 23) So we know this is an end time prophecy.

We are also told that this will happen **"in the latter time of the indignation."** (verse 19) Other translations render this as "at the final period of the indignation," (NASB) "at the latter end of the indignation," (RSV) and "in the last end of the indignation." (KJV) Comparing this with Isaiah 10:25, which we have already examined, (page 54) we again recognize **"the Assyrian,"** for **"the indignation"** will cease in his destruction. We also recognize **"the king of the North,"** because Seleucus, the first of the Seleucid kings, was one of the four that rose out of Alexander's empire.

We noticed that this **"little horn"** **"grew exceedingly great toward the south, toward the east, and toward the Glorious *Land*."** **"The Glorious *Land*"** is plainly Daniel's land, that is, Judea. But what is **"the south"** and "the east?" In identifying these areas, we must remember the point of reference. This horn represents a king. Where does this king start from? We have seen that he is **"the Assyrian."** We noticed on page 53 that he will come forth from Nineveh. (We also saw in footnote 23 on page 53 that the largest surviving community of Assyrians is in the neighborhood of ancient Nineveh, modern day Mosul.) So we realize that **"toward the south"** means south from Nineveh, or from the northern part of today's Iraq.

What is south of the northern part of today's Iraq? The ancient **"land of the Chaldeans."** We need to examine a key prophecy about this land. It begins in Jeremiah 50:1 with the words, **"The word that the LORD spoke against Babylon *and* against the land of the Chaldeans by Jeremiah the prophet."** We notice that this prophecy is not just directed **"against Babylon."** It is also directed **"against the land of the Chaldeans."**

In Jeremiah 50-51 the term **"the land of the Chaldeans"** is used no less than six times. (Jeremiah 50:1, 8, 25, 45, 51:4, 54) Also, **"Chaldea"** is used three more times. (Jeremiah 50:9, 51:24, 35) The ancient city of Babylon is gone. But **"the land of the Chaldeans"** is still there.[25]

---

25 I pass in silence over the notion that the ancient city of Babylon must be rebuilt and then destroyed again. This is based on a claim that some details prophesied about her destruction were not fulfilled. If this claim is correct, Babylon will have to be rebuilt so these prophecies can be fulfilled. But many historical facts surrounding these details are disputed. An attempt to prove which side is right would involve a long and (in my opinion) unprofitable debate.

Parts of this idea are based on questionable interpretations of scripture. For instance, Isaiah 13:19 says that **"Babylon... Will be as when God overthrew Sodom and Gomorrah."** And Jeremiah 50:40 says, **"As God overthrew Sodom and Gomorrah And their neighbors... So no one shall reside there."** Some claim these were not fulfilled because Babylon was not destroyed suddenly. It is well known that after her fall, Babylon slowly faded away over a period of several hundred years. But these scriptures do not say that **"Babylon"** would be destroyed suddenly. They say that after her destruction **"Babylon"** would be like **"Sodom and Gomorrah."** That is, that her destruction would be as complete as that of **"Sodom and Gomorrah."** Jeremiah 51:8 indeed says **"Babylon has suddenly fallen and been destroyed."** But that is immediately followed by the words **"Wail for her! Take balm for her pain; Perhaps she may be healed. We would have healed Babylon, But she is not healed."** (Jeremiah 51:8-9) These words at least imply, if not clearly stating, a delay between her fall and her final end. The next words at least imply how this was to take place. **"Forsake her, and let us go everyone to his own country."** (Jeremiah 51:9) This is exactly how Babylon was finally destroyed. Everyone just went away, until no one was left. Babylon became a ghost town, and was eventually buried by blowing sand.

Some claim Jeremiah 51:26 has not been fulfilled, because it says **"'They shall not take from you a stone for a corner Nor a stone for a foundation, But you shall be desolate forever,' says the**

In this prophecy, it is critical to notice the direction this attack comes from. Just two verses after **"the land of the Chaldeans"** was introduced in Jeremiah 50:1, we read, **"For out of the north a nation comes up against her, Which shall make her land desolate, And no one shall dwell therein. They shall move, they shall depart, Both man and beast."** (Jeremiah 50:3) The detail that this attack will come from **"the north"** is stressed by repeating it four times in the two chapters of this prophecy. (Jeremiah 50:3, 9, 41, 51:48)

This attack comes **"out of the north."** But what of the attack that conquered the ancient city of Babylon? This was made by the Medes and the Persians. Daniel 8:3 represents these kings as **"a ram which had two horns, and the two horns *were* high; but one *was* higher than the other, and the higher *one* came up last."** Daniel 8:20 specifically tells us that this ram's two horns **"*are* the kings of Media and Persia."** The first head of this alliance was **"Darius the Mede."** (Daniel 5:31) He was soon succeeded by his partner **"Cyrus the Persian."** (Daniel 6:28)[26] Cyrus was much greater than his partner Darius, and scripture speaks thus of him:

> "Thus says the Lord to His anointed,
>
> To Cyrus, whose right hand I have held—To subdue nations before him And loose the armor of kings, To open before him the double doors, So that the gates will not be shut: 'I will go before you And make the crooked places straight; I will break in pieces the gates of bronze And cut the bars of iron. I will give you the treasures of darkness And hidden riches of secret places, That you may know that I, the Lord, Who call *you* by your name, *Am* the God of Israel." (Isaiah 45:1-3)

This prophecy continues, **"'My counsel shall stand, And I will do all My pleasure,' Calling a bird of prey from the east, The man who executes**

LORD." They say this has not been fulfilled because Babylon has long been mined for bricks. But a brick is not a stone. These ruins cannot be mined for stone because ancient Babylon was not made of stone, but of brick.

26 History, not scripture, tells us this was only two years later.

My counsel, from a far country. Indeed I have spoken *it;* I will also bring it to pass. I have purposed *it;* I will also do it."** (Isaiah 46:10-11)

It calls Cyrus **"a bird of prey from the east."** Again, we read in Isaiah 41:2, **"Who raised up one from the east? Who in righteousness called him to His feet? Who gave the nations before him, And made *him* rule over kings? Who gave *them* as the dust *to* his sword, As driven stubble to his bow?"** While this passage does not name Cyrus, its parallel to Isaiah 46 makes the reference clear.

So we see that the conqueror of ancient Babylon came **"from the east."** Since the attack in Jeremiah 50-51 comes **"out of the north,"** as we noticed on page 58, this passage cannot speak of the same attack. But what attack does it speak of?

Daniel 8:9 tells us the male goat's little horn will grow **"toward the South."** Jeremiah 50-51 tells us **"the land of the Chaldeans,"** will be destroyed by a nation that comes **"out of the north."** We noticed on page 57 that the point of reference for the little horn's growth is the northern portion of today's Iraq and that **"the land of the Chaldeans"** is the southern portion of today's Iraq. It is therefore clear that if Daniel 8 and Jeremiah 50-51 refer to the same general time period, they speak of the same event.

We noticed on page 56 that the male goat's little horn represents a king that will come **"in the latter time of the indignation."** (Daniel 8:19) So we know this is an end time prophecy. But what about the attack on **"the land of the Chaldeans?"** Again, we find the answer in the opening verses of the prophecy. We read, **"'In those days and in that time,' says the LORD, 'The children of Israel shall come, They and the children of Judah together; With continual weeping they shall come, And seek the LORD their God.'"** (Jeremiah 50:4) This prophecy mentions **"the children of Israel"** and **"the children of Judah"** as two distinct groups. And it specifically says they will come **"together."** In Ezra 1:5 **"The heads of the fathers'** *houses* **of Judah and Benjamin, and the priests and the Levites, with all whose spirits God had** moved" returned to Judea. But this company did not include **"the children of Israel."** That is, as a group different from **"the children of Judah."**[27] Indeed, Israel, as distinct from Judah, has never returned to her land.

But further down in this prophecy, its timing is made even more clear. **"'In those days and in that time,' says the LORD, 'The iniquity of Israel shall be sought, but *there shall be* none; And the sins of Judah, but they shall not be found; For I will pardon those whom I preserve.'"** (Jeremiah 50:20) There can be no question that this has not yet happened. But it will happen **"In those days and at that time."**

Thus we see that Jeremiah 50-51 unquestionably refers to the same time period as Daniel 8. From this we see that the male goat's little horn, who is also **"the Assyrian"** and **"the king of the North"** is the northern power that will attack **"the land of the Chaldeans."**

We noticed on page 57 that the male goat's little horn will grow **"toward the south, toward the east, and toward the Glorious *Land*."** In the same place we also noticed that as **"the Assyrian,"** he will rise in the northern portion of today's Iraq. We have traced his growth **"toward the south."** But what of his growth **"toward the east?"** East from the northern portion of today's Iraq is the ancient nation of Media, the northern portion of today's Iran. But the meaning appears to be that he will grow **"toward the east"** after he grows **"toward the south."** That would mean he will grow into ancient Persia, rather than ancient Media. This is the southern portion of today's Iran, the area that was previously called Elam. We read concerning Elam:

> **"'Behold, I will break the bow of Elam, The foremost of their might. Against Elam I will bring the four winds From the four quarters of heaven, And scatter them toward all those winds; There shall be no nations where the outcasts of Elam will not go. For I will cause Elam to be dismayed before their enemies And before those who seek their life. I will bring disaster upon**

---
27 The prophetic difference between these terms is discussed on page 79 and in footnote 56 on page 81. See also page 212.

them, My fierce anger,' says the Lord; 'And I will send the sword after them Until I have consumed them. I will set My throne in Elam, And will destroy from there the king and the princes,' says the Lord."** (Jeremiah 49:35-38)

While the timing of this attack is not given, it seems to refer to the eastern growth of the male goat's little horn. No scripture expressly ties these two prophecies together, so this is only an interpretation. As an interpretation, it may be incorrect. But whether it is correct or not, Daniel 8:9 expressly tells us that this evil king, who will arise in the northern portion of today's Iraq, will successfully attack the area occupied by today's Iran.

Finally, Daniel's informer said: **"And in the latter time of their kingdom, When the transgressors have reached their fullness, A king shall arise, Having fierce features, Who understands sinister schemes. His power shall be mighty, but not by his own power; He shall destroy fearfully, And shall prosper and thrive; He shall destroy the mighty, and *also* the holy people ... And he shall exalt *himself* in his heart. He shall destroy many in *their* prosperity."** (Daniel 8:23-25) Compare this with the Assyrian's overwhelming attack on Immanuel's land in Isaiah 8:7-8 and his arrogance as described in Isaiah 10:7-14. Compare it also with the **"great fury"** of **"the king of the North"** as he returns from Egypt **"to destroy and annihilate many"**; (Daniel 11:44) planting **"the tents of his palace between the seas and the glorious holy mountain."** (Daniel 11:45) Thus we see that **"the male goat's little horn"** is the same as **"the Assyrian,"** who is also **"the king of the North,"** and as we shall see, the **"one who makes desolate."**

The one who makes desolate

We have already noticed (page 28) **"the prince who is to come."** in the first part of Daniel 9:27. **"Then he shall confirm a covenant with many for one week; But in the middle of the week He shall bring an end to sacrifice and offering." In the same place we also noticed the **"one who makes desolate"** in the last part of the verse. **"And on the wing of abominations shall be one who makes desolate, Even until the consummation, which is determined, Is poured out on the desolate."** But we have not specifically noticed the change in actors that occurs at this point. In the previous sentence the actor is **"he,"** clearly meaning **"the prince who is to come."** But in this sentence the actor changes to **"one."** From this we see that at this point another character is introduced. This is more than just a matter of interpretation. It is a matter of the basic structure of language. The **"one who makes desolate"** is not the same person as **"the prince who is to come."** He is someone new. But who is he?

According to Daniel 9:27, this **"one who makes desolate"** shall come **"on the wing of abominations."** We read in Jeremiah 10:22, **"Behold, the noise of the report has come, And a great commotion out of the north country, To make the cities of Judah desolate, a den of jackals."** This attack from the north will come **"Because of the evil of"** the doings of the **"men of Judah and inhabitants of Jerusalem."** (Jeremiah 4:4, see verses 6, 7, 10, and 14)

Remember that the Lord said of the Assyrian, **"I will send him against an ungodly nation, And against the people of My wrath."** (Isaiah 10:6, page 51) In Daniel 8:12 it is **"Because of transgression"** that **"an army was given over *to the horn* to oppose the daily *sacrifices.*"** The transgression mentioned in these passages is not just some kind of general evil, but a specific outrage. In Daniel 8:13 this outrage is called **"the transgression of desolation,"** and **"both the sanctuary and the host"** are given **"to be trampled under foot."**

Our Lord spoke of this in Matthew 24:15-21:

> **"Therefore when you see the *'abomination of desolation,'* spoken of by Daniel the prophet, standing in the holy place (whoever reads, let him understand), then let those who are in Judea flee to the mountains. Let him who is on the housetop not**

> go down to take anything out of his house. And let him who is in the field not go back to get his clothes. But woe to those who are pregnant and to those who are nursing babies in those days! And pray that your flight may not be in winter or on the Sabbath. For then there will be great tribulation, such as has not been since the beginning of the world until this time, no, nor ever shall be."

This is repeated in Mark 13:14-19. Can any serious student of prophecy doubt that the outrage which brings down the **"one who makes desolate"** is when **"the man of sin... the son of perdition"** **"sits as God in the temple of God, showing himself that he is God"**? (2 Thessalonians 2:4)

So we see that **"the Assyrian,"** **"the king of the North,"** the male goat's little horn, and the **"one who makes desolate,"** all represent the same individual. This can further be seen in the details of his destruction. As **"the king of the North,"** he **"shall come to his end, and no one will help him."** (Daniel 11:45) **"But I will remove far from you the northern *army*, And will drive him away into a barren and desolate land, With his face toward the eastern sea And his back toward the western sea; His stench will come up, And his foul odor will rise, Because he has done monstrous things."** (Joel 2:20) As the male goat's little horn, he **"shall be broken without *human* means."** (Daniel 8:25) As **"the Assyrian,"** he will be beaten down **"through the voice of the LORD."** (Isaiah 30:31) And finally, **"Assyria shall fall by a sword not of man, And a sword not of mankind shall devour him. But he shall flee from the sword, And his young men shall become forced labor."**[28] (Isaiah 31:8)

The widespread failure to notice this oppressor has led to many errors in interpreting Bible prophecy. Not being aware that he is a distinct individual, many apply various prophecies about him to other prophetic characters. We have noticed those who confuse him with Gog. (page 55) Others apply these

---

28 We should note in passing that although Sennacherib's army was destroyed without human means and he returned home, (2 Kings 19:35-36) neither scripture nor any ancient monument or record says anything about his young men having been made slaves.

prophecies to the Roman ruler. But we saw on page 56 that neither of these can be correct, for the male goat's little horn came **"out of one of"** the kingdoms that arose out of Alexander's empire, which did not include Rome or Russia.

We also saw (page 62) that the **"one who makes desolate"** is not the same person as **"the prince who is to come."** Since **"the prince who is to come"** is clearly the Roman ruler, the **"one who makes desolate"** has to be someone else.

Some think the Roman ruler will invade Judea because the Jews will refuse to accept his divine claims. They forget that at this time he will be in covenant with their rulers. (see page 10) This is referred to in Isaiah 28:14-15, where the Lord says, **"Therefore hear the word of the Lord, you scornful men, Who rule over this people who *are* in Jerusalem. Because you have said, 'We have made a covenant with death, And with Sheol we are in agreement. When the overflowing scourge passes through, It will not come to us, For we have made lies our refuge, And under falsehood we have hidden ourselves.'"**

From this we see that the rulers of Jerusalem will accept this ruler's wicked pretension. Their covenant will not only be with the Roman ruler, as we saw in Daniel 9:27, (page 10) but with him in his claim to be God.[29] Thus we see that the supposed reason for this attack will not even exist. The leaders of the Jews will not reject his blasphemous claims. They will accept them. Only the righteous will stand against this monstrous lie, and because of this[30] they will have to flee for their lives, as noted on pages 16, 17, 26, 62, 105.

This wicked Roman will indeed try to destroy Israel's righteous, for we read that **"the serpent spewed water out of his mouth like a flood after the woman, that he might cause her to be carried away by the flood."** (Revelation 12:15) But the next verse says that **"the earth helped the woman,**

---

[29] Some think that the words, **"Your covenant with death will be annulled, And your agreement with Sheol will not stand; When the overflowing scourge passes through, Then you will be trampled down by it."** (Isaiah 28:18) mean the Roman ruler will break this covenant. But the language of prophecy is very precise. This scripture does not say he will break the covenant, but that it will be **"annulled;"** and that it **"will not stand."**

[30] For a second reason they have to flee, see page 106.

and the earth opened its mouth and swallowed up the flood which the dragon had spewed out of his mouth." (Revelation 12:16) We saw on page 19 that the woman represents the righteous remnant of Israel, and on page 18 that the dragon portrays Satan acting through Roman power. Thus we see that although the Roman will try to destroy these few righteous Jews, he will fail. For more detail on this see pages 109 to 110.

But **"the one who makes desolate"** will succeed. Cruel and having no mercy, (Jeremiah 6:23) this plunderer will **"suddenly"** come upon the land. (Jeremiah 4:20, 6:26) There will be no strength to resist his attack, for **"He shall come against princes as *though* mortar, As the potter treads clay."** (Isaiah 41:25) **"He shall also enter the Glorious Land."** (Daniel 11:41) The daily progress of his advance on Jerusalem is detailed in Isaiah 10:28-32. (see pages 113 to 116) He will also overthrow many other countries, including Egypt and Ethiopia, (Isaiah 20:2-6; Daniel 11:41-43) but not **"Edom, Moab, and the prominent people of Ammon."** (Daniel 11:41) All this will happen **"at the time of the end."** (Daniel 11:40)

This confusion between the Roman and Assyrian rulers is compounded by the confusion between the Roman and Jewish leaders, which we discussed on pages 42 to 44. This leads to a confusion of Daniel 11, where we read:

> "At the time of the end the king of the South shall attack him; and the king of the North shall come against him like a whirlwind, with chariots, horsemen, and with many ships; and he shall enter the countries, overwhelm *them*, and pass through. He shall also enter the Glorious Land, and many *countries* shall be overthrown; but these shall escape from his hand: Edom, Moab, and the prominent people of Ammon." (Daniel 11:40-41)

Most students know that the word **"him"** in the first part of verse 40 refers to **"the king."** But those who think **"the king"** is the Roman **"prince"** fail to see the change of actors in verse 40. They think the repeated use of the word **"he"** in the last part of verse 40 and in verses 41-45 also refer to **"the king."** Some of them defend this idea by saying it all turns on how this passage is interpreted. (see page 208) But that is a serious error.

We are not free to interpret Scripture as we please. An interpretation of any part of the Bible is not correct if it disagrees with any other part of the Bible. (see page 181) If Daniel 11:40-41 were taken by itself, this interpretation would indeed be possible. But it completely fails to take into account the many scriptures about **"the Assyrian"** (pages 50 to 54) and **"the king."** (pages 42 to 44)

In the context of interpreting Daniel 11:40-41, one of the most important prophecies is Isaiah 7:17-20:

> **"'The LORD will bring the king of Assyria upon you and your people and your father's house—days that have not come since the day that Ephraim departed from Judah.'**
>
> **"And it shall come to pass in that day *That* the LORD will whistle for the fly That *is* in the farthest part of the rivers of Egypt, And for the bee that *is* in the land of Assyria. They will come, and all of them will rest In the desolate valleys and in the clefts of the rocks, And on all thorns and in all pastures. In the same day the Lord will shave with a hired razor, With those from beyond the River, with the king of Assyria, The head and the hair of the legs, And will also remove the beard."**

Here we see that the Lord will bring Assyria and Egypt upon the people of Ahaz (see verse 10) that is, upon Judah. From the way it is stated, the meaning is plainly that they will come at the same time. This cannot refer to Sennacherib's invasion of Judea, because at that time the king of Egypt was allied to Hezekiah. (see 2 Kings 18:21 and Isaiah 36:6) The Bible doesn't say much about this Egyptian king. But according to history he came to take part in the war, but was defeated by Sennacherib in the land of the Philistines before he reached Judea. History also says the same thing had happened when the Assyrian king Sargon attacked approximately

20 years earlier. Sargon also defeated the Egyptian army before it reached Judea. There has never been a time when Assyrian and Egyptian armies invaded Judea at the same time, so this prophecy remains to be fulfilled in the future.

When we realize the true identity of **"the king"** and remember **"the Assyrian,"** and the fact that Assyria and Egypt will invade Judea at the same time, we see that the only reasonable interpretation of Daniel 11:40 is that:

"The king of the South" (the king of Egypt) **"shall attack him,"** that is, **"the king"** (of Judah) and **"the king of the North"** (the Assyrian) **"shall come against him**[31] **like a whirlwind."** The actor has changed from **"the king of the South"** to **"the king of the North,"** who, coming **"like a whirlwind, with chariots, horsemen, and with many ships... shall enter the countries, overwhelm *them*, and pass through."** But **"the king"** (of Judah) remains the object of the action, for we read **"He shall also enter the Glorious Land,"** which is plainly Daniel's land Judea. (verse 41) This interpretation agrees with all the prophecies about **"the Assyrian"** and **"the king."**

So we see it is backwards to base interpretations about **"the Assyrian"** on interpretations of Daniel 11. Instead, the explicitly stated prophecies about **"the Assyrian"** must be considered when interpreting Daniel 11.

Finally, there is one more reason the Roman **"prince"** can not be the one who will attack Judah. The Roman and Jewish leaders will remain allied until the end. We read in Revelation 19:20 that **"the beast was captured, and with him the false prophet who worked signs in his presence, by which he deceived those who received the mark of the beast and those who worshiped his image. These two were cast alive into the lake of fire burning with brimstone."**

---

31 Throughout this book (see pages 68, 110, 111, 112, 122, 204) this second **"him"** is interpreted as a reference to **"the king."** If this interpretation is correct, the meaning is that **"the king of the South"** and **"the king of the North"** both attack **"the king."** But if this second **"him"** refers to **"the king of the South,"** the meaning is that when **"the king of the South"** attacks **"the king,"** **"the king of the North"** will in turn attack **"the king of the South."** To me, this interpretation seems less likely, but it is possible. But this is not a very important point, for in either case **"the king of the North"** will **"enter the glorious land."** So the only question is why he will do it.

We saw on pages 35 to 40 that **"the beast"** is the Roman ruler and on pages 47 to 48 that **"the false prophet"** is the Jewish **king**.

The Fourth Key Individual

The king of the South

The king of Egypt, the southern splinter of the empire of Alexander the Great. (Daniel 11:40) Identified in Daniel 11:2-27 by the fact that every act of **"the king of the South"** in this passage was actually committed by one of the ancient Ptolemies, a dynasty that ruled out of Alexandria in Egypt. He will attack the land of Judah, which is now called Israel, at the same time as the Assyrian, or **"the king of the North,"** (Isaiah 7:18, 10:24-25; Daniel 11:40) but the northern king will overwhelm and defeat him, (Daniel 11:42-43) becoming **"a cruel master, And a fierce king"** over Egypt. (Isaiah 19:4)

The Fifth Key Individual

Gog

The last great attacker of Israel. (For why I say this, see pages 101 to 104.) In Ezekiel 38 and 39 he leads **"a great company"** (chapter 38:4) down from **"the far north"** (38:15) **"into the land of those brought back from the sword *and* gathered from many people on the mountains of Israel."** (38:8) Gog will come down with an evil intent **"to take plunder and to take booty."** (38:12) But there will be a deeper reason for his attack. The Lord will bring him against Israel **"so that the nations may know Me, when I am hallowed in you, O Gog, before their eyes."** (38:16) The Lord himself will bring Gog down against Israel. He will, like Pharaoh of old, be used of God to display his power in such a great way that even the Gentiles will understand. (Ezekiel 39:23) The Lord says:

> "Son of man, set your face against Gog, of the land of Magog, the prince of Rosh, Meshech, and Tubal, and prophesy against him, and say, 'Thus says the Lord GOD: "Behold, I *am* against you, O Gog, the prince of Rosh, Meshech, and Tubal. I will turn you around, put hooks into your jaws, and lead you out, with all your army, horses, and horsemen, all splendidly clothed, a great company *with* bucklers and shields, all of them handling swords. Persia, Ethiopia, and Libya are with them, all of them *with* shield and helmet; Gomer and all its troops; the house of Togarmah *from* the far north and all its troops; many people *are* with you."'" (Ezekiel 38:2-6)

Who is this great company, and where do they come from? Gog is **"of the land of Magog."** Josephus said that Magog founded the Magogites, but that the Greeks called them Scythians.[32] The Scythians were a well known nomadic tribe in what is now called Russia. So this indicates Gog will come from Russia. (See the map on page 230.)

There is a problem in the translation of the next phrase. The Hebrew word *rosh* means *top, or chief.* (word number 7218 in Strong's Hebrew Dictionary) If we assume this is only a word, the proper translation is "chief prince of Meshech and Tubal." If, however, *rosh* is a name, the proper translation is, as given in our translation, **"prince of Rosh, Meshech, and Tubal."** The various translations are divided on this point, some giving one reading, some the other. Some might ask, was the R a capital letter, indicating a name? But ancient Hebrew did not have capital and small letters. We know the ancient Jews considered that a name from the Septuagint,[33] a Hebrew translation of the scriptures into Greek, believed to date from the second century B.C.

---

32 "Jewish Antiquities," by Flavius Josephus, Book 1, chapter 6, sec. 123, from "The New Complete Works of Josephus," trans. by William Whiston, revised by Paul L. Maier, Grand Rapids: Kregel, 1999, pg. 57.

33 In the Septuagint, this Hebrew word was rendered as Ros, preserving its sound as closely as possible in Greek, rather than by translating it as protos, the Greek adjective meaning chief. In translating, it is standard practice to reproduce the sound of a name as closely as possible, rather than attempting to reproduce the meaning of the name. This proves that the scholars that translated the Septuagint considered this word a name, rather than an adjective.

It is well known that this is commonly thought to mean Russia. This has been taught since the fourth and fifth centuries.[34] But is it correct? I had long heard this was commonly believed in Russia, so I decided to test this on a Russian I once knew. The man was not someone who would have had any prior instruction in the meaning of this passage. He was, in fact, an atheistic engineer trained in communist universities in the former USSR. I handed him a Russian Bible opened to this passage and asked him to read it and tell me in English what it said. He read it thus: "See, I am against you, oh Gogae, uh– uh– second step." I asked, "prince?" he answered, "Yes." He continued reading, "prince of Russia, Meshchovsk, and Tobolsk." I asked, "Russia, is that what it says?" He answered, "Well, no, not exactly, but that's what it means." Then he wrote on a slip of paper the word "Rosh" and said "people." He then wrote "Rosha" and said "country." He was therefore saying that it called Gog the "prince of the people of Russia." It is interesting that without hesitation he read Meshech as Meshchovsk[35] and Tubal as Tobolsk.[36]

Meshech and Tubal are a study in themselves. They are often seen in ancient writings and are almost always mentioned together. On the basis of ancient Greek and Persian accounts, modern historians believe the Moschi

---

34 In 378 A.D., Bishop Ambrose of Milan, wrote concerning Ezekiel 38-39, "Gog is the Goth, whose coming forth we have already seen, and over whom victory in days to come is promised, according to the word of the Lord:" ("Exposition of the Christian Faith," by Ambrose, book II, chapter XVI, section 138, tran. by H. De Romestin, M.A., asst. by E. De Romestin, M.A., and H. T. F. Duckworth, M.A. - From "Nicene and Post Nicene Fathers, Second Series," ed. Philip Schaff, D.D., LL.D. and Henry Wace, D.D., Edinburgh, 1884, reprint by Hendrickson, Peabody, 2012, vol 10, pg. 241.) It is well known that the Goths came out of what is now Russia.

Again, Proclus, who was Patriarch of Constantinople from 434 to 447, applied Ezekiel 38 to the barbarians who were invading (from what is now Russia.) "The Ecclesiastical History of Socrates Scholasticus," book VII, chapter XLIII, tran. by A. C. Zenis, D.D. (from "Nicene and Post Nicene Fathers, Second Series," ed. Philip Schaff, D.D., LL.D. and Henry Wace, D.D., Edinburgh, 1884, American Edition by A. Cleveland Coxe, D.D., Peabody, 1994, vol 2, pg. xxx.) In his highly reputed work titled "A History of Russia," pp. 138-139, (New Haven: Yale University Press, 1943,) George Vernadsky said this sermon was the earliest known usage of the name Rus in any historical document. He cited his source for this claim as Nicephorus Kallistus, XIV, 37. But as this ancient source has never been translated into English, it would be pointless to include a quotation from that book.

35 A Russian city about 135 miles southwest of Moscow. See the map on page 230.
36 A Russian city about 1200 miles east of Moscow. See the map on page 230.

(the Greek form of Meshech) lived near the Black Sea, just north of Armenia and a short distance south of the Caucasus Mountains.[37] As can be seen in the map on page 73, Ptolemy's atlas[38] shows the Mosthici Mountains in this area.

These mountains are now called the Moschii Mountains, or sometimes the Suram Mountains. The "Barrington Atlas of the Greek and Roman World" shows them as the Moschici Mountains.[39] It also shows them inhabited by the "Moschoi." This area is now in Caucasian Georgia. (Not the American Georgia, but part of the Commonwealth of Independent States, the former USSR.)

In 1944 the Soviet government deported approximately 100,000 Moslem "Meskhi" from this region to distant parts of the USSR for fear they would side with Turkey in a possible future war.[40]

But Josephus said Meshech was the Cappadocians.[41] As noted above, modern historians favor the Greek and Persian accounts. But ancient Christians considered Josephus very reliable. How could both Josephus and the Greek and Persian writers be correct about where these people lived?

As can be seen in the map on the following page. Cappadocia originally stretched all the way to the Mosthici Mountains. It therefore originally extended from southern Turkey to the area where the Greek and Persian writers located the Moschi. Pontus, which lay between these two nations at the time of Josephus, was not a different race. It had been created for political reasons from the northern part of Cappadocia. (See the map on page 230.) Thus we see that these two nations have a common root. If this were the case,

---

37 "Anatolia - Studies in Strabo," by Ronald Styme, pg. 68. Oxford University Press, Oxford, 1995.

38 This map, which shows the region between the Black (Pontus) Sea and the Caspian Sea, was originally published in Alexandria by Claudius Ptolemy in his famous atlas, "Geographia." While its exact date is unknown, this atlas was produced around 50 or 60 years after the Revelation is believed to have been written. No originals of this atlas have survived, but many libraries have reproductions of various mediaeval copies. The copy in this book was published in Venice by Giordano Ziletti in 1574.

39 "Barrington Atlas of the Greek and Roman World," ed. Richard J. A. Talbert, Princeton, Princeton University Press, 2000, Map #88. Based on the most up-to-date historical scholarship and archeological discoveries, this is the most authoritative atlas of the classical world available today.

40 "The Modern Encyclopedia of Russian and Soviet History," ed. by Joseph L. Wieczynski, vol. 22, pg. 7. Gulf Breeze: Academic International Press, 1981.

41 Josephus, on the same page as footnote 32 on page , but in section 125.

it would have been only natural for Josephus to name the largest branch of the race, that is, Cappadocia, even though the name Meshech was better preserved in a different place.

But this raises the question, how did these people end up in Russia? Cappadocia remained a nation until the Moslem invasion in the mid to late eleventh century. During this period the Moslems conquered almost all of modern day Turkey, Armenia, and Georgia. The inhabitants were forced to convert to Islam or face intolerable persecution. This caused widespread panic and most of the population fled to foreign lands. The name Moscow[42] first appears in Russian history about a hundred years later, as an entry for the year 1147[43] in "The Nikonian Chronicle." This chronicle was written in the years 1520-1550. It lists the Meschera as a tribe living along the Oka River,[44] which passes about 60 miles south of Moscow. (See the map on page 230.) "The Russian Primary Chronicle,"[45] written in 1116, also lists the tribes in this area, but this name is not included.

---

42 The connection between this name and the name Moschi is evident when we see its Russian form, Muskova.
43 "The Nikonian Chronicle," trans. by Serg A. and Betty Jean Zenkovsky, vol. 2, pg. 27. Princeton: The Kingston Press, 1982.
44 "The Nikonian Chronicle," vol. 1, pg. 7.
45 "The Russian Primary Chronicle, Laurentian Text," copied in 1377 from the 1116 text. trans. and edited by Samuel Hazzard Cross and Olgerd P. Sherbowitz-Wetzor, pg. 55. Cambridge,: The Mediaeval Academy of America, 1953.

— 73 —

Third Asian Map From Ziletti's 1574 Reproduction of Ptolemy's Second Century Atlas Titled "Geographia"

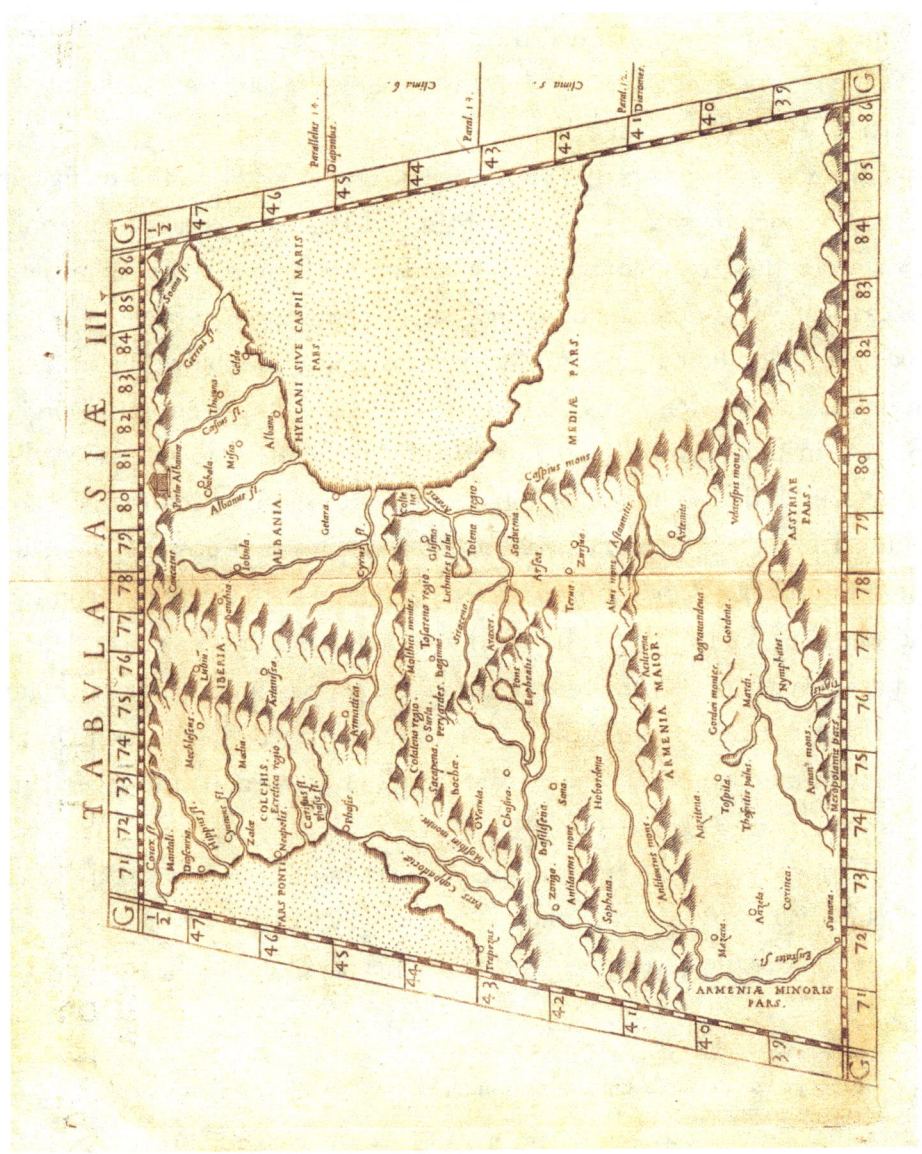

Scanned from original map in author's private library

The absence of any form of the name Meshech from a description of this area made at approximately the time of the Moslem invasion, coupled with its appearance soon after, strongly suggests that Moschi refugees from Cappadocia and Pontus settled there. As can be seen in the map on page 230, their name is still preserved in this area by the name Meshchovsk, as noted on page 70.

Josephus also wrote that Tubal was the Iberians.[46] From this we would naturally conclude that Tubal was Spain and Portugal, as it is commonly known that these two nations occupy the Iberian Peninsula. But in ancient times there was another Iberia, which can be plainly seen in Ptolemy's atlas (see page 73) and the Barrington Atlas.[47] This nation was between Armenia and the Caucasus Mountains, northeast of the Moschi in present day Georgia. (See the map on page 230.) The name Tubal is preserved to this day in the name Tbilisi, the capitol of Georgia. As the Russian city Tobolsk was not founded until the middle of the sixteenth century, it is quite possible that refugees from the Moslem invasion of Georgia settled in this region, becoming the source of the name of Tobolsk. Thus we understand that Meshech and Tubal are very possibly the root stocks of the peoples around Moscow and Tobolsk. Even if this is not correct, Meshech and Tubal definitely fled to locations within the borders of the present day Commonwealth of Independent States, the former USSR.

Armenia claims to be the house of Togarmah. This is recorded in detail in "The History of the Armenians,"[48] written by Moses of Khronosis only fifty years after the development of the Armenian alphabet. As can be seen

---

46 Josephus, on the same page as footnote 32, but in section 124.
47 "Barrington Atlas," same map as footnote 39.
48 Available in English as the "History of the Armenians," by Moses Khorenats'i, trans. Robert W. Thompson, Cambridge: Harvard University Press, 1978. See pages 74, 84, 86, and 92. In this translation Togarmah is spelled T'orgom. On page 86 he calls Armenia "the house of T'orgom," exactly the term used in Ezekiel. On page 74 he lists T'orgom as the son of T'iras, son of Gamer, son of Yapeth, son of Noah. Compare this with Genesis 10:1-3. **"Now this is the genealogy of the sons of Noah: Shem, Ham, and Japheth. And sons were born to them after the flood. The sons of Japheth were Gomer, Magog, Madai, Javan, Tubal, Meshech, and Tiras. The sons of Gomer were Ashkenaz, Riphath, and Togarmah."**

in the map on page 230, Armenia was once much larger than it is today. As was noted on page 72, when everyone was being forced to convert to Islam or face persecution, most Armenians fled to other lands. Many medieval Armenian manuscripts were copied in various places along the northern shores of the Black Sea, in the region of present day Ukraine.[49]

Many think Gomer is Germany, but Josephus clearly identified Gomer as the Galatians.[50]

From this we might think Gomer is Turkey, as Galatia is well known as a province in Asia Minor. But Galatia was so called because it was a settlement of Gauls. Further, we saw in footnote 48 (page 74) that Biblical Gomer was called Gamer in Armenia. The Assyrians called this people the Gamerraa[51] and described them sufficiently to identify them as the people whom the Greeks called Cimmerians.[52] It is common knowledge that the Gauls were descended from the Cimmerians. And that the Gauls are the ancestors of the people group that today is called Celts or Kelts. (See the map on page 229.)

As to the others, the name of Persia persisted into the twentieth century, when it was changed to Iran. And the names Ethiopia and Libya continue to the present day.

---

49 "Colophons of Armenian Manuscripts, 1301-1480," by Avedias K. Sanjian, Cambridge: Harvard University Press, 1969. (A colophon is a note added at the beginning or end of a manuscript, telling who copied it. These are of historical interest because they often included comments about the conditions under which the manuscript was copied.) Specific page numbers would be pointless because this note applies to many of the colophons included in this book.

50 Josephus, on the same page as footnote 32, section 123.

51 "The Royal Correspondence of the Assyrian Empire," translated and transliterated by Leroy Waterman, Ann Arbor: University of Michigan Press, 1930. part I, pg. 74. On pg. 75 this Assyrian word is translated "Cimmerians," with a footnote identifying them as the classical Cimmerii and Biblical Gomer. (part III, pg. 53) This is also noted on page 246 of "State Archives of Assyria, Volume V - The Correspondence of Sargon II, Part II", ed by Giovanni B. Lanfranchi and Simo Parpola, Helsinki University Press, 1990.

52 Another letter in the first reference of footnote 51 called the Gimiraa "the people of the steppe." (part II, pg. 361) It is well known that the ancient homeland of the Cimmerians was the steppe region of southern Russia. Yet another letter in this series locates the lands of Guriania and Nagiu as between the lands of Urartu and Gamirra. (part I, pg 101) This is also stated in a letter on page 75 of the second reference of footnote 51, except that the land of Nagiu was not mentioned. It is well known that Urartu is another name for Armenia, which was on Assyria's northern border, so we know the land of Gamirra, or Cimmeria, was significantly north of Armenia. That would place it somewhere in southern Russia. (The Scythians eventually drove them out of that region and they settled in central and western Europe, as shown in the map on page 229.)

From all this we can safely conclude that Gog is from the land of the Scythians, that is, present day Russia. And that Rosh, Mesech, and Tubal all refer to Russia or to lands dominated by Russia. Gog's associates include Ethiopia, Libya, Iran, Armenia, and the Celtic peoples (most of western Europe, including the British Isles, with their North American and Australian descendants).

Because Gog comes from **"the far north,"** (Ezekiel 38:6, 15; 39:2) many have confused him with **"the king of the North."** But **"the far north"** is a different term than **"the north."** Even such small differences as this are significant in Bible prophecy. We have seen that **"the king of the North"** is the king of the revived Seleucid empire, which is also the revived Assyrian empire. But Gog is king of Russia. The beast and his ten nation alliance will make a seven year (one week) treaty with Judah, which is now called Israel. But Judah's desolator attacks **"in the middle of the week."** (Daniel 9:27) If this attacker were Gog, the Celtic nations would have to withdraw from the beast's alliance to join the attackers. But as can be seen in the map on page 229, these nations will make up a very large part of that alliance. They will still be part of it when the Lord comes, for we read that **"The ten horns which you saw are ten kings who have received no kingdom as yet, but they receive authority for one hour as kings with the beast. These are of one mind, and they will give their power and authority to the beast. These will make war with the Lamb, and the Lamb will overcome them, for He is Lord of lords and King of kings; and those *who are* with Him *are* called, chosen, and faithful."** (Revelation 17:13-14) So Gog cannot be **"the king of the north."**

Again, the attack by **"the king of the North"** will usher in a **"time of trouble, such as never was since there was a nation *Even* to that time."** (Daniel 12:1) But Gog's attack will usher in the time of Israel's blessing, as we read in Ezekiel 39:28-29, **"'Then they shall know that I *am* the Lord their God, who sent them into captivity among the nations, but also brought them back to their land, and left none of them captive any longer. And I** will not hide My face from them anymore; for I shall have poured out My Spirit on the house of Israel,' says the Lord GOD." Again, we saw on page 17 that this "great tribulation, such as has not been since the beginning of the world until this time, no, nor ever shall be" will come upon Judah. (Matthew 24:16-21) But Gog will attack Israel, not Judah.[53] The two attacks could hardly be more different.

These attackers will also be destroyed in different places. The Lord tells Gog "'You shall fall upon the mountains of Israel, you and all your troops and the peoples who *are* with you; I will give you to birds of prey of every sort and *to* the beasts of the field to be devoured. You shall fall on the open field; for I have spoken,' says the Lord GOD." (Ezekiel 39:3-5) Gog will fall "upon the mountains of Israel" and "upon the open field." But these are only general. Specific detail is also given. "It will come to pass in that day *that* I will give Gog a burial place there in Israel, the valley of those who pass by east of the sea; and it will obstruct travelers, because there they will bury Gog and all his multitude. Therefore they will call *it* the Valley of Hamon Gog." (Ezekiel 39:11)

Gog will be buried in "the valley of those who pass by east of the sea." This cannot be the place where "the northern army" is destroyed, for its "stench will come up" from "a barren and desolate land" between "the eastern sea" and "the western sea." (Joel 2:20) A place in Israel between "the eastern sea" and "the western sea" and also "east of the sea" would have to be on the Mediterranean Sea coast. But the coast of the Mediterranean between "the eastern sea" and "the western sea" is a fertile plain. No part of this plain is "barren and desolate."[54] Also, Gog "shall fall upon the mountains of Israel." (Ezekiel 39:4) The fact that these two attackers will be destroyed in different places is further prove that Gog is not "the king of the North."

---

53 For the significance of this, see page 79 and footnote 56 on page 81.
54 Some translations, including the New Century Version, God's Word to the Nations, and the New Living Translation, read "east of the Dead Sea" instead of "east of the sea." This is based on a conclusion that the Hebrew text implies the Dead Sea, even though it is not named. Only a few scholars have come to this conclusion. But if correct, this is further proof that these places are different. For a valley east of the Dead Sea could not be between "the eastern sea" and "the western sea."

Gog's burial place is also not the same as **"the Valley of Jehoshaphat,"** where the nations will be destroyed. (Joel 3:2-12) The Hebrew word translated *valley* in **"the valley of those that pass by east of the sea"** is *gay'*. (word number 1516 in Strong's Hebrew Dictionary) A *gay'* is a valley with steep, high walls, like the English word *gorge*. But the Hebrew word translated *valley* in **"the Valley of Jehoshaphat"** is *'emeq*. (word number 6010 in Strong's Hebrew Dictionary) An *'emeq* is a gentle, wide valley, like the English word *vale*.

Nor is Gog buried in Armageddon. While Megiddo, or Armageddon, is called a valley in 2 Chronicles 35:22 and in some translations of Zechariah 12:11, the Hebrew word used in these places is *biq'ah*. (word number 1237 in Strong's Hebrew Dictionary) A *biq'ah* is a wide level valley between mountains, like the English word *plain*. We look at these details to clearly understand that Gog's destruction is unique, different from all other judgments of the enemies of God's people.

To learn when this unique event will happen, we first need to notice Ezekiel 38:8. **"After many days you will be visited. In the latter years you will come into the land of those brought back from the sword *and* gathered from many people on the mountains of Israel."** Again, verse 16 plainly states that **"It will be in the latter days that I will bring you against My land, so that the nations may know Me, when I am hallowed in you, O Gog, before their eyes."** This is therefore unquestionably an end time event. It will be at a time when **"My people Israel dwell safely,"** (38:14) **"all of them dwelling without walls, and having neither bars nor gates"** (38:11) See also page 214. From these scriptures we might think the time referred to is when Judah will think it is safe because it is in covenant with the beast. But after Messiah comes they will actually be safe.

We have already noticed (page 77) that this prophecy calls the land and the people Israel, not Judah. This means the time referred to is after the Lord returns, because all Israel will not return to the land until then. (See pages 149 and 213, plus footnote 105 on page 213.)

The Jews are indeed back in the land, but the word Jew refers only to descendants of the ancient kingdom of Judah, that is, members of the tribes of Judah and Benjamin. For more information of this, see page 213. The land is now called Israel, but that is not a Biblically accurate term. Scripturally, Israel means either the ten northern tribes or the entire twelve tribes. But end time prophecy does not use this name when speaking of the two southern tribes. They are always called Judah, not Israel. For more detail on this see footnote 56 on page 81.

Details in Ezekiel 39 set the time plainly. In verse 7 the Lord says that after that time He **"will not *let them* profane"** His holy name **"anymore."** This has to be after the time of **"the man of sin... the son of perdition"** (2 Thessalonians 2:3) Because at that time **"he sits as God in the temple of God, showing himself that he is God."** (2 Thessalonians 2:4) Aside from the time when they crucified their Messiah, this will be the worst profaning of His holy name in the entire sad history of this nation. So Ezekiel 39:7 sets the time of Gog's invasion as after the time of the Antichrist.

Again, in verse 22 the Lord says that **"the house of Israel shall know that I *am* the LORD their God from that day forward"** This fixes the date as after the seven years of tribulation and before the millennium. That is because during the tribulation Judah (which is the only part of **"the house of Israel"** that will be in the land at that time) will be worshiping the Antichrist, as noted above.

But during the millennium **"No more shall every man teach his neighbor, and every man his brother, saying, 'Know the Lord,' for they all shall know Me, from the least of them to the greatest of them."** (Jeremiah 31:34) So Ezekiel 39:22 places the time of Gog's defeat at the time when they cease false worship and begin to truly worship the Lord.

Again, in verse 29 we read that after this great deliverance from Gog, the Lord **"will not hide"** His **"face from them anymore."** This means the deliverance will take place after the tribulation, because during that time **"they will cry to the Lord, But He will not hear them; He will even hide His face** from them at that time, Because they have been evil in their deeds." (Micah 3:4) We know Micah's prophecy refers to the last days because it begins **"For behold, the Lord is coming out of His place. He will come down And tread on the high places of the earth. The mountains will melt under Him, And the valleys will split Like wax before the fire, Like waters poured down a steep place."** (Micah 1:3-4) So Ezekiel 39:29 shows that the deliverance from Gog will take place after the tribulation.

This can also be seen in the absence of Assyria from the list of Gog's allies. It would seem obvious that, as enemies of Judah, which is now called Israel, the Assyrians would, if they could, enthusiastically take part in such a project. Why are they missing from this alliance? As Gog's invasion will take place after Israel repents, it will take place after Assyria has been destroyed. (see page 54)

We need to realize that Israel will not truly repent until they actually see their Messiah. At that time they will ask **"What are these wounds between your arms?"**[55] **Then he will answer, 'Those with which I was wounded in the house of my friends.'"** (Zechariah 13:6) Then **"In that day there shall be a great mourning in Jerusalem, like the mourning at Hadad Rimmon in the plain of Megiddo. And the land shall mourn, every family by itself: the family of the house of David by itself, and their wives by themselves; the family of the house of Nathan by itself, and their wives by themselves; the family of the house of Levi by itself, and their wives by themselves; the family of Shimei by itself, and their wives by themselves; all the families that remain, every family by itself, and their wives by themselves."** (Zechariah 12:11-14)

We find Gog and Magog again in Revelation 20:8, but that is a thousand years later, after the millennium. (verse 7)

---

55 I am disappointed that the New King James, which we are using, joins several other modern translations in giving up the apparent reference to the crucifixion in the King James rendering of this question, **"What are these wounds in thy hands?"** (As also rendered by Young and Darby) This is because of a difficulty in the Hebrew text, which could be literally translated **"What are these wounds between your hands?"** So the NRSV reads "on your chest," while the NIV and the NCV give "on your body."

KEY EVENTS IN BIBLE PROPHECY

Early Events - Setting the Stage

The return of Judah to her land

This ongoing event, which began in the twentieth century, was not directly prophesied anywhere in scripture. But it was a necessary part of the prophetic scheme, for the scene of prophecy opens with Judah in her land, but still rebellious. As this nation had been exiled for nearly two thousand years it could not be in the land until it had returned. Although no prophecy speaks of an unrepentant Judah returning to the land, many speak of absolutely all of Israel, including Judah, returning in true repentance to both the Lord and the land.[56] (see, for instance,

---

56 It is important to understand that in the precise language of Bible prophecy, Judah and Israel are

Ezekiel 36:10-30, Zephaniah 3:11-14, and Romans 11:26) It is obvious that this has not yet happened.

The rapture of the church

For Christians of the present time, all other prophetic events pale into nothingness beside this one great event, which the scriptures speak of in numerous places.

Jesus spoke of it, saying, **"I go to prepare a place for you. And if I go and prepare a place for you, I will come again and receive you to Myself; that where I am, *there* you may be also."** (John 14:2-3)

But we also read, **"that He may establish your hearts blameless in holiness before our God and Father at the coming of our Lord Jesus Christ with all His saints."** (1 Thessalonians 3:13)

In the first passage above our Lord says **"I will come again and receive you to Myself."** The second one speaks of **"the coming of our Lord Jesus Christ with all His saints."** It is obvious that His coming to receive us to Himself has to take place before His coming **"with all His saints."** The words used by the Holy Spirit do not allow any other conclusion. But how long before **"the coming of our Lord Jesus Christ with all His saints."** will He **"come again and receive"** us to Himself?

The answer to this question begins with the promise, **"Because you have kept My command to persevere, I also will keep you from the hour of trial which shall come upon the whole world, to test those who dwell on the earth."** (Revelation 3:10) The Greek word translated *from* in this verse is *ek*, (word number 1537 in Strong's Greek Dictionary) which indeed means *from*, but in the sense of *away from* or *out of*.

---

not the same. After Judah and Ephraim divided, the term Israel applied either to Ephraim or to the entire twelve tribes, but not to Judah. So Judah does not mean Israel, and Israel does not mean Judah. This makes it possible to understand when many prophecies apply. End time prophecies that speak of Judah's rebellion and suffering apply to Daniel's seventieth week, before the Lord returns. But prophecies that speak of a delivered, restored, or victorious Judah, Ephraim, Israel, or Judah and Israel, apply to the time after the Lord has returned and brought all Israel home. For more information on this, see pages 79, and 213.

Some imagine that this only means *out of* after being *in* the "**hour of trial.**" But Thayer's Greek-English Lexicon of the New Testament defines *ek*, as it is used in Revelation 3:10, to mean *"to keep one at a distance from."* Indeed, this becomes obvious when we consider the word "**keep**" in this phrase. This word is translated from the Greek word *tereo.* (word number 5083 in Strong's Greek Dictionary) It literally means *to guard*, but in the scriptures was usually used in the sense of our English word *keep*, and is so translated more than two-thirds of the times *tereo* occurs in the Greek text of the New Testament. So it is clear that the real meaning of this promise is to be *kept out of* "**the hour of trial.**"[57]

But what is this "**the hour of trial**" that they will be *kept out of*? The Greek word translated *hour* in this passage is *hora.* (word number 5610 in Strong's Greek Dictionary) This Greek word literally means *hour*, but is often used figuratively for a short period of time.

But what **hour** are they promised to be *kept out of*? It is not just some general period of time. It is a specific one. It is "**the hour of trial.**" It is specifically called "**the hour,**" for the word "**the**" is in the Greek text, as the word *ho*.[58] (word number 3588 in Strong's Greek Dictionary) But what "**hour of trial**" is this specific time that they are they promised to be *kept out of*? It is "**the hour of trial which shall come upon the whole world, to test those who dwell on the earth.**"

---

[57] To really understand this, we need to consider another promise made concerning a part of the same time period. The Lord said to Israel and Judah, "**Ask now, and see, Whether a man is ever in labor with child? So why do I see every man with his hands on his loins Like a woman in labor, And all faces turned pale? Alas! For that day is great, So that none is like it; And it is the time of Jacob's trouble, But he shall be saved out of it.**" (Jeremiah 30:6-7) In this case, the Hebrew word translated *saved* is *yasha'*. (word number 3467 in Strong's Hebrew Dictionary) This Hebrew word means *saved* in the sense of *succor*. In the KJV, this Hebrew word is rendered *save* 149 times, *deliver* 13 times, *help* 12 times, and once as *rescue*. We notice this to clearly understand that this Hebrew word carries an entirely different sense from the Greek word *tereo* used in Revelation 3:10. In one case, the Lord promised to help some of His own get *through* a time of trouble designed for themselves. In the other, He promised to keep others of His own *out of* a time of testing designed for others, as noted on page 84.

[58] Unlike English, in both Biblical Greek and Hebrew, definite articles are normally used only for stress. If the word "the" is in the original text, it means the thing being referred to is a particular thing, not just something in general.

There is a specific **"hour of trial"** coming **"to test those who dwell on the earth."** When we see the reason this hour is coming we understand the term **"hour of trial."** For the Greek word here translated *to test* is *peirasmon*. (a singular infinitive of *peirasmos*, word number 3985 in Strong's Greek Dictionary) This literally means exactly as it is translated, *to test*. So we see that this scripture explicitly tells us that there is a particular time of testing coming, and that the purpose of that time is **"to test those who dwell on the earth."** Its purpose is not to test the saints of God, but **"those who dwell on the earth."** This is a moral class, those whose hearts are on the earth, rather than in heaven. This moral class is named in these words eight times in the Revelation,[59] and always in a negative light.

But we are also told where this time of testing will come. It **"shall come upon the whole world."** The Greek word translated *whole* in this clause is *holos*. (word number 3650 in Strong's Greek Dictionary) This Greek word literally means *whole*, or *all*, that is, *complete*. That is, there is no part of the world that will be exempted from this time of testing. So there is coming a specific time of testing, and it is coming upon the whole world. But the Lord's own are promised that they will be *kept out of* that time of testing. Now if this time is coming upon the whole world, but the Lord's own will be *kept out of* it, they cannot be in the world during that time of testing. So we see that Revelation 3:10 indicates that the Lord's own will be removed from the earth before this time of testing begins.

We see this again in a passage about Noah and Lot. **"For if God did not spare the angels who sinned, but cast them down to hell and delivered them into chains of darkness, to be reserved for judgment; and did not spare the ancient world, but saved Noah, one of eight people, a preacher of righteousness, bringing in the flood on the world of the ungodly; and turning the cities of Sodom and Gomorrah into ashes, condemned them**

---

59 See Revelation 3:10, 11:10, 13:8, 13:12, 13:14 (twice) 14:6 and 17:8 See them also as **"inhabitants of the earth"** in Revelation 12:12.

to destruction, making them an example to those who afterward would live ungodly; and delivered righteous Lot, who was oppressed by the filthy conduct of the wicked (for that righteous man, dwelling among them, tormented his righteous soul from day to day by seeing and hearing their lawless deeds)—*then* **the Lord knows how to deliver the godly out of temptations and to reserve the unjust under punishment for the day of judgment.**" (2 Peter 2:4-9)

Here the Holy Spirit gives us two specific examples, Noah and Lot, both of whom were physically removed from the scene of judgment before it took place. Then, in the context of these two examples, the He said, "*then* **the Lord knows how to deliver the godly out of temptations and to reserve the unjust under punishment for the day of judgment.**" (2 Peter 2:9)

Thus the Holy Spirit showed His intention to "**deliver the godly out of temptations**" by physically removing them from the scene "**of temptations**" before they take place, just as He did for Noah and Lot. The Greek word here translated *out of* is the same *ek* used in Revelation 3:10, which, as we saw on page 82, normally means *from* in the sense of *away from* or *out of*. And the Greek word translated *temptations* is *peirasmon*, the same word that, as we saw on page 84, was used in Revelation 3:10. There are no accidents in the precise wording of scripture. The fact that the Holy Spirit used these same two Greek words in these two parallel passages is highly significant.

Again, we read of the coming of "**the man of sin.**" The Holy Spirit said "**And now you know what is restraining, that he may be revealed in his own time. For the mystery of lawlessness is already at work; only He who now restrains *will do so* until He is taken out of the way. And then the lawless one will be revealed, whom the Lord will consume with the breath of His mouth and destroy with the brightness of His coming.**" (2 Thessalonians 2:6-8) In this scripture the Holy Spirit first clearly identified the restrainer as a personality by calling him He. Then He said "**you know what is restraining.**" He did not say "you should know," or "you ought to know." He said **"you know."** This makes it plain that he was speaking of Himself. No other possible individual could be so obvious he did not need to be named. But why should they **"know what is restraining"**? Because our Lord Himself, when he was here, had explicitly said of the Holy Spirit that **"when He has come, He will convict the world of sin, and of righteousness, and of judgment."** (John 16:8) And this **"Helper,"** as He is called in the preceding verse, 7, is explicitly called **"the Spirit of truth"** in verse 13.

We are told that **"He who now restrains *will do so* until He is taken out of the way."** How can this be, when Jesus said, **"I will pray the Father, and He will give you another Helper, that He may abide with you forever—the Spirit of truth, whom the world cannot receive, because it neither sees Him nor knows Him; but you know Him, for He dwells with you and will be in you."** (John 14:16-17) One scripture tells us **"the Spirit of truth"** is given **"that He may abide with you forever."** The other says that **"He"** will be **"taken out of the way."** How can one who will **"abide with you forever"** be **"taken out of the way?"**

We read in 1 Thessalonians 4:16-17 that **"the Lord Himself will descend from heaven with a shout, with the voice of an archangel, and with the trumpet of God. And the dead in Christ will rise first. Then we who are alive *and* remain shall be caught up together with them in the clouds to meet the Lord in the air. And thus we shall always be with the Lord."** The Holy Spirit, **"the Spirit of truth,"** is truly given **"that He may abide with you forever."** But Jesus, **"the Lord Himself,"** will also **"descend from heaven"** and catch us up **"to meet the Lord in the air. And thus we shall always be with the Lord."**

This event has to be the time when the Holy Spirit is **"taken out of the way."** This is because the Holy Spirit will be with the saints of God forever, so He cannot be **"taken out of the way"** either before or after the saints of God are removed from this earth.

It is therefore plain that the Holy Spirit will be **"taken out of the way"** at the same time the Saints of God will be **"caught up... in the clouds to meet the Lord in the air."** But it is only after that happens that **"the lawless one will be revealed."** For we remember that **"the mystery of lawlessness is already at work; only He who now restrains *will do so* until He is taken out of the way. And then the lawless one will be revealed."** (2 Thessalonians 2:6-8) So this scripture, which shows that the Holy Spirit will be **"taken out of the way"** before the Antichrist, **"the lawless one,"** will be revealed thereby shows that the rapture has to take place before that time.

We see this again in the parable of the ten virgins, where we read that **"the bridegroom came, and those who were ready went in with him to the wedding; and the door was shut. Afterward the other virgins came also, saying, 'Lord, Lord, open to us!' But he answered and said, 'Assuredly, I say to you, I do not know you.'"** (Matthew 25:10-12) here we plainly see **"those who were ready"** taken into the wedding while **"the other virgins"** are held outside a door that remains closed in spite of their pleading. The fact that the door remains closed for those that were not **"ready"** is highlighted in 2 Thessalonians 2:10-12, where we are told that **"they did not receive the love of the truth, that they might be saved. And for this reason God will send them strong delusion, that they should believe the lie, that they all may be condemned who did not believe the truth but had pleasure in unrighteousness."** (For more information on this, see pages 101 to 102.) But we need to remember that this is after **"those who were ready went in with him to the wedding."** That is, at the time of the rapture. (For more information on this, see pages 200 to 202.)

Finally, in Revelation 4:4 we read, **"Around the throne *were* twenty-four thrones, and on the thrones I saw twenty-four elders sitting, clothed in white robes; and they had crowns of gold on their heads."** As there were twelve tribes in Israel and twelve apostles, this appears to indicate the presence of all the Old Testament and New Testament saints of God already in heaven before the beginning of the seal and trumpet visions of Revelation six through nine. While this is only interpretation, it is my final *obvious* reason for putting the rapture at this point in this account, before the collapse of government throughout Europe.

There are other scriptural reasons for this which are not as obvious as these ones. Among these is the marked absence of any mention of the church in any of the prophecies about Daniel's seventieth week. Instead, these prophecies are only about God's dealings with the ancient nation of Israel, or more precisely, with Judah. For as we saw on page 8, This seventieth week was determined for Daniel's people and for Daniel's holy city, (Daniel 9:24) which are the Jews and Jerusalem, not the church. The church is not mentioned in even one of these prophesies because they apply to a time which will begin after the rapture.

The collapse of government throughout Europe

This event is directly prophesied, but only in visions that are not accompanied with an inspired interpretation. As such, it is outside the scope of this book, for our point is to concentrate on expressly stated prophecies that need only minimal interpretation. But though interpretation is required to understand the seal and trumpet visions of Revelation six through nine, no one who reads them can doubt that the subject is mass destruction. The interpretation involves only questions like what is destroyed, when, and by whom. A collapse of government throughout Europe is necessary in the prophetic scheme. This is because we are expressly told that ten kings **"shall arise from"** the ancient Roman empire. (Daniel 7:24) These ten kings (Today we call them dictators.) cannot **"arise"** until the existing European governments fall.[60]

---

[60] A number of European governments have now joined together in a common monetary system with a common currency, called the Eurodollar, or Euro for short. Because of this, these nations will now of necessity stand or fall together. If this monetary system collapses, all governments dependent on its strength will also collapse. Such a financial collapse is what caused the fall of the apparently invincible USSR.

The rise of ten kings out of the ancient Roman empire

In Daniel seven, the prophet saw a vision of four great beasts. In verse 17 he was told that **"Those great beasts, which are four, *are* four kings *which* arise out of the earth."** These kings are repeatedly seen in the prophecies of Daniel. They are first seen in chapter two, where in verses 38-40 Nebuchadnezzar was told that he was the first of them, and three more would come after him. In chapter five Nebuchadnezzar's kingdom was conquered by Darius the Mede. (verses 30-31) In chapter eight Daniel was informed that this second kingdom, which was shared by the Medes and the Persians, would fall to Greece. (verses 20-21) In verse 23 of chapter seven, Daniel was told that **"The fourth beast shall be A fourth kingdom on earth, Which shall be different from all other kingdoms, And shall devour the whole earth, Trample it and break it in pieces."** This is unquestionably Rome, the last of the great ancient empires, whose irresistible power crushed all other kingdoms throughout the known world. Rome was different from the rest of these kingdoms in that it had a Senate. (For more detail on this see page 91.) This fourth beast had ten horns, (verse 7) and Daniel's informer told him that **"The ten horns *are* ten kings *Who* shall arise from this kingdom."** (verse 24)

John saw a woman sitting on **"a scarlet beast *which was* full of names of blasphemy, having seven heads and ten horns."** (Revelation 17:3) He was told that **"The seven heads are seven mountains on which the woman sits."** (verse 9) And **"the woman whom you saw is that great city which reigns over the kings of the earth."** (verse 18) This also is unquestionably Rome, which is still called the city of seven hills, (see page 32) and which was ruling over all known kingdoms of the earth at the time this was written.

In the twelfth verse of this chapter, John was told that **"The ten horns which you saw are ten kings who have received no kingdom as yet."**

From these two passages we learn that ten kings will rise from the ancient Roman empire; and that they had not yet received any kingdom when the Revelation was given.

The ten kings unite, reviving the Roman empire

Looking now in more detail at Revelation 17:12-13; the angel told John that **"The ten horns which you saw are ten kings who have received no kingdom as yet, but they receive authority for one hour as kings with the beast. These are of one mind, and they will give their power and authority to the beast."** A few verses later the angel added that **"God has put it into their hearts to fulfill His purpose, to be of one mind, and to give their kingdom to the beast, until the words of God are fulfilled."** (verse 17) We need to realize that Daniel 7:24, which we noticed on page 32, is very specific. These ten kings will not simply arise from the world. They will arise from the ancient Roman Empire.

This prophecy does not speak of the rise of a world government. It speaks of a revival of the Roman Empire. Since the day this was written, there has never been a time when ten kings have voluntarily united to give their power to a Roman ruler. Since this has not happened, we know it will happen in the future.

We also see this beast with seven heads and ten horns in Revelation 13, where John saw **"one of his heads as if it had been mortally wounded, and his deadly wound was healed."** (verse 3) This healing of the deadly wound speaks again of a revival of the Roman empire. We have already noticed, (pages 18, 31, 89) that in Revelation 17:9, John was told; **"Here *is* the mind which has wisdom: The seven heads are seven mountains on which the woman sits."** The next verse says **"There are also seven kings. Five have fallen, one is, *and* the other has not yet come."** (verse 10) From this we see that the seven heads represent, not only seven mountains, but also seven kings. Five of these seven kings had already fallen, and one now existed. On page 33 we noticed that at the time this was written, five successive governments of Rome had fallen. Rome's current government, the line of emperors called Caesars, was a sixth. But another was coming. Clearly, the existing one must fall before a new one could come. The Roman Empire lasted hundreds of years, but it finally fell before an invading horde of Mongols. The line of emperors, the sixth government of Rome, was the mortally wounded head of the beast. Upon receiving this mortal wound, Rome fell, apparently dead. But the deadly wound will be healed. This again shows that the coming kingdom is a revival of the Roman Empire, rather than a worldwide coalition.

The last sentence of Revelation 17:10 speaks of the seventh king, saying that **"when he comes, he must continue a short time."** We thus learn that this first stage of the Roman revival will only last a short time.

An eleventh king rises out of the ancient Roman empire

In Daniel seven, as the prophet was considering the ten horns on the beast, he saw **"another horn, a little one, coming up among them, before whom three of the first horns were plucked out by the roots."** (verse 8) When this king first appears, he will seem insignificant; for when this horn first appeared, it was **"a little one."** But after telling him the ten horns represented ten kings, Daniel's informer added that **"another shall rise after them; He shall be different from the first ones, And shall subdue three kings."** (verse 24)

Here we find two more details to help in the early identification of this king. First, we are specifically told that he will **"rise after"** the first ten kings. And second, **"He shall be different from the first ones."** The Chaldean word here translated *different* is **shena**. (word number 8133 in Strong's Hebrew and Chaldee Dictionary) This word does not just mean that this king is not one of the first ten. It means that there is some kind of a basic difference between him and all of the rest. It is the same word used of the fourth beast in verse 23. (See page 89.)

The eleventh king subdues three of the first ten

As Daniel was considering the horns he saw **"three of the first horns... plucked out by the roots" "before"** the **"little"** horn (verse 8) Daniel was specifically told that the king represented by this horn **"shall subdue three kings."** (verse 24) Verse 20 says that the three **"fell"** before this one. In view of this clear language, it is amazing that many think this wicked ruler will come into power by peaceful means. The error in this view is pointed out in footnote 8 on page 30.

The rise of the beast

The last horn on Daniel's fourth beast had **"eyes like the eyes of a man, and a mouth speaking pompous words."** (Daniel 7:8) It was **"because of the sound of the pompous words which the horn was speaking"** that **"the beast was slain, and its body destroyed and given to the burning flame."** (verse 11)

We notice this to see the connection between this horn and the beast. Indeed, this horn was part of the beast, for it came up on its head. (verse 20, compare verse 8) In Revelation 13 the horn and the beast become one and the same, for **"all the world marveled and followed the beast... and they worshiped the beast, saying, 'Who *is* like the beast? Who is able to make war with him?' And he was given a mouth speaking great things and blasphemies... Then he opened his mouth in blasphemy against God, to blaspheme His name, His tabernacle, and those who dwell in heaven."** (Revelation 13:3-6)

We have already noticed (pages 33, 90) that **"There are also seven kings. Five have fallen, one is, *and* the other has not yet come. And when he comes, he must continue a short time."** (Revelation 17:10) Immediately after this, John was told that **"the beast that was, and is not, is himself** also the eighth, and is of the seven, and is going to perdition." (verse 11) The revival of the Roman empire will not be complete until this eighth king has assumed power.

The beast is allowed to persecute the saints of the Most High

In Daniel 7, this evil dictator is seen **"making war against the saints, and prevailing against them,"** (verse 21) He **"Shall persecute the saints of the Most High... Then *the saints* shall be given into his hand."** (verse 25) The same thing is said in Revelation 13. **"It was granted to him to make war with the saints and to overcome them."** (verse 7) It is important to notice that these scriptures do not just say that he will persecute the saints. They specifically say that he will be allowed to do this. We are reminded of a similar time when our Lord told those who came to arrest Him, **"this is your hour, and the power of darkness."** (Luke 22:53)

Why is the beast allowed to persecute the saints? Our Lord told the scribes and Pharisees to **"Fill up, then, the measure of your fathers' *guilt*. Serpents, brood of vipers! How can you escape the condemnation of hell? Therefore, indeed, I send you prophets, wise men, and scribes: *some* of them you will kill and crucify, and *some* of them you will scourge in your synagogues and persecute from city to city, that on you may come all the righteous blood shed on the earth, from the blood of righteous Abel to the blood of Zechariah, son of Berechiah, whom you murdered between the temple and the altar."** (Matthew 23:32-35) Even so, the Roman empire will be revived for judgment, not for blessing. It will be allowed to multiply its guilt in persecuting these future saints, that it might justly be judged for all it has done in ages past.

Babylon the great destroyed

This judgment of Rome begins with the destruction of Babylon the great. The power represented by this symbol is called a **"great harlot who sits on many waters, with whom the kings of the earth committed fornication, and the inhabitants of the earth were made drunk with the wine of her fornication."** (Revelation 17:1-2) She is **"arrayed in purple and scarlet, and adorned with gold and precious stones and pearls, having in her hand a golden cup full of abominations and the filthiness of her fornication."** (verse 4) She also was **"drunk with the blood of the saints and with the blood of the martyrs of Jesus."** (verse 6)

Who does this woman represent? Some have assumed she represents a revival of the ancient city of Babylon[61] because Revelation 17:5 says that **"on her forehead a name *was* written: MYSTERY, BABYLON THE GREAT, THE MOTHER OF HARLOTS AND OF THE ABOMINATIONS OF THE EARTH."** But the word **"MYSTERY"** indicates that she represents something else. If she represented **"BABYLON,"** this would only be a label, not a **"MYSTERY."** Her identity is plainly stated in verse 18: **"And the woman whom you saw is that great city which reigns over the kings of the earth."** This is unquestionably Rome, which was ruling over the entire known world when this was written.

We have seen that the beast is Rome. The ten horns on the beast **"will hate the harlot, make her desolate and naked, eat her flesh and burn her with fire."** (Revelation 17:16) This is not just something that will happen, for we are specifically told that **"God has put it into their hearts."** (Revelation 17:17) Why does He do this? Because **"Babylon the great is fallen, is fallen, and has become a dwelling place of demons, a prison for every foul spirit, and a cage for every unclean and hated bird! For all the nations have drunk of the wine of the wrath of her fornication, the kings of the earth have**

---

61 My reasons for doubting the notion that prophecy requires a rebuilding of ancient Babylon are given in footnote 25 on page 57.

committed fornication with her, and the merchants of the earth have become rich through the abundance of her luxury." (Revelation 18:2-3) **"For she says in her heart, 'I sit *as* queen, and am no widow, and will not see sorrow.' Therefore her plagues will come in one day; death and mourning and famine. And she will be utterly burned with fire, for strong *is* the Lord God who judges her."** (Revelation 18:7-8) **"And in her was found the blood of prophets and saints, and of all who were slain on the earth."** (verse 24)

But how can Rome destroy Rome? We understand when we notice that the Rome that is destroyed is a harlot that rides on the beast. We have seen (page 93) that the Beast represents the Roman government, that is, political Rome. But the harlot is a Roman power separate and distinct from the political power, but wickedly joined in unlawful unions with **"the kings of the earth."**

Finally, we must notice that if a man desired to get married, but a woman other than his chosen bride was claiming to be his wife, he would first need to deal with her false claim. Immediately before the marriage of the Lamb to His spotless bride in Revelation 19:6-9, we read of the harlot's destruction in chapter 18 and heaven's celebration of that destruction in the first five verses of chapter 19. We thus recognize the **"great harlot"** as the well known Roman power that claims to be the bride of Christ, but in truth is guilty of the blood of His prophets and saints.

This is, of course, an interpretation. But the meaning of the symbol seems quite clear, and without it we could never understand how Rome could destroy Rome. This interpretation becomes even more obvious when we notice that God's people are called to **"Come out of her... lest you share in her sins, and lest you receive of her plagues."** (Revelation 18:4) God would not call His people to **"come out of her"** unless some of them were in her. Sad to say, some true believers remain in the darkness of that wicked system. Let those who think to remain there and reform her take careful note of this instruction and warning: **"Come out of her... lest you share in her sins, and lest you receive of her plagues."**

The First Half of the Week

The Roman prince makes a seven year treaty with Judah.

In Daniel 9 the prophet was told that **"Seventy weeks are determined For your people and for your holy city."** (verse 24) The Old Testament term **"week"** was used to describe periods of both seven days and seven years.[62]

Daniel was then told **"*That* from the going forth of the command To restore and build Jerusalem Until Messiah the Prince, *There shall be* seven weeks and sixty-two weeks... And after the sixty-two weeks Messiah shall be cut off, but not for Himself; And the people of the prince who is to come Shall destroy the city and the sanctuary."** (Daniel 9:25-26) Notice that it does not say that **"the prince who is to come"** **"shall destroy the city and the sanctuary."** They were not to be destroyed by this prince, but by his people. History says this was done by the Romans under the command of Titus. (see page 26) By this we know **"the prince who is to come"** will be a Roman, for the people of Rome destroyed **"the city and the sanctuary."** This Roman prince **"shall confirm a covenant with many for one week."** (Daniel 9:27) As the **"Seventy weeks are determined For your people and for your holy city"** (verse 24) we understand that the **"many"** are Daniel's people, the Jews.

We therefore understand that the coming Roman prince will make a seven year treaty [63] with the people of revived Judah, which is now called Israel. The treaty clearly includes the protection of Jerusalem, but this will fail, for we read in Isaiah 28:14-18:

> **"Therefore hear the word of the LORD, you scornful men, Who rule this people who are in Jerusalem, Because you have said, 'We have made a covenant with death, And with Sheol**

---

62 This is explained in detail on pages 9 to 10.

63 It is interesting that in mid 1999 the concept of such a temporary treaty was introduced into modern international politics. A three year treaty was proposed to allow conditions to stabilize in the former Yugoslavia.

we are in agreement. When the overflowing scourge passes through, It will not come to us, For we have made lies our refuge, And under falsehood we have hidden ourselves.' Therefore thus says the Lord GOD:... 'Your covenant with death will be annulled, And your agreement with Sheol will not stand; When the overflowing scourge passes through, Then you will be trampled down by it.'"

The rebuilding of the temple and the resumption of sacrifices

Like the return of Judah to her land, these events are not directly prophesied for this time. (Although both are for the millennium.) But we know both will happen at this time.

There has to be a temple at this time because **"the man of sin"** will sit **"as God in the temple of God, showing himself that he is God."** (2 Thessalonians 2:3-4) We further read in Malachi 3:1-3:

> "'The Lord, whom you seek, Will suddenly come to His temple, Even the Messenger of the covenant, In whom you delight. Behold, He is coming,' Says the LORD of hosts. But who can endure the day of His coming? And who can stand when He appears? For He *is* like a refiner's fire And like launderer's soap. He will sit as a refiner and a purifier of silver; He will purify the sons of Levi, And purge them as gold and silver, That they may offer to the LORD An offering in righteousness."

This has not yet happened, so it has to be future. But it distinctly says that the Lord will **"suddenly come to His temple."** For this to happen, there has to be a temple. As there is not one at this time, we know one will be built.

We also know that sacrifices will be resumed before this time because we read in Daniel 8:11-12 that **"by him the daily *sacrifices* were taken away, and the place of His sanctuary was cast down. Because of transgression, an army was given over *to the horn* to oppose the daily *sacrifices*."**

Again, there will be one who **"shall bring an end to sacrifice and offering"** (Daniel 9:27) It is clearly impossible to **"bring an end"** to a practice unless it is taking place. So even though sacrifices are not presently being offered, we know the practice will be resumed before this time.

The rise of the Antichrist

In Revelation 13, after John saw the beast with seven heads and ten horns **"rising up out of the sea,"** (verse 1) he **"saw another beast coming up out of the earth."** (verse 11) We are not told how this second beast rises to power, but from the sequence of the visions, we see that this beast rises up after the first one. This is stressed by twice referring to **"the first beast"** in verse 12. This second beast **"had two horns like a lamb and spoke like a dragon."** (Revelation 13:11) From this we recognize him as the Antichrist, or false Christ, for he looked like a lamb, (**"the Lamb of God,"** John 1:29, 36) but when he spoke, he spoke like a dragon (**"the great dragon... that serpent of old, called the Devil and Satan"** Revelation 12:9).[64] This false prophet (for so he is called in Revelation 16:13, 19:20, and 20:10) **"performs great signs, so that he even makes fire come down from heaven on the earth in the sight of men."** (Revelation 13:13)

But we remember (page 97) that worship has been resumed in the temple of God. This worship, though not Christian, is directed toward the God of Israel, the one true God. Those who continue this worship now find themselves persecuted by the followers of the Antichrist. This will be a time of unparalleled hatred, treachery, and betrayal. Jesus was speaking of this time when He said, **"Then they will deliver you up to tribulation and kill you, and you will be hated by all nations for My name's sake. And then many will be offended, will betray one another, and will hate one another."** (Matthew 24:9-10)

---

64 For more detail on this, see pages 42 to 50.

In Mark 13 He added **"Now brother will betray brother to death, and a father *his* child; and children will rise up against parents and cause them to be put to death. And you will be hated by all for My name's sake. But he who endures to the end shall be saved."** (Mark 13:12-13) Micah wrote of this time, **"Do not trust in a friend; Do not put your confidence in a companion; Guard the doors of your mouth From her who lies in your bosom. For son dishonors father, Daughter rises against her mother, Daughter-in-law against her mother-in-law; A man's enemies *are* the men of his own household."** (Micah 7:5-6)

This is treated at length in the first book of the Psalms, where we read: [65] **"O LORD my God, in You I put my trust; Save me from all those who persecute me; And deliver me,"** (Psalm 7:1) and **"My times *are* in Your hand; Deliver me from the hand of my enemies, And from those who persecute me."** (Psalm 31:15) We further read, **"My enemies speak evil of me: 'When will he die, and his name perish?'"** (Psalm 41:5) But who are these enemies? The next verse shows us. **"And if he comes to see *me*, he speaks lies; His heart gathers iniquity to itself; *When* he goes out, he tells *it.*"** (Psalm 41:6) In another of these Psalms we read, **"I am a reproach among all my enemies, But especially among my neighbors, And *am* repulsive to my acquaintances; Those who see me outside flee from me."** (Psalm 31:11) Their enemies are their neighbors, those who come to visit them.

---

65 In the Hebrew original, there were five books of Psalms. The first book was Psalms 1-41; the second, 42-72; the third, 73-89; the fourth, 90-106; and the fifth, 107-150. These were combined into one in our English Bible. All such trifling with the Word of God is destructive, and this has masked the distinctive characters of these five books.

These five books of Psalms take us sequentially through the end times period. They do not give the actual events, but the feelings of the righteous remnant as they pass through them. In the first book, they are seen suffering in the midst of an ungodly nation. In the second book, they are cast out. As the Lord Jesus experienced these afflictions, He figures largely in these books. The third book bewails the destruction the enemy has wrought in the land. In the fourth book the Lord has finally arrived and the righteous are called to come and worship Him. Jesus is not seen in the third book and His suffering is not in the fourth. Finally in the fifth and last book, the righteous are back in the land and preparing to obey the Lord's command to take vengeance on those who had tried to destroy them. This is the book where we find the call for vengeance on Judas. (Psalm 109:6-20)

It seems that all have fallen away, so they cry, **"Help, LORD, for the godly man ceases! For the faithful disappear from among the sons of men."** (Psalm 12:1)

This produces a greater fear than the persecution from the enemies. They pray **"Keep back Your servant also from presumptuous *sins;* Let them not have dominion over me. Then I shall be blameless, And I shall be innocent of great transgression."** [66] (Psalm 19:13)

In keeping with this prayer, they witness boldly in the face of opposition, as they say in Psalm 40:9-10: **"I have proclaimed the good news of righteousness In the great assembly; Indeed, I do not restrain my lips, O LORD, You Yourself know. I have not hidden Your righteousness within my heart; I have declared Your faithfulness and Your salvation; I have not concealed Your lovingkindness and Your truth From the great assembly."**

Helped on by Antichrist, the beast demands worship as God

Even as Jesus, the true Christ, taught men to worship the Father, the Antichrist **"exercises all the authority of the first beast in his presence, and causes the earth and those who dwell in it to worship the first beast, whose deadly wound was healed."** (Revelation 13:12) And even as the true Christ did miracles. The Antichrist will likewise do miracles. **"And he deceives those who dwell on the earth by those signs which he was granted to do in the sight of the beast, telling those who dwell on the earth to make an image to the beast who was wounded by the sword and lived. He was granted *power* to give breath to the image of the beast, that the image of the beast should both speak and cause as many as would not worship the image of the beast to be killed."** (verses 14-15)

---

[66] I am disappointed that the New King James, which we are using, has abandoned the reading of the King James Version, "innocent from the great transgression." This seems to me to be the true sense, a prayer to be kept from the great sin that was being pressed upon them, that is, to worship the Antichrist.

All commerce linked to the worship of the beast

The second beast **"causes all, both small and great, rich and poor, free and slave, to receive a mark on their right hand or on their foreheads, and that no one may buy or sell except one who has the mark or the name of the beast, or the number of his name."** (Revelation 13:16-17)

Accepting this mark will in some way involve worshiping the beast, for mankind is clearly warned that **"If anyone worships the beast and his image, and receives *his* mark on his forehead or on his hand, he himself shall also drink of the wine of the wrath of God, which is poured out full strength into the cup of His indignation. He shall be tormented with fire and brimstone in the presence of the holy angels and in the presence of the Lamb. And the smoke of their torment ascends forever and ever; and they have no rest day or night, who worship the beast and his image, and whoever receives the mark of his name."** (Revelation 14:9-11)

Previous wilful rejecters of the gospel turned over to "the lie."[67]

This is clearly stated in 2 Thessalonians 2:9-12, where we are told that **"The coming of the *lawless one* is according to the working of Satan, with all power, signs, and lying wonders, and with all unrighteous deception among those who perish, because they did not receive the love of the truth, that they might be saved. And for this reason God will send them strong delusion, that they should believe the lie, that they all may be condemned who did not believe the truth but had pleasure in unrighteousness."**

The reason for this is distinctly stated. God will do this as a punishment **"because they did not receive the love of the truth,"** that is, because they did not wish to know the truth. This awful punishment is because, instead of receiving the truth, they **"had pleasure in unrighteousness."**

---

[67] We saw in footnote 19 on page 49 that this lie is that **"the beast"** is God, and the Antichrist is the Messiah, God's anointed messenger.

We see this again in the last chapter of Isaiah. **"Just as they have chosen their own ways, And their soul delights in their abominations, So will I choose their delusions, And bring their fears on them; Because, when I called, no one answered, When I spoke they did not hear; But they did evil before My eyes, And chose *that* in which I do not delight."** (Isaiah 66:3-4)

Two witnesses testify in Jerusalem

But even while men labor under a delusion sent by God, He still warns them through specially chosen witnesses:

> **"And I will give *power* to my two witnesses, and they will prophesy one thousand two hundred and sixty days, clothed in sackcloth. These are the two olive trees and the two lampstands standing before the God of the earth. And if anyone wants to harm them, fire proceeds from their mouth and devours their enemies. And if anyone wants to harm them, he must be killed in this manner. These have power to shut heaven, so that no rain falls in the days of their prophecy; and they have power over waters to turn them to blood, and to strike the earth with all plagues, as often as they desire. When they finish their testimony, the beast that ascends out of the bottomless pit will make war against them, overcome them, and kill them. And their dead bodies *will lie* in the street of the great city which spiritually is called Sodom and Egypt, where also our Lord was crucified."** (Revelation 11:3-8)

The comment that **"These are the two olive trees and the two lampstands standing before the God of the earth"** refers to Zechariah 4:2-3; "And he said to me, 'What do you see?' So I said, 'I am looking, and there *is* a lampstand of solid gold with a bowl on top of it, and on the *stand* seven lamps with seven pipes to the seven lamps. Two olive trees *are* by it, one at the right of the bowl and the other at its left.'" This is explained a few verses later: "**Then I answered and said to him, 'What *are* these two olive trees; at the right of the lampstand and at its left?' And I further answered and said to him, 'What *are these* two olive branches that *drip* into the receptacles of the two gold pipes from which the golden *oil* drains?' Then he answered me and said, 'Do you not know what these *are?*' And I said, 'No, my lord.' So he said, 'These *are* the two anointed ones, who stand beside the Lord of the whole earth.'"** [68] (Zechariah 4:11-14)

From this we understand that these two witnesses are specially anointed by God. They will give a solemn warning, and it will be given in such a remarkable way that everyone will know about it. But instead of heeding the warning, **"those who dwell on the earth"** will hate them and rejoice over their deaths. When these two witnesses are killed, they will **"make merry, and send gifts to one another, because these two prophets tormented those who dwell on the earth."** (Revelation 11:10)

The male goat's little horn begins his campaigns

We noticed on pages 56 to 60 that the male goat's little horn will arise in what is now northern Iraq (ancient Assyria) and attack what is now southern Iraq, **"the land of the Chaldeans."** (Jeremiah 50-51) We noticed on page 74 that he will also attack Media or Persia (Elam,) present day Iran. Scripture does not specifically say when these attacks will take place, but it implies a time in Daniel 8:9. **"And out of one of them came a little horn which grew exceedingly great toward the south, toward the east, and toward the Glorious *Land*."** This seems to mean that he will first grow **"toward the south,"** then **"toward the east,"** and then **"toward the Glorious *Land*."**

---

68 The context and grammar of the Hebrew used here indicates that these two were already standing "**beside the Lord of the whole earth**" in Zechariah's day. They can be neither angels nor resurrected men, for they will be killed. Luke 20:26 shows us that neither angels nor resurrected men can die. It is interesting to note that Scripture tells us of two men who were in heaven at that time, but have not died and are therefore not resurrected. Enoch and Elijah were taken to heaven without passing through death. (Genesis 5:24, 2 Kings 2:11)

If that was indeed the intended meaning of this statement, and I believe it was, the male goat's first two campaigns will take place before the middle of the week. That is because Daniel 9:27 clearly places his attack on **"the Glorious *Land*"** **"in the middle of the week,"** as noted on page 104.

The Middle of the Week

The abomination of desolation

We have seen (pages 10, 96) that the **"prince who is to come"** will make a seven year treaty with the people of Judah, but that Isaiah 28:18 warns them that **"Your covenant with death will be annulled, And your agreement with Sheol will not stand;"** (pages 64, 97) Why? The Lord says **"But in the middle of the week He shall bring an end to sacrifice and offering. And on the wing of abominations shall be one who makes desolate."** (Daniel 9:27) We also read of **"the transgression of desolation"** in Daniel 8:13 and of **"the abomination of desolation"** in Daniel 12:11. There can be little doubt that these passages refer to the time when **"the man of sin... the son of perdition, who opposes and exalts himself above all that is called God or that is worshiped, ... sits as God in the temple of God, showing himself that he is God."** (2 Thessalonians 2:3-4)

We note in passing that this term **"the abomination of desolation"** is also found in some English translations of Daniel 11:31. This includes The New King James Translation, which we are using. But the Hebrew word translated *desolation* in this verse is *meshomem*. This word form literally means *desolator*, not *desolation*. The form of this word which means *desolation* is *shomem*. This form was used in both Daniel 8:13 and Daniel 12:11. As these are both forms of the Hebrew word *shamem*, Strong's Hebrew Dictionary lists them both under the same index number (8074). But such slight variations are significant in Bible prophecy.

Daniel 11:31 refers to a different event than the one in Daniel 8:13 and 12:11. Daniel 11:21-32 describes the actions of the Seleucid king Antiochus Epiphanes. History says this **"vile person"** (Daniel 11:21) desecrated the altar with the sacrifice of a pig. Verse 31 literally calls this the abomination of the desolator. But Daniel 8:13 and 12:11 refer to an event which was still future when our Lord spoke of it approximately two hundred years after the time of Antiochus Epiphanes. Jesus called it **"the 'abomination of desolation,'** spoken of by Daniel the prophet." (Matthew 24:15)

The flight of the righteous

> **"When you see the *'abomination of desolation,'* spoken of by Daniel the prophet, standing in the holy place"** (whoever reads, let him understand), **then let those who are in Judea flee to the mountains. Let him who is on the housetop not go down to take anything out of his house. And let him who is in the field not go back to get his clothes."** (Matthew 24:15-18)

This is not only a prophecy, but also an instruction and a warning to those in Judea when the abomination of desolation takes place. Immediately upon hearing the news, they are to run for their lives. There can be no doubt that the warning to stop for nothing, not even to go into the house to take anything out of it, is intended to be taken literally. **"For then there will be great tribulation, such as has not been since the beginning of the world until this time, no, nor ever shall be."** (Matthew 24:21)

This part of Matthew 24 has been misapplied perhaps as grossly as any other part of scripture. Many American Christians think this is a warning to themselves, and have made extensive preparations to hide out in the wilderness. But if they had carefully read the passage, they would have known better. It specifically says **"let those who are in Judea flee to the mountains."** This is not a warning to the whole world. It is a warning to those in the land of Judea who will be heeding the Lord's words.

Scripture gives several reasons for the urgency of this warning. One is found in Daniel 9:27. **"And on the wing of abominations shall be one who makes desolate, Even until the consummation, which is determined, Is poured out on the desolate."** These words **"on the wing of"** seem to indicate speed, as we read in Jeremiah 4:20. **"Destruction upon destruction is cried, For the whole land is plundered. Suddenly my tents are plundered, *And my curtains in a moment.*"** The awesome speed of this attack is detailed in Isaiah 10:28-32, which we will examine shortly. (page 113) But an even more urgent reason for this haste in their flight is examined in the next few sections, from here through page 110.

The dragon pursues the fleeing righteous

> **"Now a great sign appeared in heaven: a woman clothed with the sun, with the moon under her feet, and on her head a garland of twelve stars. Then being with child, she cried out in labor and in pain to give birth... And the dragon stood before the woman who was ready to give birth, to devour her Child as soon as it was born. She bore a male Child who was to rule all nations with a rod of iron. And her Child was caught up to God and His throne."** (Revelation 12:1-5)

Revelation 20:2 tells us that the dragon is **"that serpent of old, who is *the* Devil and Satan."** The **"male Child who was to rule all nations with a rod of iron"** can be none other than the Lord Jesus. Satan, acting through Rome, tried to destroy Him at His birth. (Matthew 2:16) But He was caught up to God. (Acts 1:9) Pages 18 to 20 explain how we can know the woman represents the righteous remnant of Israel.

> **"Now when the dragon saw that he had been cast to the earth, he persecuted the woman who gave birth to the male *Child*. But the woman was given two wings of a great eagle, that she might fly into the wilderness to her place, where she is nourished for**

a time and times and half a time, from the presence of the serpent. So the serpent spewed water out of his mouth like a flood after the woman, that he might cause her to be carried away by the flood." (Revelation 12:13-15)

The meaning is plainly that Satan attempts to destroy the righteous as they flee. (Here we need to remember that, as we saw on pages 19 to 20, only the righteous are considered as even part of the true Israel.)

The righteous flee across the Jordan to Edom and Moab.

We have noticed the warning that the righteous should flee to the mountains. (see pages 16, 17, 26, 62, 105) The mountains just across the Jordan river from Judea (today's Israel) are the ancient home of the Edomites and the Moabites. Most of this area is in today's Jordan.

This is treated in the second book of the Psalms:

> "As the deer pants for the water brooks, So pants my soul for You, O God. My soul thirsts for God, for the living God. When shall I come and appear before God? My tears have been my food day and night, While they continually say to me, 'Where *is* your God?' When I remember these *things*, I pour out my soul within me. For I used to go with the multitude; I went with them to the house of God, With the voice of joy and praise, With a multitude that kept a pilgrim feast. Why are you cast down, O my soul? And *why* are you disquieted within me? Hope in God, for I shall yet praise Him *For* the help of His countenance. O my God, my soul is cast down within me; Therefore I will remember You from the land of the Jordan, And from the heights of Hermon, From the Hill Mizar." (Psalm 42:1-6)

> "O God, You *are* my God; Early will I seek You; My soul thirsts for You; My flesh longs for You In a dry and thirsty land Where there is no water." (Psalm 63:1)

In these Psalms we notice that the righteous long to **"come and appear before God,"** but they cannot. They **"used to go with the multitude... to the house of God,"** but this is no longer possible. Instead, they can only remember their God **"from the land of the Jordan," "from the heights of Hermon,"** and **"From the hill Mizar."** They are **"In a dry and thirsty land Where there is no water."** That is where they have fled.

Again, we read, **"Take counsel, execute judgment; Make your shadow like the night in the middle of the day; Hide the outcasts, Do not betray him who escapes. Let My outcasts dwell with you, O Moab; Be a shelter to them from the face of the spoiler. For the extortioner is at an end, Devastation ceases, The oppressors are consumed out of the land."** (Isaiah 16:3-4)

This entire area is a desolate wilderness. We see this twice in Revelation 12: **"Then the woman fled into the wilderness, where she has a place prepared by God, that they should feed her there one thousand two hundred and sixty days."** (Revelation 12:6) **"But the woman was given two wings of a great eagle, that she might fly into the wilderness to her place, where she is nourished for a time and times and half a time, from the presence of the serpent."** (Revelation 12:13)

This time of exile is part of the Lord's design for His people, for He says, **"Therefore, behold, I will allure her, Will bring her into the wilderness, And speak comfort to her."** (Hosea 2:14)

He further says that **"The people who survived the sword Found grace in the wilderness; Israel, when I went to give him rest."** (Jeremiah 31:2) Again, in Isaiah 26:20 the Lord figuratively says, **"Come, my people, enter your chambers, And shut your doors behind you; Hide yourself, as it were, for a little moment, Until the indignation is past."**

The righteous are helped as they flee.

If the nations had any understanding they would help the righteous as they flee, for when the Lord comes, He will judge them on the basis of how they have treated these refugees. Matthew 25:31-45 describes this judgment in detail. In rewarding the righteous, the King will say **"inasmuch as you did it to one of the least of these My brethren, you did it to Me."** (verse 40) Likewise, in condemning the wicked, He will say **"inasmuch as you did not do it to one of the least of these, you did not do it to Me."** (verse 45) These scriptures show that some will help these righteous Jews, but they will be the exception, not the rule. Pages 110 to 125 trace many prophetic details about how the surrounding nations, instead of helping these refugees, will join in the attack against them.

But there will be help for the righteous as they flee. We noticed on page 107 that in Revelation 13:15 **"the serpent spewed water out of his mouth like a flood after the woman, that he might cause her to be carried away by the flood."** But the next verse says, **"the earth helped the woman, and the earth opened its mouth and swallowed up the flood which the dragon had spewed out of his mouth."** (Revelation 13:16)

This might seem to contradict the many scriptures (see pages 119 to 123) that tell how many nations join in the attack on Judea. But rather than contradict this prophecy, it explains it.

We have seen on pages 18 and 65 that the dragon, or the serpent, represents Satan acting through Roman power. We have seen on pages 10 and 54 that the Beast, the Roman ruler, will be in covenant with Judea. And we saw on page 64 that the rulers of Judea, which is now called Israel, will stand with the Beast in his claim to be God. From these things we understand that the serpent's action in spewing **"water out of his mouth like a flood after the woman, that he might cause her to be carried away by the flood."** (Revelation 13:15) is a police action. This is not a foreign army invading Judea. It is the government of Rome acting with the government of Judea to suppress rebellion. There are only a handful of rebels, but they have long been a problem. In spite of intense persecution, as we saw on pages 98 to 99, they have continued to publicly stand for the One True God of Israel. (see page 100) The time has come to put an end to this rebellion. So a police action to completely stamp it out begins. This police action is the more urgent reason for haste in the flight of the righteous that we noticed on page 106. But this police action cannot be carried out. The earth opens its mouth, and swallows up **"the flood which the dragon had spewed out of his mouth."** (Revelation 13:16) What happens? At this time, suddenly (see pages 65, 106) and without warning:

The kings of the South and North attack Judah's king.

> "Then the king shall do according to his own will: he shall exalt and magnify himself above every god, shall speak blasphemies against the God of gods, and shall prosper till the wrath has been accomplished; for what has been determined shall be done. He shall regard neither the God of his fathers nor the desire of women, nor regard any god; for he shall exalt himself above *them* all. But in their place he shall honor a god of fortresses; and a god which his fathers did not know he shall honor with gold and silver, with precious stones and pleasant things. Thus he shall act against the strongest fortresses with a foreign god, which he shall acknowledge, *and* advance *its* glory; and he shall cause them to rule over many, and divide the land for gain. At the time of the end the king of the South shall attack him; and the king of the North shall come against him like a whirlwind, with chariots, horsemen, and with many ships." (Daniel 11:36-40)

Here we read of an impious king of Judah, who **"shall exalt and magnify himself above every god,"** yet he shall acknowledge **"a foreign god."**

From these details we recognize the Antichrist. Like the true Christ, this wicked one claims to be **"above every god."** Yet, again like the true Christ, he instructs his followers to worship another.

Even as Christ taught us to worship the Father, (see John 4:21-24) the Antichrist will teach men to worship the Beast. [69] His sin is punished by a two pronged attack. The kings of the South and the North attack him at the same time. But **"the king of the South"** quickly drops out of the picture. The rest of the account speaks only of **"the king of the North."**

Earlier in this chapter, the Holy Spirit used twenty-seven verses to identify **"the king of the South"** and **"the king of the North."** This passage describes a long series of wars which took place over a period of approximately 130 years. Every act of **"the king of the North"** in this account was actually committed by one of the Seleucids, a dynasty that ruled out of Antioch in Syria. This dynasty ruled essentially all the territory of the previous Assyrian empire. (See the map on page 231.) In like manner, every act of **"the king of the South"** was actually committed by one of the Ptolemies, a dynasty that ruled out of Alexandria in Egypt. Thus we see that **"the king of the North"** is the king of the Selucid Empire, which corresponds to the Assyrian empire, and that **"the king of the South"** is the king of Egypt. This is treated in more detail in pages 54 to 55.

In Daniel 8, the prophet was shown a male goat. And **"the goat had a notable horn between his eyes."** (verse 5) But **"when he became strong, the large horn was broken, and in place of it four notable ones came up toward the four winds of heaven. And out of one of them came a little horn which grew exceedingly great toward the south, toward the east, and toward the Glorious *Land.*"** (verses 8-9)

Verses 21-22 of this chapter tell us that **"the male goat *is* the kingdom of Greece. The large horn that *is* between its eyes *is* the first king. As for the broken *horn* and the four that stood up in its place, four kingdoms shall arise out of that nation, but not with its power."** Verse 17 expressly

---

69 For more detail on this, see pages to .

states **"that the vision *refers* to the time of the end."** Verses 23-24 explain that **"in the latter time of their kingdom, When the transgressors have reached their fullness, A king shall arise, Having fierce features, Who understands sinister schemes. His power shall be mighty, but not by his own power; He shall destroy fearfully, And shall prosper and thrive; He shall destroy the mighty, and *also* the holy people."** Verses 11-12 tell us that **"by him the daily *sacrifices* were taken away, and the place of His sanctuary was cast down. Because of transgression, an army was given over *to the horn* to oppose the daily *sacrifices*; and he cast truth down to the ground. He did *all this* and prospered."**

This attacker can be none other than **"the king of the North"** we find in Daniel 11. He can be neither the Russian leader nor the Roman leader, because Daniel 8:9 tells us that this **"little horn"** came **"out of one of"** the four kingdoms that would **"arise out of"** **"the kingdom of Greece."** (see pages 56, 64, 103) Upon the death of Alexander the Great, the great Greek conqueror, his four generals divided the empire, making four kingdoms. The king represented by this **"little horn"** will come **"out of one of"** these. But Alexander's empire did not include Rome or any part of Russia.

The king of the North invades the Glorious Land.

From all this we see three things. First, in **"the time of the end"** a king will attack **"the Glorious *Land.*"** (Daniel 8:9) This, of course, is clearly Daniel's land, Judea. Second, this attack will be a punishment from God **"Because of transgression."** And third, the invader will come from somewhere within the area conquered by Alexander the Great.

Again, Daniel 11:40 tells us that **"the king of the South"** and **"the king of the North"** will attack **"the king,"** as we have already noticed (on pages 66, 67, 68, 209.) The next verse continues with the account of **"the king of the North,"** saying, **"He shall also enter the Glorious Land."** (Daniel 11:41)

The daily progress of the Assyrian's attack (see map, page 231)

We have previously examined the Assyrian's attack in Isaiah 10:24-25. (page 54) That passage continues through verse 27, immediately followed by this remarkable account:

> "He has come to Aiath, He has passed Migron; At Michmash he has attended to his equipment. They have gone along the ridge, They have taken up lodging at Geba. Ramah is afraid, Gibeah of Saul has fled. Lift up your voice, O daughter of Gallim! Cause it to be heard as far as Laish; O poor Anathoth! Madmenah has fled, The inhabitants of Gebim seek refuge. As yet he will remain at Nob that day; He will shake his fist at the mount of the daughter of Zion, The hill of Jerusalem." (Isaiah 10:28-32)

The following details show the daily progress of this attack. Each stop specifically mentioned is marked by a red star in the map on page 231.

Day 1:

> "At Michmash he has attended to his equipment."

Day 2:

> "They have taken up lodging at Geba."

Day 3:

> "As yet he will remain at Nob that day."

Day 4:

> "He will shake his fist at the mount of the daughter of Zion, The hill of Jerusalem."

This passage describes a defeat of ten cities in only four days. Even by modern standards, this is remarkable progress for an advancing army. There is no strength to resist his advance, for **"he shall come against princes as *though* mortar, As the potter treads clay."** (Isaiah 41:25)

Some think this passage (Isaiah 10:28-32) refers to the ancient Sennacherib's advance on Jerusalem, but that cannot be correct.

This prophecy describes an advance on Jerusalem from the north. But 2 Kings 18:17, 2 Chronicles 32:9, and Isaiah 36:2 all say Sennacherib's forces came to Jerusalem from Lachish, which was southwest of Jerusalem. Archeologists have found extensive evidence of Assyrian presence in this southern region, but not in any part of ancient Judea north of Jerusalem. That is, not along the path described in Isaiah 10:28-32.

Further, Sennacherib boasted that he had conquered 46 of Hezekiah's fortified cities, with their neighboring small towns, by the use of siege ramps and battering rams, by boring holes and making breaches, as well as by relentlessly attacking with foot soldiers. Such a campaign would clearly take a long time. So it could not be the swift advance described in this prophecy.

Sennacherib left this boast on each of seven monuments known to modern scholars. [70] The best known of these is a prism shaped monument shown on the next page. It is often called "The Oriental Institute Prism" because it is held by the Oriental Institute. As this institute is part of the University of Chicago, the monument is also called "The Chicago Prism." But the Oriental Institute simply calls it the "Clay Prism of Sennacherib."

---

70 These seven monuments are listed on page 10 and translated on page 129 of "Sennacherib's Campaign to Judah : new studies," by William R. Gallagher, Leiden; Boston; Köln: Brill, 1999. This authoritative book clearly presents the current state of historical scholarship on this subject. Working from a purely logical basis, it demonstrates the error in many objections to the historical reliability of Biblical accounts of this campaign. It devotes well over a hundred pages to these accounts, but doesn't even mention any portion of Isaiah 10:28-32.

The Oriental Institute Prism

"Courtesy of the Oriental Institute of the University of Chicago."

This monument (and each of the others) lists the cities Sennacherib conquered in this campaign. These lists clearly show that as he invaded this area he came along the seacoast, not inland through the mountains, as indicated in Isaiah 10:28-32.

This fact is so well established that A. T. Olmstead quoted Isaiah 10:28-32 in his monumental 650 page "History of Assyria," observing that this was not the path Sennacherib followed. [71]

---

71 "History of Assyria," by A. T. Olmstead, Chicago: University of Chicago Press, 1951, pgs. 301 and 302.

Finally, it would seem the writers of the Dead Sea Scrolls would have known the route Sennacherib followed. But they plainly did not think Sennacherib followed this route, for one of them quoted this exact passage, (Isaiah 10:28-32) commenting that it referred to "the Last Days."[72]

The flight of the king

The king is fainthearted, (Jeremiah 4:9) and abandons his people, leaving them to face the invader without a king. (Micah 4:9) He does this because he does not care about them, for we read:

> **"I will raise up a shepherd in the land *who* will not care for those who are cut off, nor seek the young, nor heal those that are broken, nor feed those that still stand. But he will eat the flesh of the fat and tear their hooves in pieces. Woe to the worthless shepherd, Who leaves the flock!" (Zechariah 11:16-17)**

Our Lord contrasted himself to this king, saying:

> **"I am the good shepherd. The good shepherd gives His life for the sheep. But a hireling, *he who is* not the shepherd, one who does not own the sheep, sees the wolf coming and leaves the sheep and flees; and the wolf catches the sheep and scatters them. The hireling flees because he is a hireling and does not care about the sheep. I am the good shepherd; and I know My *sheep*, and am known by My own. As the Father knows Me, even so I know the Father; and I lay down My life for the sheep." (John 10:11-15)**

We notice that, in so contrasting himself to this evil king, Jesus, the true Messiah, was pointing him out as the Antichrist, the false messiah.

---

[72] From the commentary on Isaiah in "The Dead Sea Scrolls, a New Translation," by Michael Wise, Martin Abegg, Jr., and Edward Cook, New York: 1996, pg. 210. Scholars believe these scrolls were written between the first and third centuries B.C.

The worthless shepherd is severely wounded

We just noticed the words **"Woe to the worthless shepherd,"** because he **"leaves the flock!"** The next sentence says, **"A sword** *shall be* **against his arm And against his right eye; His arm shall completely wither, And his right eye shall be totally blinded."** (Zechariah 11:17) For more information on this, see footnote 17 on page 56.

The king escapes.

Though seriously wounded, **"the king"** escapes, for he **"shall prosper till the wrath has been accomplished."** (Daniel 11:36) We see him as **"the false prophet"** with the beast at two later times. In Revelation 16:13 these two call the armies of the world to Armageddon, and in Revelation 19:20 they are captured and punished together.

The rulers of Jerusalem attempt to flee, but are captured.

The rulers of Jerusalem also flee, but are captured, for we read in Isaiah 22:3 that **"All your rulers have fled together; They are captured by the archers. All who are found in you are bound together; They have fled from afar."**

Jerusalem falls.

"Behold, the day of the LORD is coming, And your spoil will be divided in your midst. For I will gather all the nations to battle against Jerusalem; The city shall be taken, The houses rifled, And the women ravished." (Zechariah 14:1-2) This is not just an ordinary defeat of a city. It is **"the day of the LORD;"** the day of the Lord's judgment of the whole world, beginning at Jerusalem.

The temple is cast down.

On page 56, we noticed the desolator described in Daniel 8:9 as **"a little horn which grew exceedingly great toward the south, toward the east, and toward the Glorious *Land*."** The eleventh and twelfth verses of that chapter tell us that **"He even exalted *himself* as high as the Prince of the host; and by** [73] **him the daily *sacrifices* were taken away, and the place of His sanctuary was cast down. Because of transgression, an army was given over *to the horn* to oppose the daily *sacrifices*."**

This is mourned at length in the third book of the Psalms, where we read:

> **"The enemy has damaged everything in the sanctuary. Your enemies roar in the midst of Your meeting place; They set up their banners *for* signs. They seem like men who lift up Axes among the thick trees. And now they break down its carved work, all at once, With axes and hammers. They have set fire to Your sanctuary; They have defiled the dwelling place of Your name to the ground. They said in their hearts, 'Let us destroy them altogether.' They have burned up all the meeting places of God in the land."** (Psalm 74:3-8)

> **"O God, the nations have come into Your inheritance; Your holy temple they have defiled; They have laid Jerusalem in**

---

73 This appears to contradict Daniel 9:27, which says that **"the prince who is to come"** (verse 26) **"shall bring an end to sacrifice and offering."** But the words *and by him* in the clause **"and by him the daily *sacrifices* were taken away"** (Daniel 8:11) are translated from the Hebrew word ***umimenu***, which is a combined word not included in Strong's Hebrew Dictionary. This word can also be translated ***and from him***. This reading, which is preferred by able translators including J. N. Darby, William Kelly, and the Jewish Publication Society, is given as a marginal reading in the King James Version. This translation makes the clause mean that the daily sacrifice was taken away *from* **"the Prince of the host,"** not *by* the **"little horn."** It also clarifies the last clause of the sentence, **"and the place of His sanctuary was cast down."** This last clause has to refer to **"the Prince of the host,"** because the **"little horn"** is conquering, not being cast down. The New American Standard Bible uses the sense *from him*, but adds the word *it* (from a possible rendering of the verb translated *removed*) saying "it removed the regular sacrifice from Him." This was also done in the New Revised Standard Version, the New International Version, and God's Word to the Nations.

heaps. The dead bodies of Your servants They have given *as* food for the birds of the heavens, The flesh of Your saints to the beasts of the earth. Their blood they have shed like water all around Jerusalem, And *there was* no one to bury them." (Psalm 79:1-3)

"My soul longs, yes, even faints For the courts of the LORD; My heart and my flesh cry out for the living God. Even the sparrow has found a home, And the swallow a nest for herself, Where she may lay her young; *Even* Your altars, O LORD of hosts, My King and my God." (Psalm 84:2-3)

The Lords's altars were supposed to be a place of continual fire. But the fires have gone out, and now birds have built nests in the altars!

Many nations join in the conquest of Jerusalem

In Zechariah 14:2, which we noticed on page 20, the Lord says **"I will gather all the nations [74] to battle against Jerusalem."** Like the destruction of the temple, this is mourned in the third book of the Psalms. But it is not only mourned. The specific nations making up this confederacy are named.

"Do not keep silent, O God! Do not hold Your peace, And do not be still, O God! For behold, Your enemies make a tumult;

---

[74] Some might find a problem in the words **"I will gather all the nations to battle against Jerusalem."** The prophetic scriptures tell of many nations that will be involved in this attack, but the list contains far less than **"all the nations."** This apparent difficulty disappears when we examine the Hebrew. The Hebrew word translated *all* is *kol*. (word number 3605 Strong's Hebrew Dictionary) There can be no doubt that the normal meaning of *kol* is *all* or *every*. But that is not the only way this word is used. Even in our English language, while *all* normally means *the sum total of each and every member* of a group, it is sometimes used in a more general sense. Hebrew uses the word *kol* in the same way. This more general use can be seen in 2 Samuel 6:5. **"Then David and all the house of Israel played *music* before the LORD on all kinds of *instruments of* fir wood, on harps, on stringed instruments, on tambourines, on sistrums, and on cymbals."** The Hebrew word translated *all kinds of* is *kol*. Now it should be evident to even the most casual reader that David and his people could not have been using every musical instrument in the entire world (or even in the entire city, for that matter). So from the context it is obvious that the correct translation is *all kinds of*, not *all*.

> And those who hate You have lifted up their head. They have taken crafty counsel against Your people, And consulted together against Your sheltered ones. They have said, 'Come, and let us cut them off from *being* a nation, That the name of Israel may be remembered no more.' For they have consulted together with one consent; They form a confederacy against You: The tents of Edom and the Ishmaelites; Moab and the Hagrites; Gebal, Ammon, and Amalek; Philistia with the inhabitants of Tyre; Assyria also has joined with them; They have helped the children of Lot. Selah" (Psalm 83:1-8)

The modern identities of some of these nations is not known with certainty. But it is known that they were all members of the various ethnic groups surrounding Israel. They mainly occupied the lands that make up present day Lebanon, Syria, Jordan, Iraq, the northern portion of Saudi Arabia, and the proposed Palestinian state.

Edom joins the attack.

In Obadiah 10-14 the Lord addresses Edom, saying:

> "For violence against your brother Jacob, Shame shall cover you, And you shall be cut off forever. In the day that you stood on the other side; In the day that strangers carried captive his forces, When foreigners entered his gates And cast lots for Jerusalem; Even you *were* as one of them. But you should not have gazed on the day of your brother In the day of his captivity; Nor should you have rejoiced over the children of Judah In the day of their destruction; Nor should you have spoken proudly In the day of distress. You should not have entered the gate of My people In the day of their calamity. Indeed, you should not have gazed on their affliction In the day of their calamity, Nor laid *hands* on their substance In the day of their calamity. You should not have stood at the crossroads To cut off those among them who escaped; Nor should you have delivered up those among them who remained In the day of distress."

Again, we read in Amos 1:11, **"Thus says the LORD: 'For three transgressions of Edom, and for four, I will not turn away its *punishment*, Because he pursued his brother with the sword, And cast off all pity; His anger tore perpetually, And he kept his wrath forever.'"**

We notice that both of these scriptures indicate that the Edomites will pursue those who escape. This clearly refers to the righteous remnant who will have fled just before the invasion. We remember that they will flee into the hill country of Edom and Moab. (see page 107) From this we learn that the Edomites will not help them, but will attack them as they flee. They will be severely punished for this crime, but not until later.

The Philistines help the Edomites.

The last passage we noticed about the attack by Edom (page 121) is part of Amos 1. Earlier in this chapter we read, **"Thus says the LORD: 'For three transgressions of Gaza, and for four, I will not turn away its *punishment*, Because they took captive the whole captivity To deliver *them* up to Edom. But I will send a fire upon the wall of Gaza, Which shall devour its palaces. I will cut off the inhabitant from Ashdod, And the one who holds the scepter from Ashkelon; I will turn My hand against Ekron, And the remnant of the Philistines shall perish,' Says the Lord GOD."** (Amos 1:6-8) The Palestinians of today proudly boast that they are these Philistines. It is interesting to note that Gaza has now been turned over to them.

The inhabitants of Tyre help the Edomites.

The account in Amos 1 continues, **"Thus says the LORD: 'For three transgressions of Tyre, and for four, I will not turn away its *punishment*, Because they delivered up the whole captivity to Edom, And did not remember the covenant of brotherhood.'"** (verse 9)

Sidon joins Tyre and the Philistines in this evil project.

> "Indeed, what have you to do with Me, O Tyre and Sidon, and all the coasts of Philistia? Will you retaliate against Me? But if you retaliate against Me, Swiftly and speedily I will return your retaliation upon your own head; Because you have taken My silver and My gold, And have carried into your temples My prized possessions. Also the people of Judah and the people of Jerusalem You have sold to the Greeks, That you may remove them far from their borders." (Joel 3:4-6)

In this prophecy we see that Sidon as well as Tyre (both in today's Lebanon) join with **"all the coasts of Philista"** in selling **"the people of Judah and the people of Jerusalem"** to **"the Greeks."** But how did **"the Greeks"** get into this picture. We have already noticed on pages 66, 67, 68, 208 that this war will be started by simultaneous attacks from the **"the king of the South"** and **"the king of the North."** On pages 54 and 55 we saw that these two kings ruled two of the four remnants of the kingdom of Alexander the Great, the great Greek conqueror. They are therefore called **"the Greeks."**

The three verses immediately preceding the last passage clearly show that this prophecy concerns the last days:

> "For behold, in those days and at that time, When I bring back the captives of Judah and Jerusalem, I will also gather all nations, And bring them down to the Valley of Jehoshaphat; And I will enter into judgment with them there On account of My people, My heritage Israel, Whom they have scattered among the nations; They have also divided up My land. They have cast lots for My people, Have given a boy *as payment* for a harlot, And sold a girl for wine, that they may drink." (Joel 3:1-3)

Babylon, **"The land of the Chaldeans,"** joins the attack.

> "'Behold, he shall come up like a lion from the floodplain of the Jordan Against the dwelling place of the strong; But I will

> make them suddenly run away from her. And who *is* a chosen *man that* I may appoint over her? For who *is* like Me? Who will arraign Me? And who *is* that shepherd Who will withstand Me?' Therefore hear the counsel of the LORD that He has taken against Babylon, And His purposes that He has proposed against the land of the Chaldeans: 'Surely the least of the flock shall draw them out; Surely He will make their dwelling place desolate with them. At the noise of the taking of Babylon The earth trembles, And the cry is heard among the nations.'" (Jeremiah 50:44-46)

While this prophecy is specifically about the end of the struggle, rather than the beginning, it clearly shows that **"Babylon,"** which is **"the land of the Chaldeans,"** will join in the attack. This is the southern part of today's Iraq. This has to be future, for ancient Babylon was never made to **"suddenly run away from"** anywhere, much less Jerusalem.

Even far off Elam is among the attackers.

> "For *it is* a day of trouble and treading down and perplexity By the Lord God of hosts In the Valley of Vision— Breaking down the walls And of crying to the mountain. Elam bore the quiver With chariots of men *and* horsemen, And Kir uncovered the shield. It shall come to pass *that* your choicest valleys Shall be full of chariots, And the horsemen shall set themselves in array at the gate." (Isaiah 22:5-7)

In this prophecy we find **"Elam"** specifically named among the attackers. This has to be future, for ancient **"Elam"** never attacked Judah. This ancient nation was located in what is now Iran, so far away that such an attack would have seemed unthinkable in Isaiah's day. But we understand this when we remember that the little horn of Daniel 8:9 **"grew exceedingly great toward the south, toward the east, and toward the Glorious *Land.*"**

We noticed on page 60 that this shows that, before attacking **"the Glorious Land,"** this evil king will conquer both **"Babylon,"** which is **"the land of the Chaldeans"** and **"Elam."** So he will already have full control over these lands before he begins his attack upon **"the Glorious Land."**

We also find **"Kir"** in this prophecy, but in Isaiah 15:1 we learn that **"Kir"** is a city **"of Moab,"** and we have already seen (on page 119) that Moab is among the attackers.

The Last Half of the Week

The king of the North overthrows many countries.

We have noticed (pages 65, 112) that in Daniel 11:41 **"the king of the North"** shall **"enter the Glorious Land."** this verse continues with the words **"and many *countries* shall be overthrown."** While the Assyrian found many nations useful in his attack on Judea, he is not their ally, for he turns to attack them.

Edom, Moab, and the prominent people of Ammon spared.

But some nations escape the Assyrian's wrath. Daniel 11:41 continues, **"but these shall escape from his hand: Edom, Moab, and the prominent people of Ammon."** These nations occupied most of the territory that is now called Jordan. This nation will be spared at this time. No reason for this is stated here, but we realize the reason when we remember that this is where the righteous have fled. (page 107) If the Assyrian's army overran this area, it would seek out and destroy these righteous ones. But as we have seen, (page 121) these nations will not welcome the refugees, but will try to capture or kill them. The escape of these nations will therefore be only temporary. They will be punished for these crimes when the Lord comes. (Isaiah 11:14, Ezekiel 25:1-14)

The Assyrian conquers Lebanon.

In Isaiah 10, immediately after the daily progress of the Assyrian's attack, (as noted on page 113) we read, **"Behold, the Lord, The LORD of hosts, Will lop off the bough with terror; Those of high stature *will be* hewn down, And the haughty will be humbled. He will cut down the thickets of the forest with iron, And Lebanon will fall by the Mighty One."** [75] (verses 33-34) This is (at least in part) the Lord's judgment on Tyre, a chief city of Lebanon, for its crimes in helping Edom prey upon the fleeing righteous, which we noticed in Amos 1:9. (page 121) In that prophecy the Lord said, **"But I will send a fire upon the wall of Tyre, Which shall devour its palaces."** (Amos 1:10) According to Joel 3:1-6, Sidon will also take part in this crime, but she is not mentioned here except in the general reference to Lebanon.

The Assyrian destroys Philistia (the area now called Palestine)

In Isaiah 14, just after announcing the destruction of the Assyrian, (verses 24-27) the Lord says, **"do not rejoice, all you of Philistia, Because the rod that struck you is broken; For out of the serpent's roots will come forth a viper, And its offspring *will be* a fiery flying serpent... And it will slay your remnant. Wail, O gate! Cry, O city! All you of Philistia are dissolved; For smoke will come from the north, And no one *will be* alone in his appointed times."** (verses 29-31) This destroyer will come out of the roots of one who had previously conquered Philistia. History tells us that this previous conqueror was Sennacherib, king of Assyria. Notice that in this passage the future Assyrian is referred to as a **"smoke... from the north."** This is another indication that **"the Assyrian"** is **"the king of the North."**

---

[75] The New King James, which we are using, joins a number of other modern translations in rendering the last three words of this passage as **"the Mighty One."** This indicates the translator's idea that these words refer to God. This is entirely a matter of interpretation. A number of other translations side with the old King James in rendering these words "*a mighty one.*" This indicates a persuasion that the words refer to a human conqueror. To me, this seems more likely, as the context is plainly that of the destructive campaign of **"the Assyrian."**

Even as Tyre, Sidon, and the Philistines were united in their attack upon Jerusalem, they will be destroyed together.

> "The word of the LORD that came to Jeremiah the prophet against the Philistines, before Pharaoh attacked Gaza. Thus says the LORD:
>
> 'Behold, waters rise out of the north, And shall be an overflowing flood; They shall overflow the land and all that is in it, The city and those who dwell within; Then the men shall cry, And all the inhabitants of the land shall wail. At the noise of the stamping hooves of his strong horses, At the rushing of his chariots, At the rumbling of his wheels, The fathers will not look back for their children, Lacking courage, Because of the day that comes to plunder all the Philistines, To cut off from Tyre and Sidon every helper who remains; For the LORD shall plunder the Philistines, The remnant of the country of Caphtor. Baldness has come upon Gaza, Ashkelon is cut off With the remnant of their valley." (Jeremiah 47:1-5)

We note in passing that, while this prophecy came **"before Pharaoh attacked Gaza,"** it speaks of an attack from **"the north,"** not from the south, the homeland of Pharaoh. The north, as we have seen, (pages 53 to 63) is the homeland of **"the Assyrian."** Even as we noticed in the case of Sennacherib, (page 50) Pharaoh's attack was the occasion of this prophecy, but not its only subject.

As in the case of Lebanon, and in particular the city of Tyre, and as we noticed on page 121, Amos 1:6 says the Philistines will be destroyed **"Because they took captive the whole captivity To deliver *them* up to Edom."** that passage continues:

> "'But I will send a fire upon the wall of Gaza, Which shall devour its palaces. I will cut off the inhabitant from Ashdod, And the one who holds the scepter from Ashkelon; I will turn My hand against Ekron, And the remnant of the Philistines shall perish,' Says the Lord GOD." (Amos 1:7-8)

This is again mentioned in Zechariah: **"Ashkelon shall see it and fear; Gaza also shall be very sorrowful; And Ekron, for He dried up her expectation. The king shall perish from Gaza, And Ashkelon shall not be inhabited."** (Zechariah 9:5)

The king of the North invades Egypt.

The account in Daniel 11 continues with **"the king of the North,"** saying that **"He shall stretch out his hand against the countries, and the land of Egypt shall not escape. He shall have power over the treasures of gold and silver, and over all the precious things of Egypt."** (Daniel 11:42-43)

We note in passing that Saudi Arabia, a nation along the route to Egypt, has become one of the richest nations in the world, having great treasuries of gold and silver.

The king of the North subdues Libya and Ethiopia.

The account continues with the words: **"also the Libyans and Ethiopians *shall follow* at his heels."** [76] (Daniel 11:43)

The king of the North returns to Judea.

The account continues: **"But news from the east and the north shall trouble him; therefore he shall go out with great fury to destroy and annihilate many. And he shall plant the tents of his palace between the seas and the glorious holy mountain."** (Daniel 11:44-45)

---

76 In the Hebrew original, this is a difficult sentence and there is little agreement between the various translations. While several other translations use the same words as the New King James, which we are using, nearly as many read "shall be at his steps" or "are at his steps." Others give "will surrender to him", "will submit to him", "will be his servants", "will obey him", or "in submission." However this difficult sentence is translated, the thought expressed in the last clause "***shall follow at his heels***" is definitely not willing allegiance.

There is some question as to the correct translation of the clause **"between the seas and."** Some make the sea singular instead of plural, others render the word **"and"** as "in" or "at." But **"the glorious holy mountain"** is plainly mount Zion. So we see that this evil king returns from Egypt to the land of Judea. And when he returns, he does it **"with great fury to destroy and annihilate many."** This is evidently the time spoken of in Zechariah 13:8; **"'And it shall come to pass in all the land,' Says the LORD, 'That two-thirds in it shall be cut off *and* die, But *one*-third shall be left in it:'"**

But what is the reason for this king's fury? He has returned to Judea because of **"news from the east and the north."** We are not expressly told the nature of this news, but as it comes **"from the east and from the north"** it would appear that it involves preparations for attacks from these areas. But we are not specifically told that any such attacks will occur at this time. [77]

The great tribulation

We just noticed that in Daniel 11:45 (the last verse of chapter 11) **"the king of the North"** returns to Judea. In the next verse (Daniel 12:1) the account continues: **"At that time Michael shall stand up, The great prince who stands *watch* over the sons of your people; And there shall be a time of trouble, Such as never was since there was a nation, *Even* to that time."**

We have also noticed (pages 16, 17, 26, 62, 105) our Lord's instructions to the righteous to flee when they see the abomination of desolation (Matthew 24:15-18) The next section reads:

> **"But woe to those who are pregnant and to those who are nursing babies in those days! And pray that your flight may not be in winter or on the Sabbath. For then there will be great tribulation,**

---

[77] An invasion from the east is prophesied in Revelation 16. But as that prophecy is in symbolic language not accompanied by an inspired interpretation, it is outside of the subject matter of this book.

> such as has not been since the beginning of the world until this time, no, nor ever shall be. And unless those days were shortened, no flesh would be saved; but for the elect's sake those days will be shortened." (Matthew 24:19-22)

When I was young I pondered long over these words, repeatedly saying to myself, "I cannot conceive of a war that would literally kill everyone, and everything!" Today it is common knowledge that an all out nuclear exchange would end all life on this planet. There can be no reasonable doubt that our Lord was referring to this threat when He said that **"unless those days were shortened, no flesh would be saved."** But He also added the words **"but for the elect's sake those days will be shortened."** We can therefore safely conclude that the threat of nuclear annihilation is real. In fact, it would definitely happen if our Lord did not step in. But He has promised to step in before it goes that far. The all out nuclear exchange that would end all life on this planet will not take place. But this does not mean there will not be a limited nuclear exchange.

We should also notice that the Lord said to pray that their flight should not be on the Sabbath. From this we realize that this instruction is not directed toward Christians, but Jews, for Jewish law allowed only very limited travel on the Sabbath. According to Acts 1:12, this was the distance from Mount Olivet to Jerusalem, which is only about nine tenths of a mile. The idea that this only applies to Israel and the Jews is confirmed by Jeremiah 30:5-7:

> **"We have heard a voice of trembling, Of fear, and not of peace. Ask now, and see, Whether a man is ever in labor with child? So why do I see every man *with* his hands on his loins Like a woman in labor, And all faces turned pale? Alas! For that day *is* great, So that none *is* like it; And it *is* the time of Jacob's trouble, But he shall be saved out of it."**

We thus understand that, while there will be much sorrow around the world (Matthew 24:8) this is particularly **"the time of Jacob's trouble."**

The ruins of Jerusalem fortified [78]

We noticed the fall of Jerusalem in Zechariah 14:1-2. (page 117) This passage continues with the words **"Half of the city shall go into captivity, But the remnant of the people shall not be cut off from the city."** (Zechariah 14:2)

Those who remain will fortify what is left of the city, for we read in Isaiah 22:9-11 that **"You also saw the damage to the city of David, That it was great; And you gathered together the waters of the lower pool. You numbered the houses of Jerusalem, And the houses you broke down To fortify the wall. You also made a reservoir between the two walls For the water of the old pool."**

We must remember that this is after the righteous have been forced to flee from the city. Only the wicked are now there, so this fortification is not done in faith. It is celebrated with an impious feast, for which the Lord declares a most solemn judgment.

> **"But you did not look to its Maker, Nor did you have respect for Him who fashioned it long ago. And in that day the Lord GOD of hosts Called for weeping and for mourning, For baldness and for girding with sackcloth. But instead, joy and gladness, Slaying oxen and killing sheep, Eating meat and drinking wine: 'Let us eat and drink, for tomorrow we die!' Then it was revealed in my hearing by the LORD of hosts, 'Surely for this iniquity there will be no atonement for you, Even to your death,' says the Lord GOD of hosts."** (Isaiah 22:11-14)

---

78 This event is presented at this point in this account to get its connection with the siege of Jerusalem. That is, to understand how Jerusalem could be under siege when the Lord comes, even though it had already been defeated three and a half years earlier. It would seem most likely, however, that this event will take place while **"the king of the North"** is in Egypt. Such activity would not seem to be possible either before or after that time.

Jerusalem besieged

> "Woe to Ariel, to Ariel, the city *where* David dwelt! Add year to year; Let feasts come around. Yet I will distress Ariel; There shall be heaviness and sorrow, And it shall be to Me as Ariel. I will encamp against you all around, I will lay siege against you with a mound, And I will raise siegeworks against you. You shall be brought down, You shall speak out of the ground; Your speech shall be low, out of the dust; Your voice shall be like a medium's, out of the ground; And your speech shall whisper out of the dust." (Isaiah 29:1-4)

We note in passing that the words **"add year to year"** indicate that this siege will last at least two years.

The agents of this judgment are the surrounding nations. But in this passage the Lord declares that He is Himself the one laying siege to Jerusalem. That is, this is but another of the Lord's severe judgments against this city that has still not repented. But it is important to notice that while this scripture says **"You shall be brought down,"** it does not say that the city will be taken. The pillage and rape we previously saw in Zechariah 14:1-2 (page 117) are not mentioned. As is common in a prolonged siege, Jerusalem will be reduced to the point of death, but this time it will not be overthrown.

But this siege is not only the Lord's design for the judgment of Jerusalem. It is also for the judgment of the surrounding nations, as we see in Micah 4:11-12. **"Now also many nations have gathered against you, Who say, 'Let her be defiled, And let our eye look upon Zion. But they do not know the thoughts of the LORD, Nor do they understand His counsel; For He will gather them like sheaves to the threshing floor.'"** So the Lord says in Zechariah 12:2-3 **"Behold, I will make Jerusalem a cup of drunkenness to all the surrounding peoples, when they lay siege against Judah and Jerusalem. And it shall happen in that day that I will make Jerusalem a very heavy stone for all peoples; all who would heave** it away will surely be cut in pieces, though all nations of the earth are gathered against it." We will see the result in the next section. (page 134)

Rescue - The LORD's Campaigns

The Lord of Lords comes

The physical return of the Lord to judge the earth is one of the great themes of scripture. Probably the best known reference to this earth shattering event is John's vision in Revelation 19:11-16.

> **"I saw heaven opened, and behold, a white horse. And He who sat on him *was* called Faithful and True, and in righteousness He judges and makes war. His eyes *were* like a flame of fire, and on His head *were* many crowns. He had a name written that no one knew except Himself. He *was* clothed with a robe dipped in blood, and His name is called The Word of God. And the armies in heaven, clothed in fine linen, white and clean, followed Him on white horses. Now out of His mouth goes a sharp sword, that with it He should strike the nations. And He Himself will rule them with a rod of iron. He Himself treads the winepress of the fierceness and wrath of Almighty God. And He has on *His* robe and on His thigh a name written: KING OF KINGS AND LORD OF LORDS."**

The symbolic significance of this vision is beyond the scope of this book. But there can be no doubt it indicates the Lord coming in an awesome display of power and glory.

But is this intended to be taken as a literal fact? Many other passages of scripture make this abundantly clear. In speaking of this time, our Lord himself said **"Then the sign of the Son of Man will appear in heaven, and then all the tribes of the earth will mourn, and they will see the Son of Man** coming on the clouds of heaven with power and great glory." (Matthew 24:30) Again we read in Jude, verses 14-15, **"Behold, the Lord comes with ten thousands of His saints, to execute judgment on all, to convict all who are ungodly among them of all their ungodly deeds which they have committed in an ungodly way, and of all the harsh things which ungodly sinners have spoken against Him."**

These passages, though graphic, are general in nature. But Bible prophecy is not limited to the general. Much of the widespread error in interpreting prophecy stems from a failure to understand this basic fact. Much of Bible prophecy is specific, exact, and highly detailed. This includes the Lord's campaign against the wicked. It is described in great detail. We first need to realize that when He comes, He will come in judgment. His ultimate goal is to bless the entire earth, but this cannot take place until he has judged the wicked. No more is he seen as **"Lowly and riding on a donkey, A colt, the foal of a donkey."** (Zechariah 9:9) Now he comes in power and glory as the king. We read in Psalm 45:3-5, **"Gird Your sword upon Your thigh, O Mighty One, With Your glory and Your majesty.** [79] **And in Your majesty ride prosperously because of truth, humility, and righteousness; And Your right hand shall teach You awesome things. Your arrows are sharp in the heart of the King's enemies; The peoples fall under You."**

This is like the warning of Deuteronomy 32:39-43:

> **"Now see that I, *even* I, *am* He, And *there is* no God besides Me; I kill and I make alive; I wound and I heal; Nor *is there any* who can deliver from My hand. For I raise My hand to heaven, And say, *'As* I live forever, If I whet My glittering sword, And My hand takes hold on judgment, I will render vengeance to My enemies, And repay those who hate Me. I will make My arrows drunk with blood, And My sword shall devour flesh, With the blood of the slain and the captives, From the heads of the leaders of the enemy.' 'Rejoice, O Gentiles, *with* His**

---

[79] We note in passing that, as this is in the second book of the Psalms, this is not mentioned as a present fact, but as a petition for the future.

people; For He will avenge the blood of His servants, And render vengeance to His adversaries; He will provide atonement for His land *and* His people.'"

We left Jerusalem under siege, surrounded by many nations. When the Lord appears, he will deal with this in summary manner. **"Then the LORD will go forth And fight against those nations, As He fights in the day of battle. And in that day His feet will stand on the Mount of Olives, Which faces Jerusalem on the east. And the Mount of Olives shall be split in two, From east to west,** *Making* **a very large valley; Half of the mountain shall move toward the north And half of it toward the south."** (Zechariah 14:3-4) As can be seen in the map on page 232, the Lord's campaigns start at the Mount of Olives.

Micah 1:3-5 says, **"For behold, the LORD is coming out of His place; He will come down And tread on the high places of the earth. The mountains will melt under Him, And the valleys will split Like wax before the fire, Like waters poured down a steep place. All this is for the transgression of Jacob And for the sins of the house of Israel."** What can it mean that **"all this is for the transgression of Jacob And for the sins of the house of Israel."** Isn't this the Lord's deliverance of Jerusalem? We remember that when Jerusalem was fortified, it was in unbelief. (Isaiah 22:11-14, page 130) The Lord, in His glorious appearing, drives the nations away. But Jerusalem must also be punished. She has to flee as well, not this time from an army, but from an earthquake. Zechariah 14:4, which we have just noticed, says that the earthquake will **"make a very large valley."** The next verse continues with the words **"Then you shall flee** *through* **My mountain valley, For the mountain valley shall reach to Azal. Yes, you shall flee As you fled from the earthquake In the days of Uzziah king of Judah. Thus the LORD my God will come,** *And* **all the saints with You."** (Zechariah 14:5) We also read in Zechariah 12:7 that **"The LORD will save the tents of Judah first, so that the glory of the house of David and the glory of the inhabitants of**

Jerusalem shall not become greater than that of Judah."** From this we see that Jerusalem will not be saved before **"the tents of Judah."**

The nations are driven away from Jerusalem.

We have already noticed (on page 134) that Zechariah 14:3 says, **"Then the LORD will go forth And fight against those nations, As He fights in the day of battle."** When the Lord keeps this promise, He says **"Moreover the multitude of your foes Shall be like fine dust, And the multitude of the terrible ones Like chaff that passes away; Yes, it shall be in an instant, suddenly."** (Isaiah 29:5) Again, Isaiah 17:12-13 says, **"Woe to the multitude of many people *Who* make a noise like the roar of the seas, And to the rushing of nations *That* make a rushing like the rushing of mighty waters! The nations will rush like the rushing of many waters; But *God* will rebuke them and they will flee far away, And be chased like the chaff of the mountains before the wind, Like a rolling thing before the whirlwind."** Edom is particularly noticed in this regard, for concerning him, (Jeremiah 49:17) the Lord says, **"Behold, he shall come up like a lion from the floodplain of the Jordan Against the dwelling place of the strong; But I will suddenly make him run away from her. And who *is* a chosen *man that* I may appoint over her? For who *is* like Me? Who will arraign Me? And who *is* that shepherd Who will withstand Me?"** [80] (verse 19)

Joel 3:1-2, which we noticed on page 122, says these nations will not come against Jerusalem of their own accord. They will be brought there by the Lord. But this passage also tells us where He will force them as they flee. **"For behold, in those days and at that time, When I bring back the captives of Judah and Jerusalem, I will also gather all nations,**

---

[80] As noted on page 122, these exact words are also said of **"Babylon," "the land of the Chaldeans,"** in Jeremiah 50:44.

And bring them down to the Valley of Jehoshaphat; And I will enter into judgment with them there On account of My people, My heritage Israel, Whom they have scattered among the nations; They have also divided up My land."** He will **"enter into judgment with them"** in **"the Valley of Jehoshaphat."**

Where is this **"Valley of Jehoshaphat?"** Scholars are not certain. But there are several common theories. Tradition (which is seldom reliable) identifies it with the Kidron valley. But this location does not fit some of the details we shall shortly examine. Some think it is the Valley of the son of Hinnom, on the opposite side of Jerusalem, because we are twice told that this valley will no more be called by that name, but will be called the **"Valley of Slaughter."** (Jeremiah 7:32 and 19:6) But a careful reading of these passages shows that they do not refer to a judgment of the gentile nations, but of Judah.

Scholars of today do not know of any valley that was ever called the **"Valley of Jehoshaphat"** but there is a valley that could very appropriately be called by this name. In 2 Chronicles 20, **"some came and told Jehoshaphat, saying, 'A great multitude is coming against you from beyond the sea, from Syria; and they are in Hazazon Tamar' (which *is* En Gedi)."** (verse 2)

Jehoshaphat called all Judah to fast and pray, and the Lord answered **"Do not be afraid nor dismayed because of this great multitude, for the battle *is* not yours, but God's. Tomorrow go down against them. They will surely come up by the Ascent of Ziz, and you will find them at the end of the brook before the Wilderness of Jeruel. You will not *need* to fight in this *battle*. Position yourselves, stand still and see the salvation of the LORD, who is with you, O Judah and Jerusalem!"** (verses 15-17)

Believing this promise, the people **"rose early in the morning and went out into the Wilderness of Tekoa."** (verse 20) And **"the LORD set ambushes against the people of Ammon, Moab, and Mount Seir, who had come against Judah; and they were defeated. For the people of Ammon and Moab stood up against the inhabitants of Mount Seir to utterly kill** and destroy *them*. And when they had made an end of the inhabitants of Seir, they helped to destroy one another. So when Judah came to a place overlooking the wilderness, they looked toward the multitude; and there *were* their dead bodies, fallen on the earth. No one had escaped." (verses 22-24) There was so much spoil it took three days to gather it. **"And on the fourth day they assembled in the Valley of Berachah,** [81] **for there they blessed the LORD; therefore the name of that place was called The Valley of Berachah until this day."** (verse 26)

As noted above, the **"Valley of Jehoshaphat"** would be a most appropriate name for the place where this happened. To locate this valley, we first need to locate the places named. **"En Gedi,"** the place where the invading army was encamped, is near the center of the western shore of the Dead Sea. See the map on page 232. As can be further seen in the map on page 231, the **"Ascent of Ziz"** is a ravine that rises from a lower wilderness called the **"Wilderness of Jeruel"** to an upper wilderness called the **"Wilderness of Tekoa."** [82] This upper wilderness is not the top of the mountain, but only a plateau that forms a broad valley. This valley is almost certainly where the invading army was destroyed, and is believed to be the Biblical **"Valley of Berachah."** As can be seen in the map on page 231, it runs generally east to west, from the cliffs above Ziz (about six miles north of En Gedi) to about nine miles south of Jerusalem. The prophetic name of the **"Valley of Jehoshaphat"** almost certainly refers to this valley.

The northern army is destroyed.

On page 54 we noticed that the indignation against Judah will cease, as will God's anger, in the destruction of the Assyrian. This is when the

---

81 This name is transliterated from the Hebrew word ***berakah***, which means blessing. (word number 1293 in Strong's Hebrew Dictionary)

82 Actually, there are two ravines that fit this description, but most scholars think the northern one is the Biblical **"Ascent of Ziz."**

deliverance of Judah begins. In Joel 2:20 the Lord declares **"But I will remove far from you the northern *army*, And will drive him away into a barren and desolate land, With his face toward the eastern sea And his back toward the western sea; His stench will come up, And his foul odor will rise, Because he has done monstrous things."** The valley we have been discussing runs through **"a barren and desolate land."** An army driven away from Jerusalem and fleeing down this valley would have its **"face toward the eastern sea"** and its **"back toward the western sea."** Thus we see that this valley fits both the name **"the Valley of Jehoshaphat,"** and also the description of where the Lord will deal with **"the northern *army*."** So the map on page 231 shows the path of the Assyrian ending in this valley.

We can now understand why the Kidron valley does not fit this description. It fails on several counts. First, **"the northern army"** will be **"removed far from"** Jerusalem. The Kidron valley begins just under the walls of Jerusalem. An army driven into this valley would not be **"far from"** Jerusalem. Second, the Hebrew word translated *valley* in both the **"valley of Berachah"** and the **"valley of Jehoshaphat"** is *'emeq.* (word number 6010 in Strong's Hebrew Dictionary) This is also the Hebrew word used in the **"valley of decision,"** which Joel uses to describe the **"valley of Jehoshaphat."** (Joel 3:14) (see page 140) As we noticed on page 78, this Hebrew word indicates a broad valley, rather than a narrow one. But the Hebrew word translated *brook* in each place where the **"Brook Kidron"** is mentioned is *nachal.* (word number 5158 in Strong's Hebrew Dictionary) This word means either a brook or a narrow valley. This is very suitable, for the Kidron valley is indeed narrow.

This reason applies even more strongly to the **"Valley of the son of Hinnom."** The Hebrew word used for this valley is *gay'.* (word number 1516 in Strong's Hebrew Dictionary) This Hebrew word means a *gorge*, that is, a valley even narrower than a *nachal.* We need to remember that on page 137 we noticed that the **"Wilderness of Tekoa,"** Which scholars think is the Biblical **"Valley of Berachah,"** is a broad valley, that is an *'emeq*. So this is the only one of these valleys that even could be the Biblical **"valley of Jehoshaphat."**

A final reason, based on logic rather than the Biblical description, is that the Kidron valley is between the Mount of Olives, where the Lord will appear, and Jerusalem. Unless the besieging army was actually on the Mount of Olives, it would have to run toward the Lord, rather than away from Him, to get into the Kidron valley. But we remember that the Mount of Olives will split when the Lord's feet touch it, half of it moving toward the south and half toward the north. (Zechariah 14:4, page 134) If the army was actually on the mountain as it split, it would seem that such a violent earthquake would destroy it so completely it would be unable to flee.

This geographical discussion is a departure from the general theme of this book, which is to concentrate on expressly stated prophecies that need only minimal interpretation. I have done this because knowing the locations of these events helps in understanding them. While the reasons for concluding that the **"Valley of Jehoshaphat"** is the **"Valley of Berachah"** seem very strong, this is only an interpretation of scripture.

Since this is only an interpretation, it may not be correct. But the events that will take place in this valley are not interpretations. These are not things that might happen, but things that will most certainly happen. For **"The LORD of hosts has sworn, saying, 'Surely, as I have thought, so it shall come to pass, And as I have purposed,** *so* **it shall stand: That I will break the Assyrian in My land, And on My mountains tread him underfoot. Then his yoke shall be removed from them, And his burden removed from their shoulders. This** *is* **the purpose that is purposed against the whole earth, And this** *is* **the hand that is stretched out over all the nations. For the LORD of hosts has purposed, And who will annul** *it?* **His hand** *is* **stretched out, And who will turn it back?'"** (Isaiah 14:24-27)

The king of Assyria will escape at this time, for we read in Isaiah 31:8-9 that **"Assyria shall fall by a sword not of man, And a sword not of mankind shall devour him. But he shall flee from the sword, And his young men shall become forced labor. He shall cross over to his stronghold for fear, And his princes shall be afraid of the banner,' Says the LORD, Whose fire** *is* **in Zion And whose furnace** *is* **in Jerusalem."**

The nations are destroyed.

But it is not only **"the northern *army*"** that is destroyed in this valley. Though men make much more of Armageddon, and that will indeed be a great battle, the **"Valley of Jehoshaphat"** is **"the valley of decision."**

> **"Proclaim this among the nations: 'Prepare for war! Wake up the mighty men, Let all the men of war draw near, Let them come up. Beat your plowshares into swords And your pruning hooks into spears; Let the weak say, "I** *am* **strong."' Assemble and come, all you nations, And gather together all around. Cause Your mighty ones to go down there, O LORD. 'Let the nations be wakened, and come up to the Valley of Jehoshaphat; For there I will sit to judge all the surrounding nations. Put in the sickle, for the harvest is ripe. Come, go down; For the winepress is full, The vats overflow; For their wickedness** *is* **great.' Multitudes, multitudes in the valley of decision! For the day of the LORD** *is* **near in the valley of decision."** (Joel 3:9-14)

We should notice that this is not the great judgment of the nations described in Matthew 25:31-46. At that judgment there will be reward as well as punishment. Here, there is no blessing, but only unsparing destruction of the enemies of God's chosen people.

Edom is destroyed.

In the mad flight of the nations, Edom appears to be pushed by the armies behind them, for we read in Obadiah 7 that **"All the men in your confederacy Shall force you to the border; The men at peace with you Shall deceive you *and* prevail against you. *Those who eat* your bread shall lay a trap for you. No one is aware of it."** [83] So the map on page 231 shows Edom continuing through the Valley of Jehoshaphat, where the rest of the armies will be destroyed, down the Ascent of Ziz, and along the shore of the Dead sea toward their homeland. Edom reaches home, but not safety, for Jeremiah 49:8 says, **"Flee, turn back, dwell in the depths, O inhabitants of Dedan! For I will bring the calamity of Esau upon him, The time *that* I will punish him."**

We have noticed (page 120) the Lord's prophecy **"concerning Edom"** (Obadiah 1) **"For violence against your brother Jacob, Shame shall cover you, And you shall be cut off forever."** (verse 10) Verse 15 concludes this section with the words, **"For the day of the LORD upon all the nations *is* near; As you have done, it shall be done to you; Your reprisal shall return upon your own head."**

When we previously noticed this prophecy, it was in regard to what Edom did to Judah, but now we must notice it in a different light. Edom's crimes against Judah are the reason for the terrible judgment that now falls on this land. We also noticed Amos 1:11, (page 121) where we read

"Thus says the LORD: 'For three transgressions of Edom, and for four, I will not turn away its *punishment*, Because he pursued his brother with the sword, And cast off all pity; His anger tore perpetually, And he kept his wrath forever.'" The next verse reads, **"But I will send a fire upon Teman, Which shall devour the palaces of Bozrah."**

---

83 The wording of our translation and numerous others implies that this will be an intentional plot by Edom's confederates. But this is not necessarily the meaning of this passage, as we see in Young's Literal Translation (by the Dr. Young of Young's Concordance fame): "Unto the border sent thee have all thine allies, Forgotten thee, prevailed over thee, have thy friends, Thy bread they make a snare under thee, There is no understanding in him!" This seems to imply carelessness or recklessness, as would occur in a state of panic, rather than intent.

Isaiah and Jeremiah describe this judgment in detail.

> "For My sword shall be bathed in heaven; Indeed it shall come down on Edom, And on the people of My curse, for judgment. The sword of the LORD is filled with blood, It is made overflowing with fatness, With the blood of lambs and goats, With the fat of the kidneys of rams. For the LORD has a sacrifice in Bozrah, And a great slaughter in the land of Edom. The wild oxen shall come down with them, And the young bulls with the mighty bulls; Their land shall be soaked with blood, And their dust saturated with fatness. For *it is* the day of the Lord's vengeance, The year of recompense for the cause of Zion. Its streams shall be turned into pitch, And its dust into brimstone; Its land shall become burning pitch. It shall not be quenched night or day; Its smoke shall ascend forever. From generation to generation it shall lie waste; No one shall pass through it forever and ever." (Isaiah 34:5-10)

> "Therefore hear the counsel of the LORD that He has taken against Edom, And His purposes that He has proposed against the inhabitants of Teman: Surely the least of the flock shall draw them out; Surely He shall make their dwelling places desolate with them. The earth shakes at the noise of their fall; At the cry its noise is heard at the Red Sea. Behold, He shall come up and fly like the eagle, And spread His wings over Bozrah; The heart of the mighty men of Edom in that day shall be Like the heart of a woman in birth pangs." (Jeremiah 49:20-22)

As can be seen in the map on page 232, this judgment begins at Bozrah, about thirty miles south of the Dead Sea. It then goes some twenty-five miles south to Teman, and from there to within hearing distance of the Red Sea. Habakkuk 3:3, which we will examine shortly, (page 143) mentions His coming from Mount Paran, which is approximately one hundred and sixty miles southeast of Teman, and is on the shore of the Red Sea. This entire area will receive the same judgment as Sodom and Gomorrah.

God returns from destroying Edom.

> "Who *is* this who comes from Edom, With dyed garments from Bozrah, This *One who is* glorious in His apparel, Traveling in the greatness of His strength?; 'I who speak in righteousness, mighty to save.' Why *is* Your apparel red, And Your garments like one who treads in the winepress? 'I have trodden the winepress alone, And from the peoples no one *was* with Me. For I have trodden them in My anger, And trampled them in My fury; Their blood is sprinkled upon My garments, And I have stained all My robes. For the day of vengeance *is* in My heart, And the year of My redeemed has come. I looked, but *there was* no one to help, And I wondered That *there was* no one to uphold; Therefore My own arm brought salvation for Me; And My own fury, it sustained Me. I have trodden down the peoples in My anger, Made them drunk in My fury, And brought down their strength to the earth.'" (Isaiah 63:1-6)

But the work is now only well started, **"For the indignation of the LORD *is* against all nations, And *His* fury against all their armies."** (Isaiah 34:2) As can be further seen in the map on page 232, God returns to Jerusalem after destroying Edom. But when He returns, it is not yet in blessing. It is still in judgment, for we read in Habakkuk 3:3-6 that **"God came from Teman, The Holy One from Mount Paran. Selah. His glory covered the heavens, And the earth was full of His praise. *His* brightness was like the light; He had rays *flashing* from His hand, And there His power *was* hidden. Before Him went pestilence, And fever followed at His feet. He stood and measured the earth; He looked and startled the nations. And the everlasting mountains were scattered, The perpetual hills bowed. His ways *are* everlasting."**

The Lord comes to His Temple.

We see this again in Malachi 3:1-3, **"And the Lord, whom you seek, Will suddenly come to His temple, Even the Messenger of the covenant, In whom you delight. Behold, He is coming,' Says the LORD of hosts. 'But who can endure the day of His coming? And who can stand when He appears? For He *is* like a refiner's fire And like launderer's soap. He will sit as a refiner and a purifier of silver; He will purify the sons of Levi, And purge them as gold and silver, That they may offer to the LORD An offering in righteousness.'"** But we remember that the righteous had been cast out three and a half years earlier. (see page 105) All who are left are wicked. So this coming is not deliverance, but a terror, as we read in Isaiah 66:6. **"The sound of noise from the city! A voice from the temple! The voice of the LORD, Who fully repays His enemies!"**

Armageddon

Such events could not fail to get the world's attention. **"The kings of the earth and of the whole world"** [84] respond to this new threat. **"The kings from the east"** are particularly noticed. The Euphrates River is dried up so they can cross it. In light of this detail, it is interesting to note that a dam has now been built on the Euphrates River, so this has become possible by mere human means.

> "Then the sixth angel poured out his bowl on the great river Euphrates, and its water was dried up, so that the way of the kings from the east might be prepared. And I saw three unclean spirits like frogs *coming* out of the mouth of the dragon, out of the mouth of the beast, and out of the mouth of the false prophet. For they are spirits of demons, performing signs,

---

[84] We should note in passing that this expression **"the kings of the earth and of the whole world"** shows that in Bible prophecy the terms **"the earth"** and **"the whole world"** have different meanings.

which **go out to the kings of the earth and of the whole world, to gather them to the battle of that great day of God Almighty. 'Behold, I am coming as a thief. Blessed** *is* **he who watches, and keeps his garments, lest he walk naked and they see his shame.' And they gathered them together to the place called in Hebrew, Armageddon."** (Revelation 16:12-16)

As can be seen in the map on page 232, Armageddon is on the edge of the plain of Megiddo, about 55 miles north of Jerusalem. Some call it the "valley of Armageddon," but it is not so called in scripture. There is a reference to the **"Valley of Megiddo"** in 2 Chronicles 35:22 and in some translations of Zechariah 12:11. But it is important to realize that the Hebrew word translated *valley* in these places is distinctly different from the Hebrew word used for the **"valley of Jehoshaphat."** Megiddo is a *biq'ah.* (word number 1237 in Strong's Hebrew Dictionary) This indicates a wide level valley between mountains, or a *plain*. This Hebrew word is also used for Megiddo in Zechariah 12:11, where our translation renders it as a **"plain,"** rather than a *valley*.

We saw (on page 78) that the **"valley of Jehoshaphat"** is an *'emeq*, that is, a *vale*. This plainly shows that these are different valleys. We therefore understand that the prophesied judgment in the **"valley of Jehoshaphat"** is not just another description of the battle of Armageddon.

Demons go out performing signs, to gather all the nations. (Revelation 16:13-14) The ten kings allied with the Beast are particularly noticed. **"The ten horns which you saw are ten kings who have received no kingdom as yet, but they receive authority for one hour as kings with the beast. These are of one mind, and they will give their power and authority to the beast. These will make war with the Lamb, and the Lamb will overcome them, for He is Lord of lords and King of kings; and those** *who are* **with Him** *are* **called, chosen, and faithful."** (Revelation 17:12-14)

But it is not only **"the kings of the earth"** that prepare for this battle. The Lord makes preparations of his own. **"Then I saw an angel standing in** the sun; and he cried with a loud voice, saying to all the birds that fly in the midst of heaven, 'Come and gather together for the supper of the great God, that you may eat the flesh of kings, the flesh of captains, the flesh of mighty men, the flesh of horses and of those who sit on them, and the flesh of all *people*, free and slave, both small and great.'" (Revelation 19:17-18)

The beast and the false prophet cast into the lake of fire

There can only be one outcome in such an uneven contest. **"And I saw the beast, the kings of the earth, and their armies, gathered together to make war against Him who sat on the horse and against His army. Then the beast was captured, and with him the false prophet who worked signs in his presence, by which he deceived those who received the mark of the beast and those who worshiped his image. These two were cast alive into the lake of fire burning with brimstone. And the rest were killed with the sword which proceeded from the mouth of Him who sat on the horse. And all the birds were filled with their flesh."** (Revelation 19:19-21)

The survivors from this battle sent to call all Israel home.

This is explicitly stated in Isaiah 66:15-20, where the Lord says:

> "For behold, the Lord will come with fire And with His chariots, like a whirlwind, To render His anger with fury, And His rebuke with flames of fire. For by fire and by His sword The Lord will judge all flesh; And the slain of the Lord shall be many. 'Those who sanctify themselves and purify themselves, To go to the gardens After an *idol* in the midst, Eating swine's flesh and the abomination and the mouse, Shall be consumed together," says the Lord.
>
> 'For I *know* their works and their thoughts. It shall be that I will gather all nations and tongues; and they shall come and

see My glory. I will set a sign among them; and those among them who escape I will send to the nations: *to* Tarshish and Pul and Lud, who draw the bow, and Tubal and Javan, *to* the coastlands afar off who have not heard My fame nor seen My glory. And they shall declare My glory among the Gentiles. Then they shall bring all your brethren for an offering to the LORD out of all nations, on horses and in chariots and in litters, on mules and on camels, to My holy mountain Jerusalem,' says the LORD, 'as the children of Israel bring an offering in a clean vessel into the house of the LORD.'"

We see this again in Jeremiah 16:14-16, where we read:

"'Therefore behold, the days are coming,' says the LORD, 'that it shall no more be said, "The LORD lives who brought up the children of Israel from the land of Egypt," but, "The LORD lives who brought up the children of Israel from the land of the north and from all the lands where He had driven them."' For I will bring them back into their land which I gave to their fathers. 'Behold, I will send for many fishermen,' says the LORD, 'and they shall fish them; and afterward I will send for many hunters, and they shall hunt them from every mountain and every hill, and out of the holes of the rocks.'"

This is celebrated in Isaiah 52:7. **"How beautiful upon the mountains Are the feet of him who brings good news, Who proclaims peace, Who brings glad tidings of good *things*, Who proclaims salvation, Who says to Zion, 'Your God reigns!'"** It is also celebrated in the fourth book of the Psalms. Psalm 93:1, 96:10, 97:1, and 99:1 announce the wondrous news that **"The Lord reigns."** Psalm 95:2 and 100:2 sound the call to **"come before His presence"** and Psalm 96:8 invites them to **"come into His courts."**

Restoration - The Ancient Promises Fulfilled

All Israel brought back to the land

The return of all Israel to their land is one of the great themes of prophecy, and is found in too many places to cite them all. One of them is Jeremiah 31:7-9:

> **"Sing with gladness for Jacob, And shout among the chief of the nations; Proclaim, give praise, and say, 'O LORD, save Your people, The remnant of Israel!' Behold, I will bring them from the north country, And gather them from the ends of the earth,** *Among* **them the blind and the lame, The woman with child And the one who labors with child, together; A great throng shall return there. They shall come with weeping, And with supplications I will lead them. I will cause them to walk by the rivers of waters, In a straight way in which they shall not stumble; For I am a Father to Israel, And Ephraim** *is* **My firstborn."**

We need to notice that this prophecy has to refer to the future because it has never been fulfilled. For it explicitly speaks of Ephraim, the northern kingdom of Israel after its division in the days of Rehoboam, the foolish son of the wise Solomon. (2 Chronicles 10) A small portion of Judah, the southern kingdom, returned to their land after the Babylonian captivity. But, as a nation, Ephraim never returned. For more information on this, see pages 79, 81 and 212.

Unlike the previous return of Judah to her land, this is not a partial return. All Israel will be gathered. We see this in Ezekiel 36:10, where the Lord tells the **"mountains of Israel"** (verse 8) that He **"will multiply men upon you, all the house of Israel, all** [85] **of it; and the cities shall be**

---

[85] Footnote 74 on page 119 pointed out that the Hebrew word for ***all***, ***kol***, (word number 3605 in Strong's Hebrew dictionary) does not always mean ***the sum total of each and every member*** of a group. But the fact that the word ***all*** is repeated makes it plain that this is the meaning intended here.

inhabited and the ruins rebuilt." We see it again in Micah 2:12, where the Lord says **"I will surely assemble all of you, O Jacob, I will surely gather the remnant of Israel; I will put them together like sheep of the fold, Like a flock in the midst of their pasture; They shall make a loud noise because of** *so many* **people."**

The nations bring the children of Israel home.

> "They shall bring your sons in *their* arms, And your daughters shall be carried on *their* shoulders; Kings shall be your foster fathers, And their queens your nursing mothers; They shall bow down to you with *their* faces to the earth, And lick up the dust of your feet. Then you will know that I *am* the LORD, For they shall not be ashamed who wait for Me." (Isaiah 49:22-23)

The rebels purged from among Israel.

But many of the children of Israel are rebels. To such, the Lord's appearing does not mean blessing, but judgment. These will be removed from among the people.

> "'As I live,' says the Lord GOD, 'surely with a mighty hand, with an outstretched arm, and with fury poured out, I will rule over you. I will bring you out from the peoples and gather you out of the countries where you are scattered, with a mighty hand, with an outstretched arm, and with fury poured out. And I will bring you into the wilderness of the peoples, and there I will plead My case with you face to face. Just as I pleaded My case with your fathers in the wilderness of the land of Egypt, so I will plead My case with you,' says the Lord GOD. 'I will make you pass under the rod, and I will bring you into the bond of the covenant; I will purge the rebels from among you, and those who transgress against Me; I will bring them

out of the country where they dwell, but they shall not enter the land of Israel. Then you will know that I am the LORD.'" (Ezekiel 20:33-38)

"In that day you shall not be shamed for any of your deeds In which you transgress against Me; For then I will take away from your midst Those who rejoice in your pride, And you shall no longer be haughty In My holy mountain. I will leave in your midst A meek and humble people, And they shall trust in the name of the LORD." (Zephaniah 3:11-12)

This is how **"it shall come to pass that *he who is* left in Zion and remains in Jerusalem will be called holy; everyone who is recorded among the living in Jerusalem. When the Lord has washed away the filth of the daughters of Zion, and purged the blood of Jerusalem from her midst, by the spirit of judgment and by the spirit of burning."** (Isaiah 4:3-4)

Israel repents of their rejection of Jesus as their Messiah.

When Israel finally sees their long awaited Messiah, **"*one* will say to him, 'What are these wounds between your arms?'** [86] **Then he will answer, '*Those* with which I was wounded in the house of my friends.'** (Zechariah 13:6) The result is that **"In that day there shall be a great mourning in Jerusalem, like the mourning at Hadad Rimmon in the plain of Megiddo. And the land shall mourn, every family by itself: the family of the house of David by itself, and their wives by themselves; the family of the house of Nathan by itself, and their wives by themselves; the family of the house of Levi by itself, and their wives by themselves; the family of Shimei by itself, and their wives by themselves; all the families that remain, every family by itself, and their wives by themselves."** (Zechariah 12:11-14)

---

86 As noted in footnote 54 on page 80, I am disappointed that the New King James, which we are using, has joined a number of other modern translations in abandoning the apparent reference to our Lord's crucifixion in the King James reading, "What *are* these wounds in thine hands?"

Again, we read, "Then I will give them a heart to know Me, that I *am* the LORD; and they shall be My people, and I will be their God, for they shall return to Me with their whole heart." (Jeremiah 24:7) "And so all Israel will be saved" (Romans 11:26)

Ephraim and Judah reunited

This is detailed in Ezekiel 37, in which the Lord says: **"As for you, son of man, take a stick for yourself and write on it: 'For Judah and for the children of Israel, his companions.' Then take another stick and write on it, 'For Joseph, the stick of Ephraim, and *for* all the house of Israel, his companions.' Then join them one to another for yourself into one stick, and they will become one in your hand."** (Ezekiel 37:16-17) The Lord then told Ezekiel that when the children of his people asked him what this meant, he should answer them that **"the Lord GOD"** says: **"Surely I will take the children of Israel from among the nations, wherever they have gone, and will gather them from every side and bring them into their own land; and I will make them one nation in the land, on the mountains of Israel; and one king shall be king over them all; they shall no longer be two nations, nor shall they ever be divided into two kingdoms again."** (Ezekiel 37:21-22)

Isaiah also speaks of this, saying:

> "It shall come to pass in that day That the Lord shall set His hand again the second time To recover the remnant of His people who are left, From Assyria and Egypt, From Pathros and Cush, From Elam and Shinar, From Hamath and the islands of the sea. He will set up a banner for the nations, and will assemble the outcasts of Israel, And gather together the dispersed of Judah From the four corners of the earth. Also the envy of Ephraim shall depart, And the adversaries of Judah shall be cut off; Ephraim shall not envy Judah, And Judah shall not harass Ephraim." (Isaiah 11:11-13)

This is celebrated in the fifth book of the Psalms:

> "Behold, how good and how pleasant *it is* For brethren to dwell together in unity! *It is* like the precious oil upon the head, Running down on the beard, The beard of Aaron, Running down on the edge of his garments. *It is* like the dew of Hermon, Descending upon the mountains of Zion; For there the LORD commanded the blessing; Life forevermore." (Psalm 133:1-3)

And again:

> "When the LORD brought back the captivity of Zion, We were like those who dream. Then our mouth was filled with laughter, And our tongue with singing. Then they said among the nations, 'The LORD has done great things for them.' The LORD has done great things for us, *And* we are glad." (Psalm 126:1-3)

The Lord sends united Israel to war.

But the Lord has come to judge the nations, and His work is not yet finished. The nations that have hated Israel must now be punished. The Lord, in His justice, decrees that this must be done by the very ones they have so long tried to destroy. He commands Israel to destroy them.

The justice of this is pointed out in Habakkuk 2:8; **"Because you have plundered many nations, All the remnant of the people shall plunder you, Because of men's blood And the violence of the land *and* the city, And of all who dwell in it."**

We see this again in Isaiah 49:26. **"I will feed those who oppress you with their own flesh, And they shall be drunk with their own blood as with sweet wine. All flesh shall know That I, the LORD, *am* your Savior, And your Redeemer, the Mighty One of Jacob ."** Again, in Isaiah 51:22-23, the

Lord says, **"See, I have taken out of your hand The cup of trembling, The dregs of the cup of My fury; You shall no longer drink it. But I will put it into the hand of those who afflict you, Who have said to you, 'Lie down, that we may walk over you.' And you have laid your body like the ground, And as the street, for those who walk over."**

In keeping with this decree, the Lord gives Israel a most awesome charge: **"Cursed** *is* **he who does the work of the LORD deceitfully, And cursed** *is* **he who keeps back his sword from blood."** (Jeremiah 48:10) This may seem unlike the gracious God we know, but we must remember that the present age of grace is over, and it is now **"the Day of the LORD."** As we read in the fifth book of the Psalms, **"The Lord** *is* **at Your right hand; He shall execute kings in the day of His wrath. He shall judge among the nations, He shall fill** *the places* **with dead bodies, He shall execute the heads of many countries."** (Psalm 110:6)

This same fifth book of the Psalms goes on to give Israel's response to the Lord's instructions:

> "All nations surrounded me, But in the name of the LORD I will destroy them. They surrounded me, Yes, they surrounded me; But in the name of the LORD I will destroy them. They surrounded me like bees; They were quenched like a fire of thorns; For in the name of the LORD I will destroy them." (Psalm 118:10-12)

> "Let the saints be joyful in glory; Let them sing aloud on their beds. *Let* the high praises of God *be* in their mouth, And a two-edged sword in their hand, To execute vengeance on the nations, And punishments on the peoples; To bind their kings with chains, And their nobles with fetters of iron; To execute on them the written judgment; This honor have all His saints. Praise the LORD!" (Psalm 149:5-9)

So we read that **"In that day I will make the governors of Judah like a firepan in the woodpile, and like a fiery torch in the sheaves; they shall devour** all the surrounding peoples on the right hand and on the left... In that day the LORD will defend the inhabitants of Jerusalem; the one who is feeble among them in that day shall be like David, and the house of David *shall be like God, like the Angel of the LORD before them.*" (Zechariah 12:6-8) And "the governors of Judah shall say in their heart, 'The inhabitants of Jerusalem *are* my strength in the LORD of hosts, their God.'" (Zechariah 12:5)

Israel conquers the Philistines, Edom, Moab, and Ammon

We noticed the prophecy about Ephraim being reconciled with Judah. (page 151) The rest of that prophecy says, **"Ephraim shall not envy Judah, And Judah shall not harass Ephraim. But they shall fly down upon the shoulder of the Philistines toward the west; Together they shall plunder the people of the East; They shall lay their hand on Edom and Moab; And the people of Ammon shall obey them."** (Isaiah 11:13-14)

We see this again in Ezekiel 25:14, where the Lord God says, **"I will lay My vengeance on Edom by the hand of My people Israel, that they may do in Edom according to My anger and according to My fury; and they shall know My vengeance."**

The destruction of these lands will be complete.

> **"For Gaza shall be forsaken, And Ashkelon desolate; They shall drive out Ashdod at noon-day, And Ekron shall be uprooted. Woe to the inhabitants of the seacoast, The nation of the Cherethites! The word of the LORD *is* against you, O Canaan, land of the Philistines: 'I will destroy you; So there shall be no inhabitant.' The seacoast shall be pastures, With shelters for shepherds and folds for flocks. The coast shall be for the remnant of the house of Judah; They shall feed *their* flocks there; In the houses of Ashkelon they shall lie down at evening. For the LORD their God will intervene for them, And return their captives."** (Zephaniah 2:4-7)

> "'Therefore, as I live,' Says the LORD of hosts, the God of Israel, 'Surely Moab shall be like Sodom, And the people of Ammon like Gomorrah; Overrun with weeds and saltpits, And a perpetual desolation. The residue of My people shall plunder them, And the remnant of My people shall possess them.'" (Zephaniah 2:9)

All this must of necessity be future, for since the days of Isaiah, Ephraim and Judah have never joined together in a successful military operation. Ezekiel wrote after all of Ephraim and most of Judah had been carried away captive. And Israel has never completely destroyed any of these nations, as is so clearly stated in Zephaniah.

The Lord sends Israel against the Grecian kings. [87]

> "For I have bent Judah, My *bow*, Fitted the bow with Ephraim, And raised up your sons, O Zion, Against your sons, O Greece, And made you like the sword of a mighty man. Then the LORD will be seen over them, And His arrow will go forth like lightning. The Lord GOD will blow the trumpet, And go with whirlwinds from the south. The LORD of hosts will defend them; They shall devour and subdue with slingstones. They shall drink *and* roar as if with wine; They shall be filled *with blood* like basins, Like the corners of the altar." (Zechariah 9:13-15)

Israel wastes the land of Assyria with the sword.

This is expressly stated in Micah 5. This has to be future, for Israel has never invaded Assyria.

---

[87] We noticed on page 122 that this term refers to **"the king of the North"** (Assyria) and **"the king of the South"** (Egypt), two of the four splinters from the breakup of the kingdom of the Greek king Alexander the Great.

> "And this *One* shall be peace. When the Assyrian comes into our land, And when he treads in our palaces, Then we will raise against him Seven shepherds and eight princely men. They shall waste with the sword the land of Assyria, And the land of Nimrod at its entrances; Thus He shall deliver *us* from the Assyrian, When he comes into our land And when he treads within our borders." (Micah 5:5-6)

All Israel settled in the land

All Israel is now settled in the land. This is described in the last two chapters of Ezekiel, beginning with the details of the boundaries of the land. (Ezekiel 47:15-20) These boundaries are shown in the map on page 232.

Next come specific instructions as to how the land is to be divided. Strangers who dwell among them are not left out.

> "Thus you shall divide this land among yourselves according to the tribes of Israel. It shall be that you will divide it by lot as an inheritance for yourselves, and for the strangers who dwell among you and who bear children among you. They shall be to you as native-born among the children of Israel; they shall have an inheritance with you among the tribes of Israel. And it shall be *that* in whatever tribe the stranger dwells, there you shall give *him* his inheritance," says the Lord GOD." (Ezekiel 47:21-23)

Finally, the Lord names each of the twelve tribes, stating which portion of the land is to be given to each of them. (Ezekiel 48:1-7 and 23-29) Between these last two passages is another highly detailed instruction regarding a plot reserved for the Temple, the Levites, and the king.

Many imagine that this is only figurative speech, that it does not mean literal Israel, but only the people of God generally. In this regard it is important to examine a most remarkable prophecy addressed to a piece of real estate.

> "But you, O mountains of Israel, you shall shoot forth your branches and yield your fruit to My people Israel, for they are about to come. For indeed I *am* for you, and I will turn to you, and you shall be tilled and sown. I will multiply men upon you, all the house of Israel, all of it; and the cities shall be inhabited and the ruins rebuilt. I will multiply upon you man and beast; and they shall increase and bear young; I will make you inhabited as in former times, and do better *for you* than at your beginnings. Then you shall know that I *am* the LORD. Yes, I will cause men to walk on you, My people Israel; they shall take possession of you, and you shall be their inheritance" (Ezekiel 36:8-12)

In view of all this explicit detail, it is simple unbelief to deny that this refers to a physical restoration of the natural offspring of the ancient nation of Israel. The only way to escape this conclusion is to deny that the scriptures mean what they explicitly say.

Sodom and Samaria restored

Some nations will joyfully attack Judah because of their hatred. These, as we have seen, (pages 154, 155) will be destroyed. But less guilty nations, though also punished, will afterward be blessed along with Israel. In Ezekiel 16:53-55 the Lord says **"When I bring back their captives, the captives of Sodom and her daughters, and the captives of Samaria and her daughters, then *I will also bring back* the captives of your captivity among them, that you may bear your own shame and be disgraced by all that you did when you comforted them. When your sisters, Sodom and her daughters, return to their former state, and Samaria and her daughters return to their former state, then you and your daughters will return to your former state."**

Egypt and Assyria restored

So with Egypt and Assyria. **"And the LORD will strike Egypt, He will strike and heal** *it;* **they will return to the LORD, and He will be entreated by them and heal them. In that day there will be a highway from Egypt to Assyria, and the Assyrian will come into Egypt and the Egyptian into Assyria, and the Egyptians will serve with the Assyrians. In that day Israel will be one of three with Egypt and Assyria; a blessing in the midst of the land."** (Isaiah 19:22-24)

Moab, Ammon, and Elam restored

These are stated in highly similar passages. **"'Yet I will bring back the captives of Moab In the latter days,' says the Lord."** (Jeremiah 48:47) **"But afterward I will bring back The captives of the people of Ammon,' says the Lord."** (Jeremiah 49:6) **"'But it shall come to pass in the latter days: I will bring back the captives of Elam,' says the Lord."** (Jeremiah 49:39)

The invasion and defeat of Gog

But the nations will still not be completely subdued. One final battle must take place. Gog will come down after the Lord has brought Israel **"back from the sword,"** after they have been **"brought out of the nations."** (Ezekiel 38:8) Gog's thought will only be evil, but it will be the Lord Himself who brings him down. Why? **"So that the nations may know Me, when I am hallowed in you, O Gog, before their eyes."** (verse 16)

The millennium is about to begin. It is time to put an end to all thought of rebellion. To do this, the Lord needs one final display of His power. He says **"Thus I will magnify Myself and sanctify Myself, and I will be known in the eyes of many nations. Then they shall know that I** *am* **the LORD."** (Ezekiel 38:23)

Gog will provide the occasion, but **"all the nations shall see My judgment which I have executed, and My hand which I have laid on them."** (Ezekiel 39:21)

The Lord will strike down this rebellion in an awesome display of power.

> "'Surely in that day there shall be a great earthquake in the land of Israel, so that the fish of the sea, the birds of the heavens, the beasts of the field, all creeping things that creep on the earth, and all men who *are* on the face of the earth shall shake at My presence. The mountains shall be thrown down, the steep places shall fall, and every wall shall fall to the ground. I will call for a sword against Gog throughout all My mountains,' says the Lord GOD. 'Every man's sword will be against his brother. And I will bring him to judgment with pestilence and bloodshed; I will rain down on him, on his troops, and on the many peoples who *are* with him, flooding rain, great hailstones, fire, and brimstone.'" (Ezekiel 38:18-22)

The destruction will be so great that Israel will burn their weapons as fuel for seven years. See the chart on page 6.

> "Then those who dwell in the cities of Israel will go out and set on fire and burn the weapons, both the shields and bucklers, the bows and arrows, the javelins and spears; and they will make fires with them for seven years. They will not take wood from the field nor cut down *any* from the forests, because they will make fires with the weapons; and they will plunder those who plundered them, and pillage those who pillaged them," says the Lord GOD." (Ezekiel 39:9-10)

It will take seven months to bury the dead. (See chart, page 6)

> "'For seven months the house of Israel will be burying them, in order to cleanse the land. Indeed all the people of the land will be burying, and they will gain renown for it on the day that I am glorified,' says the Lord GOD. 'They will set apart men regularly employed, with the help of a search party, to

pass through the land and bury those bodies remaining on the ground, in order to cleanse it. At the end of seven months they will make a search. The search party will pass through the land; and when anyone sees a man's bone, he shall set up a marker by it, till the buriers have buried it in the Valley of Hamon Gog."' [88] (Ezekiel 39:12-15)

The Millennium

See the chart on page 6.

The kingdom of God set up on earth.

Scripture could not be more clear in this matter. The God of heaven will most assuredly come to this earth and set up a kingdom. Some imagine this will eventually come about through human effort. The many scriptures we have examined clearly show the error of this notion. But we are not left to conclude this from other scriptures. It is expressly stated that God will do this Himself. He will not leave it in the hands of others.

---

[88] It has been argued that Gog's attack could not be at the end of the seventieth week because that would make this period of burial stretch into the millennium. But this actually proves that the attack cannot come in the middle of the week, when many think it will occur. We have noticed (page 119) that at the time of that attack there will be no one left to bury the dead. We have also seen (page 131) that during the last half of this week, Judah will be under siege in the fortified remains of Jerusalem. Each of these would clearly make it impossible for **"the house of Israel"** to **"set apart men regularly employed, with the help of a search party, to pass through the land and bury those bodies remaining on the ground."** (Ezekiel 39:12-14) These same conditions also show that, aside from the few under siege in Jerusalem, there would be none left **"who dwell in the cities of Israel."** And these few would not be able to **"go out and set on fire and burn the weapons, both the shields and bucklers, the bows and arrows, the javelins and spears; and... make fires with them for seven years."** (Ezekiel 39:9) This detail also shows that this attack cannot come just before the seventieth week, when many think it will occur. For the seven years would then stretch into this last half of the week. Further, we saw on pages 146 to 147 that Israel will be called home after the Lord returns. As pointed out in footnote 56 on page 81, this shows that this prophecy refers to a time after the Lord returns. For in these two chapters (Ezekiel 38-39) the name Israel occurs 17 times, but Judah is never mentioned. For more details that prove this is when Gog will attack, see pages 78 to 80.

> "And in the days of these kings the God of heaven will set up a kingdom which shall never be destroyed; and the kingdom shall not be left to other people; it shall break in pieces and consume all these kingdoms, and it shall stand forever." (Daniel 2:44)

The nations judged

The Ancient of Days will judge the kingdoms of the world.

> "I watched till thrones were put in place, And the Ancient of Days was seated; His garment *was* white as snow, And the hair of His head *was* like pure wool. His throne *was* a fiery flame, Its wheels a burning fire; A fiery stream issued And came forth from before Him. A thousand thousands ministered to Him; Ten thousand times ten thousand stood before Him. The court was seated, And the books were opened.
>
> I watched then because of the sound of the pompous words which the horn was speaking; I watched till the beast was slain, and its body destroyed and given to the burning flame. As for the rest of the beasts, they had their dominion taken away, yet their lives were prolonged for a season and a time." (Daniel 7:9-12)

Jesus described this judgment in Matthew 25:31-45, saying the nations will be judged on the basis of how they have treated His own. In rewarding the righteous, the King will say **"inasmuch as you did it to one of the least of these My brethren, you did it to Me."** (verse 40) Likewise, in condemning the wicked, He will say **"inasmuch as you did not do it to one of the least of these, you did not do it to Me."** (verse 45)

This is a formal judgment before a throne. It is therefore not the same as the Lord's destructive judgments while He conquers the nations. This is an eternal judgment, for **"these will go away into everlasting punishment, but the righteous into eternal life."** (Matthew 25:46)

Satan imprisoned

Many think Satan is just a symbolic personification of evil, but in the Holy Scriptures he is a specific living being, a person, an individual. This wicked individual will be imprisoned.

> **"Then I saw an angel coming down from heaven, having the key to the bottomless pit and a great chain in his hand. He laid hold of the dragon, that serpent of old, who is *the* Devil and Satan, and bound him for a thousand years; and he cast him into the bottomless pit, and shut him up, and set a seal on him, so that he should deceive the nations no more till the thousand years were finished."** (Revelation 20:1-3)

Satan will be imprisoned **"so that he should deceive the nations no more till the thousand years were finished."** While the scriptures do not state the timing of this event, it is presented in the Revelation after the beast and the false prophet are cast into the lake of fire (Revelation 19:20) and before judgment is committed to the saints. (Revelation 20:4)

The resurrection and reign of the righteous

> **"And I saw thrones, and they sat on them, and judgment was committed to them. Then *I saw* the souls of those who had been beheaded for their witness to Jesus and for the word of God, who had not worshiped the beast or his image, and had not received *his* mark on their foreheads or on their hands. And they lived and reigned with Christ for a thousand years. But the rest of the dead lived not again until the thousand years were finished. This *is* the first resurrection. Blessed and holy *is* he that hath part in the first resurrection: on such the second death hath no power, but they shall be priests of God and of Christ, and shall reign with him a thousand years."** (Revelation 20:4-6)

Judgment is committed to the saints.

In Daniel 7, the prophet was watching **"until the Ancient of Days came, and a judgment was made *in favor* of the saints of the Most High, and the time came for the saints to possess the kingdom."** (verses 21-22) Daniel's interpreter told him, **"Then the kingdom and dominion, And the greatness of the kingdoms under the whole heaven, Shall be given to the people, the saints of the Most High. His kingdom *is* an everlasting kingdom, And all dominions shall serve and obey Him."** (verse 27)

A new temple is built.

This is distinctly prophesied in words too plain to misunderstand. In Zechariah 6:12-13 we read, **"Behold, the Man whose name *is* the BRANCH! From His place He shall branch out, And He shall build the temple of the LORD; Yes, He shall build the temple of the LORD. He shall bear the glory, And shall sit and rule on His throne; So He shall be a priest on His throne, And the counsel of peace shall be between them both."**

In Ezekiel 40 through 42, the prophet was shown a vision of a temple, in which a man with a measuring line took him everywhere, measuring all the details of a temple unlike anything that has ever been built. Finally, in chapter 43, Ezekiel was told, **"Son of man, *this is* the place of My throne and the place of the soles of My feet, where I will dwell in the midst of the children of Israel forever. No more shall the house of Israel defile My holy name, they nor their kings, by their harlotry or with the carcasses of their kings on their high places."** (Ezekiel 43:7)

Temple worship resumed, with animal sacrifices.

Many think this cannot happen, because it seems contrary to scriptures such as Hebrews 10; **"by one offering He has perfected forever those who are being sanctified."** (verse 14) and **"Now where there is remission of these, *there is* no longer an offering for sin."** (verse 18) But our understanding of the meaning of one scripture cannot set aside the express statement of another. When the scriptures tell us something in plain words, they mean exactly what they say. Like the construction of the new temple, worship in the form of animal sacrifice is prophesied in crystal clear language. It begins in Ezekiel 43:12, with the words, **"This *is* the law of the temple: The whole area surrounding the mountaintop *is* most holy. Behold, this *is* the law of the temple."** An altar is then described, and Ezekiel is told **"These *are* the ordinances for the altar on the day when it is made, for sacrificing burnt offerings on it, and for sprinkling blood on it."** (Ezekiel 43:18)

Next follows a long and detailed description of various animal sacrifices that are to be offered on this altar. This goes into chapter 46. The language is all future, and is very explicit and detailed. The instructions in this section include every sacrifice specified as perpetual in the law of Moses, as well as most of the ordinances specified the same way.

These include a renewal of the command to keep the **"Sabbath,"** as given in Ezekiel 44:24, Ezekiel 45:17, and Ezekiel 46:1-5 and 12. This had been commanded as **"a perpetual covenant"** with **"the children of Israel"** in Exodus 31:16. Again, in Ezekiel 45:21-25 we find the keeping of the **"Passover,"** with its accompanying **"unleavened bread."** This had been commanded as **"an everlasting ordinance"** in Exodus 12:14 and 17, and **"forever"** in Exodus 12:24. In addition to these, we find the keeping of **"the appointed feasts"** in Ezekiel 46:9-11. These are detailed in Leviticus 23:4-43, where they are commanded to be kept **"forever"** in verses 14, 21, 31, and 41.

The last of these **"appointed feasts"** was a command to **"dwell in booths for seven days."** (Leviticus 23:42) This came to be called **"the Feast of Tabernacles."** (John 7:2) This is not named in Ezekiel, but Zechariah 14:16-19 goes into some detail about it, saying that not only Israel, but all the surrounding nations, will come up to Jerusalem to keep it every year, and that every **"family"** that fails to come up to that feast will be severely punished, either by lack of rain or by plague, that is, by God himself.

We find the same thing in the renewed laws of the priesthood. Ezekiel 44:15 explicitly limits this to **"the sons of Zadok,"** because he was the only priest that remained faithful **"when the children of Israel went astray from"** the Lord. Zadok's descent from Aaron through Phineas is traced in 1 Chronicles 6:3-8. This is significant because the priesthood was given to Aaron and his sons **"for a perpetual statute"** in Exodus 29:9, and with **"an everlasting priesthood"** in Exodus 40:15. Then Aaron's son Phineas and **"his descendants after him"** were additionally given **"a covenant of an everlasting priesthood"** in Numbers 25:13. So a future appointment of **"the sons of Zadok"** as priests is a fulfillment of this eternal pledge.

Other perpetual laws about the priests are also repeated here. Their holy garments are mentioned in Ezekiel 42:14 and 44:17-19. These had been commanded to be worn **"always"** in Exodus 28:38 and as **"a statute forever"** in Exodus 28:43. Again, Ezekiel 44:21 says, **"No priest shall drink wine when he enters the inner court."** This is the same as in Leviticus 10:9, where it is commanded as **"a statute forever throughout your generations."** And Ezekiel 48:14 forbids them to sell their land. This might seem strange to us, but this was to preserve the land to them and their children for ever. This, again, is a repeat of what we find in Leviticus 25:32-34, where the priests could only sell their houses until **"the Jubilee"** (an equivalent of what we call a lease,) but they could not sell their land at all **"for it is their perpetual possession."**

Likewise, **"every sacrifice of any kind,"** including **"the best of all first-fruits of any kind"** were reserved as food for the priests in Ezekiel 44:29-30.

These had been reserved as food for the priests **as "a statute forever"** in Exodus 29:28, Leviticus 6:18, 7:34 and 36, and 10:15, **"as an ordinance forever"** in Numbers 18:11 and 19, and **"by a perpetual statute"** in Leviticus 24:9.

Thus we see that the commandments for this future worship repeat the perpetual ordinances originally given through Moses. But they are not a reinstitution of that law. For some of the laws here are different from those given through Moses. For instance, the daily **"burnt offering"** of a lamb every morning and every evening, with flour and oil, is commanded **"continually"** in Exodus 29:38 and 42, as well as **"throughout your generations"** in Exodus 29:42. This command is repeated in Ezekiel 46:13-15, but there it is only every morning, and the amount of flour and of oil is different.

Another radical difference between this future worship and that under the law of Moses can be seen by referring to 1 Samuel 13. In this chapter Saul, God's anointed king over Israel, offered up a burnt offering. **"And Samuel said to Saul, 'You have done foolishly. You have not kept the commandment of the LORD your God, which He commanded you. For now the LORD would have established your kingdom over Israel forever. But now your kingdom shall not continue. The LORD has sought for Himself a man after His own heart, and the LORD has commanded him *to be* commander over His people, because you have not kept what the LORD commanded you.'"** (1 Samuel 13:13-14) Under the law of Moses, offerings were not to be made by rulers, but by priests. Again, in 2 Chronicles 26:16-21, king Uzziah was struck with leprosy because he offered incense. But the law of this future temple will be different:

> "Then it shall be the prince's part *to give* burnt offerings, grain offerings, and drink offerings, at the feasts, the New Moons, the Sabbaths, and at all the appointed seasons of the house of Israel. He shall prepare the sin offering, the grain offering, the burnt offering, and the peace offerings to make atonement for the house of Israel." (Ezekiel 45:17)

As punishment for presuming to act as priests, Saul lost his kingdom and Uzziah was struck with leprosy. But as we noticed on page 163, this coming prince **"shall be a priest on His throne."** (Zechariah 6:13)

These clear and well defined differences between this future law and the one given by Moses are absolute proof that this was never intended to apply to a time before Jesus came. For when Jesus was here, He said, **"Do not think that I came to destroy the Law or the Prophets. I did not come to destroy but to fulfill. For assuredly, I say to you, till heaven and earth pass away, one jot or one tittle will by no means pass from the law till all is fulfilled."** (Matthew 5:17-18) So, long after Ezekiel was given, Jesus himself said that not even the tiniest detail of the law would pass until He had fulfilled all of it.

A further and very marked difference between this future worship and that in the old system is clearly stated in Jeremiah 3:16.

> **"'Then it shall come to pass, when you are multiplied and increased in the land in those days,' says the LORD, 'that they will say no more, "The ark of the covenant of the LORD." It shall not come to mind, nor shall they remember it, nor shall they visit *it*, nor shall it be made anymore.'"**

Some have made a great point of a need to find the ark, in order that prophecy can be fulfilled. But this scripture explicitly states that **"the ark of the covenant of the LORD"** will no longer even **"come to mind,"** much less be visited.

All the surrounding nations worship the LORD.

This, again, is prophesied in crystal clear language:

> **"And it shall come to pass *that* everyone who is left of all the nations which came against Jerusalem shall go up from year**

to year to worship the King, the LORD of hosts, and to keep the Feast of Tabernacles. And it shall be *that* whichever of the families of the earth do not come up to Jerusalem to worship the King, the LORD of hosts, on them there will be no rain. If the family of Egypt will not come up and enter in, they *shall have* no *rain;* they shall receive the plague with which the LORD strikes the nations who do not come up to keep the Feast of Tabernacles. This shall be the punishment of Egypt and the punishment of all the nations that do not come up to keep the Feast of Tabernacles." (Zechariah 14:16-19)

"Peoples shall yet come, Inhabitants of many cities; The inhabitants of one *city* shall go to another, saying, 'Let us continue to go and pray before the LORD, And seek the LORD of hosts. I myself will go also.' Yes, many peoples and strong nations Shall come to seek the LORD of hosts in Jerusalem, And to pray before the LORD." (Zechariah 8:20-22)

A healing river flows out of the temple.

In Ezekiel 47, the prophet was shown a river flowing from the temple of God. His informer then told him:

"This water flows toward the eastern region, goes down into the valley, and enters the sea. *When it* reaches the sea, *its* waters are healed. And it shall be *that* every living thing that moves, wherever the rivers go, will live. There will be a very great multitude of fish, because these waters go there; for they will be healed, and everything will live wherever the river goes. It shall be *that* fishermen will stand by it from En Gedi to En Eglaim; they will be *places* for spreading their nets. Their fish will be of the same kinds as the fish of the Great Sea, exceedingly many. But its swamps and marshes will not be healed; they will be given over to salt. Along the bank of the river, on this side and that, will grow all *kinds of* trees used for food;

their leaves will not wither, and their fruit will not fail. They will bear fruit every month, because their water flows from the sanctuary. Their fruit will be for food, and their leaves for medicine." (Ezekiel 47:8-12)

The whole world blessed

Like the river from the temple, the blessing of this age, though centered in Jerusalem, flows out to the whole world.

We are told concerning Israel that **"if their being cast away *is* the reconciling of the world, what *will* their acceptance *be* but life from the dead?"** (Romans 11:15) So we read of this day that **"there shall be no more curse."** (Revelation 22:3) This refers to Genesis 3:17, where the Lord told Adam, **"Because you have heeded the voice of your wife, and have eaten from the tree of which I commanded you, saying, 'You shall not eat of it': Cursed *is* the ground for your sake; In toil you shall eat *of* it All the days of your life."**

We see this again in Romans 8:19, where we read that **"the earnest expectation of the creation eagerly waits for the revealing of the sons of God."** The blessings of this wonderful day are described in glowing terms such as:

> "The wolf also shall dwell with the lamb, The leopard shall lie down with the young goat, The calf and the young lion and the fatling together; And a little child shall lead them. The cow and the bear shall graze; Their young ones shall lie down together; And the lion shall eat straw like the ox. The nursing child shall play by the cobra's hole, And the weaned child shall put his hand in the viper's den. They shall not hurt nor destroy in all My holy mountain, For the earth shall be full of the knowledge of the LORD As the waters cover the sea." (Isaiah 11:6-9)

"'No more shall an infant from there *live but a few* days, Nor an old man who has not fulfilled his days; For the child shall die one hundred years old, But the sinner *being* one hundred years old shall be accursed. They shall build houses and inhabit *them;* They shall plant vineyards and eat their fruit. They shall not build and another inhabit; They shall not plant and another eat; For as the days of a tree, *so shall be* the days of My people, And My elect shall long enjoy the work of their hands. They shall not labor in vain, Nor bring forth children for trouble; For they *shall be* the descendants of the blessed of the LORD, And their offspring with them. It shall come to pass That before they call, I will answer; And while they are still speaking, I will hear. The wolf and the lamb shall feed together, The lion shall eat straw like the ox, And dust *shall be* the serpent's food. They shall not hurt nor destroy in all My holy mountain,' Says the LORD." (Isaiah 65:20-25)**

Finally, we read of this day that **"They shall beat their swords into plowshares, And their spears into pruning hooks; Nation shall not lift up sword against nation, Neither shall they learn war anymore."** (Isaiah 2:4) This is so important it is repeated in Micah 4:3.

After the Millennium

Satan released

Many think that Satan, in his rebellion, is merely doing as he wishes, using any method possible in his attempt to overthrow God. But such is not the case. While Satan is indeed a rebel, and his acts are sin, yet he is still under the control of the Almighty God, who continually thwarts his plans and turns them against himself.

The clearest example of this is the crucifixion of our Lord Jesus Christ. This appeared to have been Satan's greatest victory. He had succeeded in persuading mankind to reject and crucify the Lord of glory. But in truth it was God's greatest victory, at least in regard to the portion of this struggle that has been revealed to us. For in yielding to this outrage, our Lord Jesus took the punishment for our sins and made the way clear for a just pardon to be offered to all mankind. Even so, God in His wisdom will allow Satan one final act of rebellion, for **"when the thousand years have expired, Satan will be released from his prison"** (Revelation 20:7)

Mankind's final rebellion

This final release of Satan will fully expose the rebellious heart, not only of Satan, but of mankind, for when Satan is released, he **"will go out to deceive the nations which are in the four corners of the earth, Gog and Magog, to gather them together to battle, whose number *is* as the sand of the sea."** (Revelation 20:8)

By this time God will have reigned a full thousand years. Mankind will have no memory of a time when things were less than perfect. But contrary to the notions of mankind, a thousand years will not be long enough to cure the rebellion in man's heart, for **"They went up on the breadth of the earth and surrounded the camp of the saints and the beloved city."** (Revelation 20:9)

The rebellion crushed

There is nothing more to prove, nothing more to demonstrate. Unlike Gog's previous attack, this rebellion will not be met with an awesome display of power. There is no word of a great and terrible earthquake, of pestilence or of flooding rain and hailstones. (As in Ezekiel 38:19-22) We are not even told that God goes out to fight with them, but only that **"fire came down from God out of heaven, and devoured them."** (Revelation 20:9)

The devil cast into the lake of fire

Satan had previously been imprisoned temporarily, but it is now time for evil to be finally put away. This begins with the final judgment of the devil. **"The devil, who deceived them, was cast into the lake of fire and brimstone where the beast and the false prophet *are*. And they will be tormented day and night forever and ever."** (Revelation 20:10)

The wicked dead judged

The Beast and the false prophet, men of particular wickedness, had been cast into the lake of fire a thousand years earlier, to be recently joined by Satan. Now the rest of the wicked dead receive the same eternal punishment.

> **"And I saw a great white throne, and him that sat on it, from whose face the earth and the heaven fled away; and there was found no place for them. And I saw the dead, small and great, stand before God; and the books were opened: and another book was opened, which is *the book* of life: and the dead were judged out of those things which were written in the books, according to their works. And the sea gave up the dead which were in it; and death and hell delivered up the dead which were in them: and they were judged every man according to their works. And death and hell were cast into the lake of fire. This is the second death. And whosoever was not found written in the book of life was cast into the lake of fire."** (Revelation 20:11-15)

Many think of this judgment as if there will be some question as to the outcome. They have the notion that some at this time will be condemned, while others will be justified. But this is a serious error. We remember that the righteous dead will have already been resurrected a thousand years earlier. (page 162) The only ones still dead at this time will be the wicked. These will be judged **"every man according to their works."** Without a pardon, no man can stand before such judgment. They will all be condemned, **"for all have sinned and fall short of the glory of God."** (Romans 3:23)

Many hope to earn a pardon by doing good deeds. But the Holy Scriptures say that **"a man is not justified by the works of the law but by faith in Jesus Christ."** (Galatians 2:16) This passage continues by saying **"we have believed in Christ Jesus, that we might be justified by faith in Christ and not by the works of the law; for by the works of the law no flesh shall be justified."** Man imagines that good deeds will cancel the evil they have done. But this is not what God says. In God's sight **"we are all like an unclean thing, And all our righteousnesses are like filthy rags."** (Isaiah 64:6) Nothing we can do can ever cancel the evil we have done. **"For the wages of sin is death."** (Romans 6:23) And God **"by no means clears the guilty."** (Numbers 14:18)

A pardon is available to all because the Lord Jesus took the punishment we deserve when He **"bore our sins in His own body on the tree."** (1 Peter 2:24) Romans 5:16-18 says justification from God is available as a **"free gift."** Because of this, **"everyone who believes is justified from all things."** (Acts 13:39) **"For God so loved the world that He gave His only begotten Son, that whoever believes in Him should not perish but have everlasting life. For God did not send His Son into the world to condemn the world, but that the world through Him might be saved. He who believes in Him is not condemned; but he who does not believe is condemned already, because he has not believed in the name of the only begotten Son of God."** (John 3:16-18)

So we realize that we can never earn a pardon, but we can have one at no cost to ourselves if we choose to believe that Jesus is truly **"the only begotten Son of God,"** and that:

1. Each of us is individually guilty before a Holy God.

2. Nothing we can do can ever take this guilt away.

3. But Jesus took the punishment we deserve.
4. And because of this, we are offered a free pardon.

Jesus promised that **"he who hears My word and believes in Him who sent Me has everlasting life, and shall not come into judgment, but has passed from death into life."** (John 5:24) The judgment He was speaking of is the judgment of the wicked dead. Those who believe are pardoned, and will not have to face this judgment. But **"he who does not believe is condemned already."** Let all who read these words take careful note of this, for **"It is a fearful thing to fall into the hands of the living God."** (Hebrews 10:31)

There will also be a judgment of the righteous, for **"we shall all stand before the judgment seat of Christ."** (Romans 14:10) But this will be a judgment for reward, not for condemnation, as we read in Revelation 22:12, **"behold, I am coming quickly, and My reward *is* with Me, to give to every one according to his work."** We further read in Hebrews 6:10 that **"God *is* not unjust to forget your work and labor of love which you have shown toward His name, *in that* you have ministered to the saints, and do minister."** Again, we read that the works of the righteous **"follow them."** (Revelation 14:13) At this judgment **"each one's praise will come from God."** (1 Corinthians 4:5)

Heaven and earth remade

In Hebrews 12:26-27 the Holy Spirit quotes from His previous words in Haggai 2:6. *"Yet once more I shake not only the earth, but also heaven."* He then continues; **"Now this, *'Yet once more,'* indicates the removal of those things that are being shaken, as of things that are made, that the things which cannot be shaken may remain."** 2 Peter 3:7 says **"the heavens and the earth... are reserved for fire until the day of judgment and perdition of ungodly men."** A few verses later we read that **"the day of the Lord will come as a thief in the night, in which the heavens will pass away with a** great noise, and the elements will melt with fervent heat; both the earth and the works that are in it will be burned up. Therefore, since all these things will be dissolved, what manner *of persons* ought you to be in holy conduct and godliness, looking for and hastening the coming of the day of God, because of which the heavens will be dissolved, being on fire, and the elements will melt with fervent heat?"** (2 Peter 3:10-12)

These scriptures plainly tell us the heavens and the earth will be destroyed. But that is not the end of the story. The passage above goes on, **"Nevertheless we, according to His promise, look for new heavens and a new earth in which righteousness dwells."** (2 Peter 3:13) We read in Hebrews 1:10-12, **"You, LORD, in the beginning laid the foundation of the earth, And the heavens are the work of Your hands. They will perish, but You remain; And they will all grow old like a garment; Like a cloak You will fold them up, And they will be changed. But You are the same, And Your years will not fail."**

In Revelation 21:1-2 John said, **"I saw a new heaven and a new earth, for the first heaven and the first earth had passed away. Also there was no more sea. Then I, John, saw the holy city, New Jerusalem, coming down out of heaven from God, prepared as a bride adorned for her husband."** After the first heaven and the first earth have passed away and been remade, New Jerusalem comes down out of heaven from God. We are not told how the saints will be protected while the first heaven and the first earth pass away. But this scripture plainly shows they will not be destroyed when this happens.

The kingdom surrendered to God the Father

When Jesus appeared to the disciples after His resurrection, He said, **"All authority has been given to Me in heaven and on earth."** (Matthew 28:18) But when all resistance has been put down, He will yield this authority back to the Father. For in 1 Corinthians 15:24-28 we read:

> "Then *comes* the end, when He delivers the kingdom to God the Father, when He puts an end to all rule and all authority and power. For He must reign till He has put all enemies under His feet. The last enemy *that* will be destroyed *is* death. For *'He has put all things under His feet.'* But when He says *'all things are put under Him' it is* evident that He who put all things under Him is excepted. Now when all things are made subject to Him, then the Son Himself will also be subject to Him who put all things under Him, that God may be all in all."

The eternal state

What will the new earth be like? We have already seen two details. In Revelation 21:1 we read that **"there was no more sea."** The physical change will therefore be very great. But the moral change will be even greater, for 2 Peter 3:13 tells us that **"righteousness dwells"** there. In the millennium evil had been restrained, but now it has been put away, and righteousness dwells. But there is more.

> "And I heard a loud voice from heaven saying, 'Behold, the tabernacle of God *is* with men, and He will dwell with them, and they shall be His people. God Himself will be with them *and be* their God. And God will wipe away every tear from their eyes; there shall be no more death, nor sorrow, nor crying. There shall be no more pain, for the former things have passed away.'" (Revelation 21:3-4)

Evil being permanently put away, it is now possible for God to dwell in the midst of His people. He **"Himself will be with them *and be* their God."** Truly it will be heaven on earth. And **"there shall be no more death, nor sorrow, nor crying. There shall be no more pain, for the former things have passed away."**

"Then He who sat on the throne said, 'Behold, I make all things new.' And He said to me, 'Write, for these words are true and faithful.' And He said to me, 'It is done! I am the Alpha and the Omega, the Beginning and the End. I will give of the fountain of the water of life freely to him who thirsts. He who overcomes shall inherit all things, and I will be his God and he shall be My son. But the cowardly, unbelieving, abominable, murderers, sexually immoral, sorcerers, idolaters, and all liars shall have their part in the lake which burns with fire and brimstone, which is the second death.'" (Revelation 21:5-8)

"He who testifies to these things says, 'Surely I am coming quickly.' Amen. Even so, come, Lord Jesus!" (Revelation 22:20)

Amen and amen.

APPENDIX

Key Concepts for Interpreting Bible Prophecy

Draw a clear line between what the scriptures say and what you think they mean.

It would be difficult to overstress the importance of this concept. Failure to clearly define this line is one of the most common errors in interpreting scripture. We know what the scriptures say, and that is all we really know. We often think we understand what a scripture means. If we are truly being led of the Holy Spirit, we interpret correctly. But we often think we are being subject to the Holy Spirit when we are really only trying to prove our own ideas. **"He who trusts in his own heart is a fool."** (Proverbs 28:26)

Don't bring your ideas to the Bible, get your ideas from the Bible.

This concept is closely related to the previous one. The moment you realize you are looking for proof that your idea is correct, stop. You are probably only being willful.

Do not speculate on the meaning of scripture.

Certain men repeatedly make such statements as "this may be a fulfillment of" such-and-such a prophecy, or "this could mean" so-and-so. All such speculation is unprofitable and vain. If we cannot speak assuredly on the meaning of a scripture, it is better to remain silent.

> **"Walk prudently when you go to the house of God; and draw near to hear rather than to give the sacrifice of fools, for they do not know that they do evil. Do not be rash with your mouth, And let not your heart utter anything hastily before God. For God *is* in heaven, and you on earth; Therefore let your words be few."** (Ecclesiastes 5:1-2)

Disregard all prophecy from any source other than the Bible.

"All Scripture *is* given by inspiration of God, and *is* profitable for doctrine, for reproof, for correction, for instruction in righteousness, that the man of God may be complete, thoroughly equipped for every good work." (2 Timothy 3:16-17) If we know the scriptures, we are complete and thoroughly equipped. Proverbs 30:6 warns us **"Do not add to His words, Lest He rebuke you, and you be found a liar."** Revelation, the last book of the Bible was also the last one to be written. It closes with this solemn warning:

"For I testify to everyone who hears the words of the prophecy of this book: If anyone adds to these things, God will add to him the plagues that are written in this book; and if anyone takes away from the words of the book of this prophecy, God shall take away his part from the Book of Life, from the holy city, and *from* the things which are written in this book." (Revelation 22:18-19)

Key Principles of Prophetic Interpretation

Principle #1: The key to the Bible is the Bible.

Except in rare questions such as the meaning of ancient words or the identity of ancient places or nations, we do not gain an understanding of the Bible from external information, we gain an understanding of external information from the Bible.

Principle #2: The Bible agrees with itself.

An interpretation of any part of the Bible is not correct if it disagrees with any other part of the Bible.

Principle #3: Biblical language is precise.

Israel does not mean *the church*, and *the church* does not mean *Israel*. *Israel* does not mean *Judah*, and *Judah* does not mean *Israel*. *The king* does not mean *the prince*, and *the prince* does not mean *the king*.

Principle #4: Every detail in the Bible is significant.

God does not waste words. *The far north* is not the same as *the north*.

Principle #5: The Bible means what it says.

Express statements of coming events mean exactly what they say.

Principle #6: Biblical visions are symbolic.

Prophetic visions in the Bible are not scenes of coming events. They are visual symbols of these events.

Principle #7: Biblical symbolism is moral.

The subject of a Biblical vision is something that has a moral similarity to what the prophet saw.

Principle #8: Human reasoning is useless.

We know the meaning of Biblical symbols only through Biblical statements about their meanings.

Principle #9: Biblical symbolism is consistent.

If the Bible gives us the meaning of a symbol in one passage, it has the same meaning in other passages.

Principle #10: Bible prophecy concerns the time of the end.

Many prophecies have had a partial fulfillment in the past, and may thus appear to apply only to that time; but unless every detail of a prophecy has been fulfilled, it also concerns the future.

Common Errors in Prophetic Interpretation

1. Many interpret the many Biblical prophecies about the future blessing of Israel to mean the Church. This is called Replacement Theology, from the idea that the Church has replaced Israel in the promises of God. But Romans 11 clearly states that God has not cast Israel away, (verse 1) that Israel's fall is only temporary, (verses 11-25) and that **"all Israel will Be saved"** (verse 26) because **"the gifts and calling of God are irrevocable."** (verse 29) Zechariah 10:6 tells us that **"the house of Judah"** and **"the house of Joseph"** **"shall be as though I had not cast them aside,"** and the next verse (7) extends this to include **"Ephraim."** We should

note here that no scripture even hints at an idea that the church is ever referred to by any of these three names. This national restoration of Israel is described often in the prophets, but nowhere as clearly or as fully as in the last twelve chapters of Ezekiel.

A most unusual prophecy in Ezekiel 36 is addressed to a piece of real estate. **"The mountains of Israel,"** along with **"the hills, the rivers, the valleys, the desolate wastes, and the cities that have been forsaken,"** are promised that they will again be inhabited by **"all the house of Israel, all of it."** (verses 1-15) **"The house of Israel"** is then promised that they will be taken **"from among the nations,"** gathered **"out of all countries,"** and brought into their own land. (verses 16-36) In chapter 37 **"the children of Israel"** are promised that they will be brought back **"into their own land"** and made into **"one nation in the land,"** **"nor shall they ever be divided into two kingdoms again."** (verses 15-28)

In chapter 38 Gog comes **"against my people Israel like a cloud, to cover the land."** (verse 16) In chapter 39 **"the house of Israel"** is occupied seven months burying Gog's dead. (verse 12) Chapter 40 begins a highly detailed description of a temple unlike any that has ever been built. This continues into chapter 43, where the Lord says *"this is* **the place of My throne and the place of the soles of My feet, where I will dwell in the midst of the children of Israel forever."** (verse 7) Then the eighteenth verse of chapter 43 begins a similarly detailed account of **"the ordinances for the altar on the day when it is made,"** which continue through chapter 44. Chapters 45 and 46 specify various laws which will apply when all this takes place. Finally, chapters 47 and 48 return to the real estate of chapter 36, describing in detail **"the borders by which you shall divide the land as an inheritance among the twelve tribes of Israel."** (47:13-20 - see map, page 232) Then they state what portion of the land will be inherited by each of the twelve tribes. (48:1-29) All this detail makes it abundantly clear that the meaning is literal Israel, not the Church.

This can also be seen in Jeremiah 32:6-33:14. In this passage, just as Jerusalem was about to be destroyed, the Lord told Jeremiah to purchase a piece of land. (chapter 32, verses 7-9 and 25) He then explained the reason for this strange instruction, saying **"concerning this city"** (verse 36) that He would **"gather them out of all countries where I have driven them in My anger, in My fury, and in great wrath; I will bring them back to this place, and I will cause them to dwell safely."** (verse 37) While some of the people returned to the land in ancient times, they have never been able to **"dwell safely."** So this prophecy remains to be fulfilled.

The prophecy continues with the words, **"'fields will be bought in this land of which you say, "It is desolate, without man or beast; it has been given into the hand of the Chaldeans." Men will buy fields for money, sign deeds and seal them, and take witnesses, in the land of Benjamin, in the places around Jerusalem, in the cities of Judah, in the cities of the mountains, in the cities of the lowland, and in the cities of the South; for I will cause their captives to return,' says the LORD."** (verses 43-44)

In chapter 33 the Lord says **"concerning the houses of this city and the houses of the kings of Judah,"** (verse 4) that He **"will cause the captives of Judah and the captives of Israel to return, and will rebuild those places as at the first."** (verse 7) He concludes with the words **"'In this place which is desolate, without man and without beast, and in all its cities, there shall again be a dwelling place of shepherds causing their flocks to lie down. In the cities of the mountains, in the cities of the lowland, in the cities of the South, in the land of Benjamin, in the places around Jerusalem, and in the cities of Judah, the flocks shall again pass under the hands of him who counts them,' says the LORD. 'Behold, the days are coming,' says the LORD, 'that I will perform that good thing which I have promised to the house of Israel and to the house of Judah:'"** (Jeremiah 33:12-14) Again, in Jeremiah 30:18, the Lord says **"Behold, I will bring back the captivity of Jacob's tents, And have mercy on his** dwelling places; The city shall be built upon its own mound, And the palace shall remain according to its own plan."

Yet again, we read in Isaiah 66:15-16 that **"the LORD will come with fire And with His chariots, like a whirlwind, To render His anger with fury, And His rebuke with flames of fire. For by fire and by His sword The LORD will judge all flesh; And the slain of the LORD shall be many."** In verses 18 to 22 the Lord continues, **"'It shall be that I will gather all nations and tongues; and they shall come and see My glory. I will set a sign among them; and those among them who escape I will send to the nations: to Tarshish and Pul and Lud, who draw the bow, and Tubal and Javan, to the coastlands afar off who have not heard My fame nor seen My glory. And they shall declare My glory among the Gentiles. Then they shall bring all your brethren for an offering to the LORD out of all nations, on horses and in chariots and in litters, on mules and on camels, to My holy mountain Jerusalem,' says the LORD, 'as the children of Israel bring an offering in a clean vessel into the house of the LORD. And I will also take some of them for priests and Levites,' says the LORD. 'For as the new heavens and the new earth Which I will make shall remain before Me,' says the LORD, 'So shall your descendants and your name remain.'"** The words **"your descendants"** are final proof that the meaning is the physical offspring of the ancient nation of Israel.

2. A modified version of Replacement Theology says the modern day Jews are not Israelites at all. It says the true Israelites are European, particularly British, and through them, the Americans. It claims the so-called lost tribes of Israel migrated to this area after Assyria was defeated. But it is well known that the British are descended from the Celts, and that their ancestors were the Cimmerians. On page 75 we noticed a number of ancient sources that identify this ethnic group as Biblical Gomer, not as Israel. Two of these sources were from the Assyrian empire. This proves that Cimmeria already existed when Assyria was in power, that is, before

Assyria carried away the ten northern tribes of Israel. So this theory cannot even possibly be correct.

Further, we noticed on pages 16, 17, 26, 62, 105, that those in Judea are instructed to flee when they see the abomination of desolation. Zechariah prophesied of the times following this event.

> **"Behold, I will make Jerusalem a cup of drunkenness to all the surrounding peoples, when they lay siege against Judah and Jerusalem. And it shall happen in that day that I will make Jerusalem a very heavy stone for all peoples; all who would heave it away will surely be cut in pieces, though all nations of the earth are gathered against it."** (Zechariah 12:2-3)

> **"For I will gather all the nations to battle against Jerusalem; The city shall be taken, The houses rifled, And the women ravished. Half of the city shall go into captivity, But the remnant of the people shall not be cut off from the city. Then the LORD will go forth And fight against those nations, As He fights in the day of battle."** (Zechariah 14:2-3)

> **"'And it shall come to pass in all the land,' Says the LORD, '*That* two-thirds in it shall be cut off *and* die, But *one*-thirds shall be left in it: I will bring the *one*-third through the fire, Will refine them as silver is refined, And test them as gold is tested. They will call on My name, And I will answer them. I will say, "This *is* My people"; And each one will say, "The LORD *is* my God."'"** (Zechariah 13:8-9)

Since these words were written, there has never been a time when siege was laid to Jerusalem, and the Lord came to her rescue. Nor has there ever been a time when half the city was led away captive, but the other half remained there. Nor has there ever been a time when two thirds of those in the land were killed, but one third were saved and restored to faith in the Lord. Thus we see that these prophecies unquestionably refer to the future. But they are about Jerusalem, Judea, and the land. In the last section we saw many specific details proving these prophecies refer to the physical descendants of the ancient nation of Israel. But that is not all they prove. They also prove these prophecies refer to the physical land of Judea (the land now called Israel) and to the physical city of Jerusalem.

We therefore understand that Judah, that is, the real Jews, will be in their ancient homeland when all this happens, as noted on page 81. Yet the ones who live in this land are not the British or the Americans, but the modern day Jews. Thus we see that this doctrine, which is sometimes called British Israelism, is contrary to both history and scripture.

3. Closely allied to Replacement Theology is the so-called Preterist notion that most of Bible prophecy was fulfilled in ancient times. This idea is based on the many New Testament passages that say things like **"Blessed is he who reads and those who hear the words of this prophecy, and keep those things which are written in it; for the time *is* near."** (Revelation 1:3) and **"Behold, I am coming quickly! Blessed *is* he who keeps the words of the prophecy of this book."** (Revelation 22:7) Preterists insist that these scriptures, and many others like them, prove that the predicted events were to happen very soon after the prophecies were given.

There can be no doubt that this is correct, for the scriptures plainly declare it, not only here, but in many other places. The prophesied events **"must shortly take place."** (Revelation 1:1) But words such as **"shortly"** and **"quickly"** should be interpreted on a divine time scale, not a human one. For **"with the Lord one day *is* as a thousand years, and a thousand years as one day."** (2 Peter 3:8)

Preterists complain that this answer is "unsatisfying." But this is not a *human* answer. When this statement is examined in its context, its meaning becomes absolutely clear. The Holy Spirit said this in answer to **"scoffers"** who **"will come in the last days, walking according to their own lusts, and saying, 'Where is the promise of His coming? For since the fathers fell** asleep, all things continue as *they were* from the beginning of creation.'"[89] (2 Peter 3:3-4) The Holy Spirit's answer was:

> **"For this they willfully forget: that by the word of God the heavens were of old, and the earth standing out of water and in the water, by which the world *that* then existed perished, being flooded with water. But the heavens and the earth *which* are now preserved by the same word, are reserved for fire until the day of judgment and perdition of ungodly men. But, beloved, do not forget this one thing, that with the Lord one day *is* as a thousand years, and a thousand years as one day. The Lord is not slack concerning *His* promise, as some count slackness, but is longsuffering toward us, not willing that any should perish but that all should come to repentance. But the day of the Lord will come as a thief in the night, in which the heavens will pass away with a great noise, and the elements will melt with fervent heat; both the earth and the works that are in it will be burned up."** (2 Peter 3:5-10)

Thus we see that the statement **"with the Lord one day *is* as a thousand years, and a thousand years as one day"** was a *divine* explanation for apparent delay in the fulfillment of prophecy. This is also stated in the Old Testament, where, in speaking of judgment, the Holy Spirit said, **"a thousand years in Your sight *Are* like yesterday when it is past, And *like* a watch in the night."** (Psalm 90:4, see verses 3-9) So *God's* answer concerning this scoffing is that **"The Lord is not slack concerning *His* promise, as some count slackness, but is longsuffering toward us, not willing that any should perish but that all should come to repentance."**

A second argument often pressed by Preterists is that the New Testament taught that its prophecies were to be fulfilled within the lifetimes of those who first received them. They quote many passages such as

---

89 This scoffing is one of the chief arguments of Preterists. They claim that if we admit that New Testament prophecies were not fulfilled in ancient times, we justify such scoffing. But the Holy Spirit gives them an entirely different answer, as we see in the next passage above.

"Then we who are alive *and* remain shall be caught up together with them in the clouds to meet the Lord in the air." (1 Thessalonians 4:17) "and to *give* you who are troubled rest with us when the Lord Jesus is revealed from heaven with His mighty angels." (2 Thessalonians 1:7) They claim that the **"we"** and **"you"** in these and many similar prophecies refer to the individuals who first received them. Taken by themselves, such passages could well have this meaning. But other interpretations are also possible. The **"we"** and **"you"** in these passages could also refer to the church as a whole. We can only learn which of these interpretations is correct by examining the rest of scripture.

This also applies to the two proof texts they quote more often than any other. In the prophecy called the Olivet discourse, Jesus said, **"this generation will by no means pass away till all these things take place."** (Matthew 24:34) Again, He said, **"there are some standing here who shall not taste death till they see the Son of Man coming in His kingdom."** (Matthew 16:28) When taken out of their contexts, each of these statements appears to conclusively prove that many events commonly expected in the end times were to take place within the current generation. But when they are examined in their contexts, we see this as error.

Looking first at the passage in Matthew 24, we read:

> **"Learn this parable from the fig tree: When its branch has already become tender and puts forth leaves, you know that summer *is* near. So you also, when you see all these things, know that it is near; at the doors! Assuredly, I say to you, this generation will by no means pass away till all these things take place."** (Matthew 24:32-34)

This passage could mean that the generation our Lord was addressing would not **"pass away till all these things take place."** But it could also mean that this applied to the generation that would **"see all these things."** We can only tell which of these interpretations is correct by examining the rest of scripture.

And looking at the second passage in its context we read:

> **"For the Son of Man will come in the glory of His Father with His angels, and then He will reward each according to his works. Assuredly, I say to you, there are some standing here who shall not taste death till they see the Son of Man coming in His kingdom.**
>
> **"Now after six days Jesus took Peter, James, and John his brother, led them up on a high mountain by themselves; and He was transfigured before them. His face shone like the sun, and His clothes became as white as the light."** (Matthew 16:27-17:2)

We need to notice the very next words after our Lord said **"there are some standing here who shall not taste death till they see the Son of Man coming in His kingdom."** These words were **"Now after six days... He was transfigured before them. His face shone like the sun, and His clothes became as white as the light."** Only six days after the Lord said this, **"Peter, James, and John his brother"** saw Him **"in the glory of His Father,"** the glory of **"His Kingdom."** It is important to notice that this context is preserved in both of the other gospels that present this account. (See Mark 9:1-4 and Luke 9:27-29) Peter said of this event that **"we did not follow cunningly devised fables when we made known to you the power and coming of our Lord Jesus Christ, but were eyewitnesses of His majesty. For He received from God the Father honor and glory when such a voice came to Him from the Excellent Glory: 'This is My beloved Son, in whom I am well pleased.' And we heard this voice which came from heaven when we were with Him on the holy mountain."** (2 Peter 1:16-18)

From all this it seems that Jesus was speaking of this event when He said **"there are some standing here who shall not taste death till they see the Son of Man coming in His kingdom."** While this is only an interpretation, it is a possible interpretation. So again, the only way we can determine if it is correct is by examining the rest of scripture.

"The rest of scripture" is too big a subject to cover in this answer. But this book is filled with prophecies that definitely were not fulfilled in ancient times. Preterists go to great lengths to prove that many of them were, but their alleged "proofs" fall far short of the mark. While claiming these events took place long ago, they minimize or ignore differences between details of the prophecies and testimonies of history. As an example, in "The Parousia," a book many Preterists consider a classic, the author, J. Stuart Russell, insisted that ancient Jerusalem was built on seven hills, even after admitting that Josephus spoke only of four or five such hills. [90] The truth is that Josephus said Jerusalem was built on two hills, not four or five, much less seven. [91] (For the true import of the seven hills, see page 32.)

Again, on page 502 of the same book, Russell argued that the ten kings mentioned in Revelation 17:12 were princes or chiefs who helped the Romans attack Jerusalem. This cannot be correct, for the armies that destroyed Jerusalem were the Lord's armies. In Matthew 22:7 our Lord prophetically said that **"when the king heard *about it*, he was furious. And he sent out his armies, destroyed those murderers, and burned up their city."** But the ten kings will be the Lord's enemies, for they **"will make war with the Lamb, and the Lamb will overcome them, for He is Lord of lords and King of kings."** (Revelation 17:14) In his argument, Russell was only able to name four such chiefs; Antiochus, Sohemus, Agrippa, and Malchus. [92] He dismissed this with the comment that there were doubtless others. But then claimed that the number ten appeared to be mystic or symbolic, so there was no need to prove that there were exactly ten of them.

---

90 "The Parousia," by J. Stuart Russell, Grand Rapids: Baker, 1999, pg.492. Originally published London: T. Fisher Unwin, 1878. All page numbers cited are from the Baker edition.

91 "The Jewish War", by Flavius Josephus, Book 5, chapter 4, sec. 1, from "The New Complete Works of Josephus," translated by William Whiston, revised by Paul L. Maier, Grand Rapids: Kregel, 1999, pg. 851.

92 Russell made no attempt to show that any of these came into power after the Revelation was given, as clearly stated in Revelation 17:12.

Russell used these arguments to prove that Jerusalem was the **"BABYLON THE GREAT"** of Revelation 17:5, whose utter destruction was prophesied in Revelation 18. But Revelation 11:8 expressly states the spiritual names of Jerusalem; **"the great city which spiritually is called Sodom and Egypt, where also our Lord was crucified."** Russell dismissed this by claiming that there was no reason why Jerusalem might not also be called Babylon. (pg. 486)

On page 371 he argued that the Revelation was written before the destruction of Jerusalem in A.D. 70, even after admitting that the "weight of authority" indicates that the Revelation was written after Jerusalem was destroyed.

Preterists call this date a "much debated" issue, but the debate is essentially all on their side. Only Preterists care when it was written. But what is this "weight of authority" Russell spoke of?

First, Irenaeus wrote:

> "We will not, however, incur the risk of pronouncing positively as to the name of Antichrist; for if it were necessary that his name should be distinctly revealed in this present time, it would have been announced by him who beheld the apocalyptic vision. For that was seen no very long time since, but almost in our day, towards the end of Domitian's reign." [93]

Preterists claim that the words "That was seen no very long time since, but almost in our day, towards the end of Domation's reign." Refer to John, rather than to his vision. But when we consider the point Irenaeus was making, we see that this cannot be correct. He told us why he had decided not to name the Antichrist. It was because if that knowledge was needed at that time, it would have been announced in John's vision. "For that was seen

---

[93] "Against Heresies," by Irenaeus, Book 5, Chapter 30, paragraph 3. From "Ante-Nicene Fathers," ed. Alexander Roberts, D.D. and James Donaldson, D.D., Edinburgh, 1884, American Edition by A. Ceveland Coxe. D.D., Peabody, 1995, vol 1, pp. 559-560.

no very long time since, but almost in our day." Irenaeus was saying that John's vision had been so recent that if there was any need to know the Antichrist's name at that time, it would have been announced in the vision. This clearly demonstrates that Irenaeus was refering to the time the Revelation was written, not to the last time John had been seen.

Preterists often claim that all other ancient writers that say the Revelation was given in the reign of Domitian were simply relying on the word of Irenaeus. But Victornius wrote:

> "'And He says unto me, Thou must again prophesy to the peoples, and to the tongues, and to the nations, and to many kings.' He says this, because when John said these things he was in the island of Patmos, condemned to the labour of the mines by Cæsar Domitian. There, therefore, he saw the Apocalypse; and when grown old, he thought that he should at length receive his quittance by suffering, Domitian being killed, all his judgments were discharged. And John being dismissed from the mines, thus subsequently delivered the same Apocalypse which he had received from God." [94]

We need to notice two details in this statement. Victorinus said that "when John said these things he was in the island of Patmos, condemned to the labour of the mines by Cæsar Domitian," and that "John being dismissed from the mines, thus subsequently delivered the same Apocalypse." Since Irenaeus did not state either of these details, they are conclusive proof that this statement by Victorinus was based on information other than the statement by Irenaeus.

Again, the "Acts of the Holy Apostle and Evangelist John" gives a long and detailed account of John's arrest and trial, including the fact that Domitian was the son of Vespasian and reigned after him. And then it says:

---

[94] "Commentary on the Apocalypse of the Blessed John," comments on Revelation 10:11, by Victorinus, tran. Rev. Robert Ernest Wallis, Ph.D. From "Ante-Nicene Fathers," ed. Alexander Roberts, D.D. and James Donaldson, D.D., Edinburgh, 1884, American Edition by A. Cleveland Coxe, D.D., Peabody, 1995, vol 7, pg. 353.

> "And when all were glorifying God, and wondering at the faith of John, Domitian said to him: I have put forth a decree of the senate, that all such persons should be summarily dealt with, without trial; but since I find from thee that they are innocent, and that their religion is rather beneficial, I banish thee to an island, that I may not seem myself to do away with my own decrees." [95]

The extreme detail of this account is proof that it is not based on either of the other two statements we have examined. But this account does not mention the fact that John was condemned to work in the mines or the fact that he published the Revelation after he was released, as we noticed on page 193. So even as the statements of Victornius have to be based on a source other than Irenaeus, they also have to be based on a source other than the "Acts of the Holy Apostle and Evangelist John."

In addition to these three ante-Nicean accounts, in the post-Nicene period Jerome said concerning John:

> "In the fourteenth year then after Nero, Domitian having raised a second persecution he was banished to the island of Patmos, and wrote the ***Apocalypse***, on which Justin Martyr and Irenæus afterwards wrote commentaries. But Domitian having been put to death and his acts, on account of his excessive cruelty, having been annulled by the senate, he returned to Ephesus under Pertinax and continuing there until the time of the emperor Trajan, founded and built churches throughout all Asia, and, worn out by old age, died in the sixty-eighth year after our Lord's passion and was buried near the same city." [96]

We must notice that none of the three earlier accounts mentioned John returning to Ephesus under Pertinax. Thus, Jerome's account was based,

---

[95] "Acts of the Holy Apostle and Evangelist John," author unknown, translated by Alexander Walker, Esq. From "Ante-Nicene Fathers," ed. Alexander Roberts, D.D. and James Donaldson, D.D., Edinburgh, 1884, in the American Edition by A. Cleveland Coxe, D.D., Peabody, 1995, vol 8, pp. 561-562.

[96] "Lives of Illustrious Men," by Jerome, chapter 9. - From "Nicene and Post-Nicene Fathers," Second Series, ed. by Philip Schaff, D.D., LL.D. and Henry Wace, D.D., vol.3, pp. 364-365.

at least in part, on information that did not come from any of the three ante-Nicene accounts we have examined.

So now we have the same information from four ancient sources, every one of which included at least some details that none of the others contained. This is conclusive proof that, contrary to the claims of Preterists, there were, at the very least, four independent ancient sources that indicated that the Revelation was written during the reign of Domatian.

This was also clearly stated in a work attributed to Hippolytus [97] and was stated by Sulpitius Severus. [98] But neither of these included any details that prove they were not basing their conclusions on sources other than one of the other four.

To call such overwhelming testimony the "weight of authority," as we noticed (page 192) was done by Russell, borders on dishonesty, as does the claim we noticed on page 193, that all other ancient writers that say the Revelation was given in the reign of Domitian were simply relying on Irenaeus. These independent ancient testimonies, speaking in unison as they do, totally destroy the Preterist system of interpretation. For if the Revelation was written after Jerusalem was destroyed, it could not be about the events of that time. The Preterist's only choice is to attack the sources, which is what they systematically, but inaccurately, do.

In addition to this, the famous church historian Eusebius said it was Domitian who condemned John to live on the island of Patmos. [99]

All this proves the Revelation could not have been written before Domation rose to power. For the apocalyptic vision occurred while John **"was on the island that is called Patmos for the word of God and for the testimony of Jesus Christ."** (Revelation 1:9)

---

[97] "Appendix to the Works of Hippolytus, Containing Dubious and Spurious Pieces," item 49, section 3. From "Ante-Nicean Fathers," ed. Alexander Roberts, D.D. and James Donaldson, D.D., Edinburgh, 1884, in the American edition ed. by Cleveland Coxe, D.D, vol 5, pg. 254.

[98] "The Sacred History Of Sulpitius Severus," book 2, chapter 31. - From "Nicene and Post-Nicene Fathers," Second Series, ed. by Philip Schaff, D.D., LL.D. and Henry Wace, D.D., vol. 11, pg. 112.

[99] "The Church History," by Eusebius, book 3, chapters 17 and 18. Taken from pg. 107 of "Eusebius – The Church History: A New Translation with Commentary" by Paul L. Maier, LL. D., Copyright 1999 © Kregel Publications, Grand Rapids, MI. Used by permission.

At the time Jerusalem was destroyed, the emperor of Rome was Vespasian. About nine years later he was succeeded by his son Titus, the one who had previously conquered Jerusalem. Titus ruled from approximately A.D. 79 to 81, to be succeeded by Domitian about eleven years after Jerusalem was destroyed. Domitian ruled until approximately A.D. 96, some 26 years after Jerusalem was destroyed. "Toward the end of Domitian's reign," as Irenaeus put it, would be a few years earlier. This, along with other evidence, leads most scholars to conclude that the Revelation was written sometime between A.D. 92 and 94, with most favoring the later date.

How do Preterists "prove" the Revelation was written earlier than this? By its "internal evidence." On page 373 of his book, Russell argued that the Revelation had to have been written before Jerusalem was destroyed because it spoke of both the city and the temple as still existing. This argument neglects the possibility that they could be rebuilt in the future. But his main argument, further down the same page, is that supposing the Revelation had been written after Jerusalem was destroyed would rob it of its prophetic character. He claimed that such an idea made the Revelation impossible to interpret. This argument involves a serious logical error. Russell attempted to prove his point by assuming it was true. This circular logic is a basic error at the very root of the Preterist system of interpretation. Although Russell's book was written over a hundred years ago, all of his arguments cited here are still commonly made by Preterists.

Both the Preterist notion and Replacement Theology destroy all possibility of even beginning to understand Bible prophecy. All prophecies that do not fit these systems of interpretation are assumed to be symbolic that is, that they do not mean what they say. But what they do mean is seldom proposed. Indeed, some who teach these ideas insist that many prophecies of the Bible cannot be understood with our present state of knowledge.

4. Others teach that no prophecy can be understood until it is fulfilled. This idea is based on the fact that Daniel was told to **"shut up the words,**

and seal the book until the time of the end" (Daniel 12:4) and that **"the words are closed up and sealed till the time of the end."** (verse 9) But in Revelation six to eight the sealed book was opened, [100] and John was told **"do not seal the words of the prophecy of this book, for the time is at hand."** (Revelation 22:10)

In speaking of **"the day of the Lord,"** 1 Thessalonians 5:4 tells us that **"you, brethren, are not in darkness, so that this Day should overtake you as a thief."** Again, Hebrews 10:25 instructs us to exhort one another, **"and so much the more as you see the Day approaching."** And the first verse of Revelation says that its purpose is **"to show His servants;** [101] **things which must shortly take place."** These and many other scriptures plainly show that the prophetic scriptures were intended to be understood before the time of their fulfillment.

5. Many say that the rapture cannot be until after the tribulation because of scriptures like:

> **"Immediately after the tribulation of those days the sun will be darkened, and the moon will not give its light; the stars will fall from heaven, and the powers of the heavens will be shaken. Then the sign of the Son of Man will appear in heaven, and then all the tribes of the earth will mourn, and they**

---

100 While it is actually outside of the scope of this book, we should notice here that although Daniel was told to **"seal the book until the time of the end,"** (Daniel 12:4) **"the last hour"** had already come in John's day. (1 John 2:18) As the Lamb opened the seven seals of the **"scroll written inside and on the back,"** (Revelation 5:1) there came a series of visions showing massive destruction of the existing world order. This destruction opens the way for the ancient world order to rise again. This shows how the prophecies of Daniel can still come to pass, even though many of the nations mentioned in them seem to have disappeared. After the seals were opened, the prophet was given a vision of a **"little book"** that was **"open."** (Revelation 10:2, 8) In verse 9 John was told to eat the book, which he did in verse 10. Throughout the rest of the Revelation, most of the symbols are from the book of Daniel. From this I conclude that the instruction to eat the little book means to go back at this point and learn (digest) the book of Daniel, for it is needed to understand the rest of the book of Revelation. But the book of Daniel could not be understood until its seals were opened in Revelation 6-9. If this interpretation is correct, no part of the revealed word of God remains sealed. All of it has now been opened to the eye of faith.

101 This break is not in the original Greek, as ancient Greek included no punctuation. It is included in some translations and omitted in others. It seems to me that this semicolon interrupts the manifest meaning of the sentence, that God gave the Revelation to Jesus **"to show His servants things which must shortly take place."**

will see the Son of Man coming on the clouds of heaven with power and great glory." (Matthew 24:29-30)

Since this has the Lord coming after the tribulation, they think it proves a post tribulation rapture. For they claim the Lord is only returning once. To prove this they point out that every scripture about the return of Jesus is always in the singular, and no scripture speaks of him returning more than once.

While this is correct, we must remember that not even one Old Testament prophecy about the Messiah said anything about Him coming more than once. But these prophecies contained many details that appeared to be contradictions. Some of them described Him as a great conquering warrior, but others showed Him as a suffering servant. The Holy Spirit told us that the prophets who uttered these prophecies noticed this.

> **"Of this salvation the prophets have inquired and searched carefully, who prophesied of the grace *that would come* to you, searching what, or what manner of time, the Spirit of Christ who was in them was indicating when He testified beforehand the sufferings of Christ and the glories that would follow."** (1 Peter 1:10-11)

The scholars of Jesus' day loved the prophecies about Israel's future glory, so they concentrated on them, neglecting the equally important prophecies about how their deliverer would suffer. This contributed to their failure to recognize Him as their Messiah.

Now that the suffering is over, and the rest of the Holy Scriptures have been given to us, we realize that these prophecies spoke of two comings of Messiah, at two different times. From this we see that the Holy Spirit established a precedent in the Old Testament. That precedent is that apparent contradictions in prophecies about the Lord's coming show that He is coming more than just once. We find many such apparent contradictions in the prophecies about our Lord's return. The precedent established in the Old Testament shows that the resolution of these apparent contradictions is that He is returning more than just once.

An examination of these apparent contradictions must begin with the radical difference between the scriptures about **"the Day of the Lord"** and those about the Lord's appearing for his own, which is commonly called the rapture. **"The Day of the Lord"** is **"cruel"** (Isaiah 13:9) and a **"very terrible"** (Joel 2:11) **"day of vengeance."** (Jeremiah 46:10) Amos 5:18-20 pronounces **"woe to you that desire the day of the Lord,"** saying it is **"very dark, with no brightness in it."**

On the other hand, 2 Timothy 4:8 tells us that the Lord will give **"the crown of righteousness... to all who have loved His appearing,"** Titus 2:13 calls it **"the blessed hope."** And Hebrews 9:28 says that **"To those who eagerly wait for Him He will appear a second time, apart from sin, for salvation."**

There could hardly be a more radical contrast between **"woe to you that desire the day of the Lord,"** and the promise of a great reward **"to all who have loved His appearing."** Likewise, a day **"with no brightness in it"** cannot be a **"blessed hope."** If these scriptures spoke of the same future event, these would be contradictions.

Again, in the parable of the ten virgins (Matthew 25:1-12) we read that **"the bridegroom came, and those who were ready went in with him to the wedding; and the door was shut. Afterward the other virgins came also, saying, 'Lord, Lord, open to us!' But he answered and said, 'Assuredly, I say to you, I do not know you.'"** (Matthew 25:10-12) here, as we noticed on page 87, we plainly see the righteous taken into the Lord's presence while the wicked are left outside a door that remains closed in spite of their pleading. But that is not all we see here. The word **"afterward"** in this parable indicates a delay between the time when **"they that were ready went in with him"** and the time when **"other virgins came also."**

This is significant because it indicates that the **"other virgins"** were not destroyed at the time when **"they that were ready went in with him."** It was only **"afterward"** that the **"other virgins"** came, begging for admission. But their pleas were rejected.

But in the parable of the wheat and the tares (Matthew 13:24-30) we read that at the time of harvest the owner of the field will say, **"First gather together the tares and bind them in bundles to burn them, but gather the wheat into my barn."** (Matthew 13:30) The word **"first"** in this command clearly indicates that the wicked are destroyed before the righteous are gathered. This order of events is exactly the opposite of the order stated in Matthew 25. So the contrast between them clearly indicates that the two parables are speaking of different events that take place at different times. And yes, the Greek text of these two parables has the words **"afterward"** and **"first."** The Greek word translated *afterward* in Matthew 25:11 is *hysteron*. (word number 5305 in Strong's Greek dictionary) And the Greek word translated *first* in Matthew 13:30 is *proton*. (word number 4412 in Strong's Greek dictionary)

In the explanation of the parable of the wheat and the tares, (Matthew 13:37-43) Jesus explicitly said it meant that **"The Son of Man will send out His angels, and they will gather out of His kingdom all things that offend, and those who practice lawlessness, and will cast them into the furnace of fire. There will be wailing and gnashing of teeth. Then the righteous will shine forth as the sun in the kingdom of their Father."** (Matthew 13:41-43) He then added, **"Again, the kingdom of heaven is like a dragnet that was cast into the sea and gathered some of every kind, which, when it was full, they drew to shore; and they sat down and gathered the good into vessels, but threw the bad away. So it will be at the end of the age. The angels will come forth, separate the wicked from among the just, and cast them into the furnace of fire. There will be wailing and gnashing of teeth."** (Matthew 13:47-50)

The last words of this explanation again highlight the radical difference between these two events. In the parable of the ten virgins, the righteous, **"those who were ready," "went in with him to the wedding."** Thus we see that the just were separated from among the wicked. But in the explanation of the parable of the wheat and the tares, Jesus explicitly said that **"the angels"** will **"separate the wicked from among the just."** It is physically impossible to perform these two separations at the same time, for the other details of these two parables show that the ones not removed at each event will be left where they were.

Again, we read that **"the Lord Himself will descend from heaven with a shout, with the voice of an archangel, and with the trumpet of God. And the dead in Christ will rise first. Then we who are alive *and* remain shall be caught up together with them in the clouds to meet the Lord in the air. And thus we shall always be with the Lord."** (1 Thessalonians 4:16-17) It is critical to notice that in Matthew 13:49 we are told that the ones who will **"separate the wicked from among the just"** will be **"the angels."** But in 1 Thessalonians 4:16-17 it will be **"The Lord himself"** who will come, and the just **"shall be caught up... in the clouds to meet the Lord in the air."**

In one case the wicked will be removed by **"the angels,"** and in the other case the righteous **"shall be caught up"** by **"The Lord himself."** If these scriptures spoke of the same event, these would be contradictions.

There are also numerous other apparent contradictions between the various comments about our Lord's return. But we have examined enough of these to plainly see that the scriptures indeed show that our Lord will return more than just once. So the fact that the Lord will come after the tribulation, as we saw in Matthew 24:29-30 (page 198) simply does not prove that the rapture will be after the tribulation.

But the very next verse says **"And He will send His angels with a great sound of a trumpet, and they will gather together His elect from the four winds, from one end of heaven to the other."** (Matthew 24:31)

Many correctly point out that here the Lord is seen gathering His own after the tribulation. So they conclude that this is the rapture. But we have seen that Our Lord himself spoke of two different events in which He will separate the righteous and the wicked. These people insist that the words **"His elect"** in this passage have to mean "the church." But this is clearly incorrect. For Isaiah 65:9 says, **"I will bring forth descendants from Jacob, And from Judah an heir of My mountains; My elect shall inherit it, And My servants shall dwell there."** Again, in verse 22 of the same chapter, we read, **"They shall not build and another inhabit; They shall not plant and another eat; For as the days of a tree,** *so shall be* **the days of My people, And My elect shall long enjoy the work of their hands."** In these two passages, the Holy Spirit twice called these Israelites **"My elect.'** This is conclusive proof that the term **"His elect"** does not necessarily mean "the church." And thus that our Lord's gathering **"His elect" "after the tribulation"** does not necessarily mean the rapture is after the tribulation.

Again, many people point to 1 Corinthians 15:52-52, in which we read, **"Behold, I tell you a mystery: We shall not all sleep, but we shall all be changed— in a moment, in the twinkling of an eye, at the last trumpet. For the trumpet will sound, and the dead will be raised incorruptible, and we shall be changed."** These people think the words **"at the last trumpet"** mean *at the last trumpet that will ever be blown.* Since trumpets are mentioned in the Revelation, they think this proves that the rapture cannot be before the time of these trumpets. But we read in Zechariah 9:13-14, **"'For I have bent Judah, My** *bow***, Fitted the bow with Ephraim, And raised up your sons, O Zion, Against your sons, O Greece, And made you like the sword of a mighty man.' Then the Lord will be seen over them, And His arrow will go forth like lightning. The Lord GOD will blow the trumpet, And go with whirlwinds from the south."** So we see **"The Lord GOD"** Himself blowing **"the trumpet"** over **"Judah"** and **"Ephraim"** as they go together to fight against the **"sons"** of **"Greece."** But Isaiah 11:11-14 and Ezekiel 37:21-22 both show that the reunion of Judah and Ephraim, and their united military campaigns, will be after the Lord has brought them back to the land. (For more detail on this, see pages 151 to 155.) And Isaiah 66 shows it is only after the Lord has **"come with fire... To render His anger with fury, And His rebuke with flames of fire"** (Isaiah 66:15) that all Israel will be brought back to their land. (For more detail on this see pages 146 to 147.) Now it is clear that the rapture cannot be after the Lord has **"come with fire... To render His anger with fury, And His rebuke with flames of fire."** So the Bible explicitly speaks of a trumpet that will be blown after the time of the rapture. Thus we see that the words **"at the last trumpet"** cannot mean that the rapture takes place *at the last trumpet that will ever be blown*. So they do not prove that the rapture will be after the tribulation.

Closely related to this is an argument these same people make about Revelation 20:4-6, where we read, **"Then *I saw* the souls of those who had been beheaded for their witness to Jesus and for the word of God, who had not worshiped the beast or his image, and had not received *his* mark on their foreheads or on their hands. And they lived and reigned with Christ for a thousand years. But the rest of the dead did not live again until the thousand years were finished. This *is* the first resurrection. Blessed and holy *is* he who has part in the first resurrection. Over such the second death has no power, but they shall be priests of God and of Christ, and shall reign with Him a thousand years."** These people say that this passage clearly says the first resurrection is after the tribulation, so the rapture cannot be before that time.

But these people are failing to notice the use and force of the words, **"this *is* the first resurrection."** These words are contrasting the resurrection of the just, which takes place before the thousand years, with the resurrection of the damned, which does not take place until after the thousand years. These words cannot mean that there was no resurrection previous to that of **"the souls of those who had been beheaded for their witness to Jesus and for the word of God,"** for we are specifically told of numerous resurrections that took place in the times of Elisha, Jesus, and the Apostles. We are also told of two witnesses that will be resurrected after the beast kills them in Revelation 11. So the words **"this *is* the first resurrection"** do not prove that the rapture will be after the tribulation.

6. Many point out that the rider on the white horse in Revelation 6:2 has a bow, but there is no mention of any arrows. They think this means he comes in peacefully, but this prophecy expressly says he will come **"conquering and to conquer."** These words mean war, not peace. Again, those who say this interpret this prophecy to mean the future Roman ruler will come into power through peaceful means, forgetting that Daniel 7:24 specifically tells us that he **"shall subdue three kings."**

This notion appears to have its roots in Daniel 11:21, which speaks of one who **"shall come in peaceably, and seize the kingdom by intrigue."** But this is part of a long passage, Daniel 11:5-32, which gives a detailed account of a (then future) series of wars between the Seleucids, (the kings of the North) and the Ptolemies (the kings of the South). These wars took place exactly as prophesied over a period of approximately 130 years. The point of this passage is to identify **"the king of the North"** and **"the king of the South"** who will attack Judah in **"the time of the end."** (Daniel 11:40) The king who came in **"peaceably,"** and seized the kingdom **"by intrigue"** was Antiochus Epiphanes, the last of the ancient Seleucid kings mentioned in this account. This has nothing to do with the coming Roman prince.

7. Many call this king of the revived Roman Empire the **"Antichrist,"** but in Revelation 13 John saw **"a beast rising up out of the sea, having seven heads and ten horns."** (verse 1) This was followed by **"another beast coming up out of the earth, and he had two horns like a lamb and spoke like a dragon."** (verse 11)

The beast with **"seven heads and ten horns"** is a well known symbol of Rome. (Daniel 7:7, 17, 19-25; Revelation 17:3-18) But the second beast looks **"like a lamb,"** that is, it looks like **"the Lamb of God,"** the

Christ, (John 1:29 and 36) but when it speaks it betrays itself as **"like a dragon,"** that is, like **"the dragon,"** or Satan. (Revelation 12:9) This second beast is thus seen to be the **"Antichrist."** For more detail on this see pages 42 to 50.

8. Many think this future Roman leader will become the ruler of the entire world. This is based on a statement in Revelation 13:7 that **"authority was given him over every tribe, tongue, and nation."** When taken by itself, this scripture could easily mean he will become king of the world. But that is not its only possible meaning. The Greek word translated **"every"** is this passage is *pas*. (word number 3956 in Strong's Greek Dictionary) Like the Hebrew word *kol*, [102] which is discussed in footnote 74 on page 119, this Greek word means *all* in a general sense, but like our English word *all*, it is not necessarily absolute. *Pas* is the Greek word used in Matthew 27:1, where we read that **"all the chief priests and elders of the people plotted against Jesus to put Him to death."** But Luke 23:50 says that Joseph of Arimathea was a member of the council, and verse 51 specifically says that **"He had not consented to their decision and deed."** Also, **Nicodemus** opposed the council in John 7:50-51 and came with Joseph to bury Jesus in John 19:39.

In English we add the word *absolutely* to the word *all* to make it absolute. In the Greek this was done by adding a syllable to the word *pas*, making it *hapas*. (word number 537 in Strong's Greek Dictionary) This is the word used in Luke 17:27, where we read that **"Noah entered the ark, and the flood came and destroyed them all."** If the Holy Spirit had meant that the beast would be given authority over *absolutely* all tribes, tongues, and nations, it would seem that He would have used the word *hapas*. But the word He used in Revelation 13:7 is *pas*, not *hapas*. So also in verses 3 and 8 of the same chapter, where we read that **"all the world marveled and followed the beast."** And **"All who dwell on the earth will worship him...."**

---

[102] The Greek word *pas* in Acts 2:17, *"I will pour out of My Spirit on all flesh;"* is an inspired translation of the Hebrew word *kol* in quoting **"I will pour out My Spirit on all flesh"** from Joel 2:28.

The Holy Spirit did not use the absolute form, *hapas*, of the Greek word *pas*, that is, *all*, in any of these places.

Further, the Greek word translated **"authority"** in this passage is *exousia*. (word number 1849 in Strong's Greek Dictionary) While this word is often used of *official authority*, it is also used to indicate nothing more than *power*, as in the ability to control. For this use of *exousia* see Romans 9:21 and 1 Corinthians 7:37. From these facts we see that this statement does not *necessarily* mean any more than that the beast will be able to impose his will over essentially all tribes, tongues, and nations. [103]

In addition to this, other scriptures clearly show that rival governments will continue to exist after this ruler rises to power. In Ezekiel 39, after describing Gog's destruction, the Lord says: **"So the house of Israel shall know that I *am* the LORD their God from that day forward."** (verse 22) As noted on page 79, this sets the date of Gog's destruction at the time of Israel's conversion, that is, after the end of Daniel's seventieth week, but before the millennium, as shown in the chart on page 6. Again, in Isaiah 10:25 the Lord says **"the indignation will cease, as will My anger"** in the destruction of **"the Assyrian."** As noted on pages 54 and 137, this sets the date of the Assyrian's destruction at the end of this week. If neither Gog nor the Assyrian are destroyed until the end of the week; they will both be in power during the Roman ruler's reign. Finally, in Revelation 16, while this **"beast"** is gathering his last great army, we see **"the kings of the East"** (verse 12) and **"the kings of the earth and of the whole world."** (verse 14) For more information on this, see pages 35 to 37, particularly footnote 12 on page 36.

The time of the Roman's unchallenged control is limited. The shortness of his reign is figuratively stated in Revelation 17:12, where we read that **"The ten horns which you saw are ten kings who have received no kingdom as yet, but**

---

[103] Footnote 13 on page 38 explains how the proposed cashless society could give the Beast essentially universal control without having any kind of *official* authority. But even without such a system, he could still have the influence needed to force his will upon the rest of the world. We often see various Presidents of the United States do this, without even the slightest pretension of any official authority anywhere outside of the actual borders of the United States.

they receive authority for one hour as kings with the beast." Revelation 13:5 tells us that **"he was given authority to continue for forty-two months."** As noted in pages 13 to 15 and the chart on page 6, this forty-two month period is the first half of Daniel's seventieth week. The **"one who makes desolate"** successfully challenges his authority **"in the middle of the week."** After this event, the Beast most certainly does not have universal control.

But he continues to have worldwide influence, for in Revelation 16:13-14 John **"saw three unclean spirits like frogs coming out of the mouth of the dragon, out of the mouth of the beast, and out of the mouth of the false prophet. For they are spirits of demons, performing signs,** *which* **go out to the kings of the earth and of the whole world, to gather them to the battle of that great day of God Almighty."**

While it is not extremely important in itself, this error leads to other errors which make it nearly impossible to understand numerous prophecies in the Bible.

9. One of these errors is the notion that this Roman ruler will attack Judah. Because they are persuaded he will be the official ruler of the entire world, many think he has to be **"the king"** of Daniel 11:36-40 and also the attacker described in verses 40-45. But we read in verses 40-41:

> **"At the time of the end the king of the South shall attack him; and the king of the North shall come against him like a whirlwind, with chariots, horsemen, and with many ships; and he shall enter the countries, overwhelm** *them,* **and pass through. He shall also enter the Glorious Land, and many** *countries* **shall be overthrown; but these shall escape from his hand: Edom, Moab, and the prominent people of Ammon."**

Most students realize the word **"him"** in the first part of verse 40 refers to **"the king,"** who is the subject of the four previous verses. In this verse **"the king"** is attacked by **"the king of the South."** Then **"the king of the North"** attacks, becoming the subject of the rest of verse 40 and the four following verses. (41-45)

But those who think the Roman is **"the king"** fail to see this. They think the repeated uses of the word **"he"** in the last part of verse 40 and in verses 41-45 refer to **"the king."**

Many defend this idea by saying, "It all depends on how you interpret Daniel 11:40-45." But this is a serious error. If this passage were taken by itself, it could well be interpreted this way. But many other scriptures show this cannot be correct. Chief among these are the scriptures about the end time "Assyrian" discussed in pages 50 to 54. This interpretation totally neglects all of these.

In this context, one of the most important of these prophecies is Isaiah 7:17-20:

> **"'The LORD will bring the king of Assyria upon you and your people and your father's house— days that have not come since the day that Ephraim departed from Judah.'**
>
> **"And it shall come to pass in that day *That* the LORD will whistle for the fly That *is* in the farthest part of the rivers of Egypt, And for the bee that *is* in the land of Assyria. They will come, and all of them will rest In the desolate valleys and in the clefts of the rocks, And on all thorns and in all pastures. In the same day the Lord will shave with a hired razor, With those from beyond the River, with the king of Assyria, The head and the hair of the legs, And will also remove the beard."**

Here we see that the Lord will bring Assyria and Egypt upon the people of Ahaz (see verse 7:10) that is, upon Judah. From the way it is stated, the meaning is plainly that they will come at the same time. There has never been a time when Assyrian and Egyptian armies invaded Judea at the same time, so this prophecy remains to be fulfilled in the future. (For more detail on this, see page 66.)

Returning now to the notion that the attacker of Daniel 11:40-45 is the Roman ruler, this interpretation also neglects the male goat's little horn of Daniel 8:9. The attacker represented by this horn will come **"out of one of"** the four kingdoms resulting from the breakup of the empire of Alexander the Great. Thus he cannot be either the Roman or the Russian ruler, for none of these four kingdoms ever included either Rome or any part of Russia. (see pages 56 to 61)

We saw on page 42 that **"the king"** is a literal translation of the Hebrew word *melek*. But the ruler of the revived Roman empire (called **"the prince"** in our translation) is called a *nagiyd* in the Hebrew (see page 25). The language of the Bible is very precise. Every detail has meaning. Even such a small difference as whether someone is called a *melek* or a *nagiyd* is important. *Nagiyd* is distinctly different from *melek*. It means a *leader* or a *commander* but not a *king* (although we saw on page 25 that it is sometimes used of kings).

Further, this Roman prince cannot be the attacker of verses 40-45 because he will be in covenant with Judah. In Daniel 9:27 we read that **"he shall confirm a covenant with many for one week."** Revelation 19:20 shows us this covenant will hold until the Lord comes, for it says **"the beast was captured, and with him the false prophet who worked signs in his presence, by which he deceived those who received the mark of the beast and those who worshiped his image. These two were cast alive into the lake of fire burning with brimstone."** We saw on pages 35 to 40 that **"the beast"** is a prophetic name for this Roman ruler and on pages 47 to 48 that **"the false prophet"** is the ruler of revived Judah.

Many think the Roman ruler will attack Judah because the Jews will reject his divine pretensions. But in Isaiah 28:14-15 we read:

> **"Therefore hear the word of the Lord, you scornful men, Who rule over this people who *are* in Jerusalem. Because you have said, We have made a covenant with death, And with Sheol we are in agreement. When the overflowing scourge passes through, It will not come to us, For we have made lies**

our refuge, And under falsehood we have hidden ourselves.'" (see verses 5:18-19)

Again, in John 5:43 our Lord told the Jews;

"I have come in My Father's name, and you do not receive Me; if another comes in his own name, him you will receive."

Many think this could not happen, but long before the Lord said this, He had told them,

"Just as they have chosen their own ways, And their soul delights in their abominations, So will I choose their delusions, And bring their fears on them; Because, when I called, no one answered, When I spoke they did not hear; But they did evil before My eyes, And chose that in which I do not delight." (Isaiah 66:3-4)

Again, 2 Thessalonians 2:9-12 says that:

"The coming of the lawless one is according to the working of Satan, with all power, signs, and lying wonders, and with all unrighteous deception among those who perish, because they did not receive the love of the truth, that they might be saved. And for this reason God will send them strong delusion, that they should believe the lie, that they all may be condemned who did not believe the truth but had pleasure in unrighteousness."

These prophecies clearly show that the Jews in general, with the rulers of Jerusalem, will be among those who have rejected **"the love of the truth"** and will therefore be turned over to believe the Roman leader's lies. [104] Thus we see that the supposed reason for such a Roman attack will not even exist. The Jews and their leaders will not reject the Roman's pretensions, but will

---

104 For more detail on this see pages 49 and 101.

accept them. Only the righteous will reject this horrible blasphemy, and for this they will have to flee for their lives, as we read:

> "Now when the dragon saw that he had been cast to the earth, he persecuted the woman who gave birth to the man *Child*. But the woman was given two wings of a great eagle, that she might *fly* into the wilderness to her place, where she is nourished for a time, and times, and half a time from the presence of the serpent. So the serpent spewed water out of his mouth like a flood after the woman, that he might cause her to be carried away by the flood." (Revelation 12:13-15)

"But the earth helped the woman, and the earth opened its mouth and swallowed up the flood which the dragon had spewed out of his mouth." (Revelation 12:16) The flood spewed out of the serpent's mouth cannot be the attack in Daniel 11:40-41, for there the attacker **"shall enter the countries, overwhelm *them*, and pass through. He shall also enter the Glorious Land, and many *countries* shall be overthrown."** In one case **"the earth helped the woman, and... swallowed up the flood."** In the other, many countries, including **"the Glorious Land"** shall be overwhelmed and overthrown. The results could hardly be more different. For more detail on this see pages 109 and 110.

10. This notion that the Roman ruler will become king of the entire world leads to another widespread error. Many who hold this idea realize this could not happen while Gog was still in power. So they conclude Gog will have to be destroyed before the time of the Roman. That is, before Daniel's seventieth week, the time commonly called the tribulation. But many details in the prophecy about Gog's destruction (Ezekiel 38-39) show this cannot be correct.

The first of these (although not the most obvious) is that throughout this prophecy the land and the people are called ***Israel***, not ***Judah***. In prophecies about Daniel's seventieth week, the word ***Israel*** is almost never used.

(For more information on this, see page 79.) This is because only Judah will be in the land during that seventieth week. (See footnote 56, page 81.) All Israel will not be in the land until Messiah comes. [105]

This agrees perfectly with the fact that those who have now returned to the land are called Jews. The word Jew does not mean an Israelite. It means a descendant of the ancient kingdom of Judah, that is, a member of either the tribe of Judah or the tribe of Benjamin. (See page 79.) This can be seen from the Hebrew words translated "Jew" in the Old Testament. The most commonly used one is *yeudiy*. (word number 3064 in Strong's Hebrew Dictionary) The meaning of this word becomes obvious when we see the word it is derived from, *yehudah*. (word number 3063 in Strong's Hebrew Dictionary) This is the name transliterated *Judah*, the name of the tribe and kingdom of Judah. Thus we see that the original form of the word Jew was Judie, or a citizen of Judah.

There is a second detail, only slightly more obvious, which shows that Gog's attack cannot be before Daniel's seventieth week. The prophecy repeatedly states that at the time of the attack, the people of Israel will be dwelling

---

[105] In Ezekiel 36:10, the Lord tells the **"mountains of Israel"** (verse 8) that He **"will multiply men upon you, all the house of Israel, all of it."** Again, in Micah 2:12, the Lord says **"I will surely assemble all of you, O Jacob, I will surely gather the remnant of Israel; I will put them together like sheep of the fold."** It is clear that this has not yet happened, for there are still Jews everywhere in the world. But when will it happen?

We see this in Isaiah 66:15-20, where the Lord says, **"For behold, the Lord will come with fire And with His chariots, like a whirlwind, To render His anger with fury, And His rebuke with flames of fire. For by fire and by His sword The Lord will judge all flesh; And the slain of the Lord shall be many... 'It shall be that I will gather all nations and tongues; and they shall come and see My glory. I will set a sign among them; and those among them who escape I will send to the nations: *to* Tarshish and Pul and Lud, who draw the bow, and Tubal and Javan, *to* the coastlands afar off who have not heard My fame nor seen My glory. And they shall declare My glory among the Gentiles. Then they shall bring all your brethren for an offering to the LORD out of all nations, on horses and in chariots and in litters, on mules and on camels, to My holy mountain Jerusalem,' says the LORD."**

Thus we see that promised return of **"all the house of Israel, all of it,"** will be after the Lord has come **"with fire And with His chariots, like a whirlwind, To render His anger with fury, And His rebuke with flames of fire."** And after He has gathered **"all nations and tongues,"** and they have come, and seen his glory, and He has sent **"those among them who escape"** **"to the nations."** It is only then that **"they shall bring all your brethren"** **"to My holy mountain Jerusalem."** For more information on this see pages 146 and 185.

"safely." (Ezekiel 38:8,11,14) The Hebrew word translated *safely* in each of these places is ***betach.*** (word number 983 in Strong's Hebrew Dictionary)

This word doesn't only refer to the actual fact of safety. It also refers to a feeling of being safe. Whether the word refers to the fact or the feeling of safety can only be determined from the context. In this case, the meaning is plainly the feeling of safety, rather than the actual fact. (see page 78) This can be seen from verse 14: **"Therefore, son of man, prophesy and say to Gog, 'Thus says the Lord GOD: "On that day when My people Israel dwell safely, will you not know *it?*"'"** If the meaning was that Gog knew the people were actually safe, this would not make him decide to attack. But if the meaning was that Gog knew they *felt* safe, it would encourage him to attack. We see this more clearly in verse 11: **"You will say, 'I will go up against a land of unwalled villages; I will go to a peaceful people, who dwell safely, all of them dwelling without walls, and having neither bars nor gates'"** Thus we see that the word *safely* in this prophecy refers to *feeling* safe, not actually *being* safe.

We have seen (page 10) that the Roman prince will make a seven year covenant with Judah, and that this seven year period will be Daniel's seventieth week. (Daniel 9:27) We have also seen (page 97) that this covenant will give them a false sense of security. (Isaiah 28:14-18)

It seems obvious that those who dwell in present day Israel will never feel safe until the Roman prince's treaty is confirmed. But we cannot interpret prophecy on the basis of current events. We need scripture for even this. In Amos 1:11 we read, **"For three transgressions of Edom, and for four, I will not turn away its punishent, Because he pursued his brother with the sword, And cast off all pity; His anger tore perpetually, And he kept his wrath forever."** The anger and wrath of Edom will never cease. The ancient land of Edom covered the southern portion of present day Jordan and the northern part of today's Saudi Arabia. Again, in Amos 1:6 we read **"For three transgressions of Gaza, and for four, I will not turn away its *punishment,***

Because they took captive the whole captivity To deliver *them* **up to Edom,"** clearly showing that Gaza will join Edom in their wickedness. The next verse, 8, mentions that this is the land of the Philistines. (that is, the Palestinians) And verse 9 adds that Tyre (in present day Lebanon) will join in as well. Thus we see that until Edom is destroyed there will never be a time when Judah (which is now called Israel) will have reasonable cause to feel safe. This shows that the people will not **"dwell safely"** until the Roman prince confirms his treaty, so Gog's attack cannot be before that time.

The first two reasons given here, while real, are not obvious. But there are also very obvious reasons. In Ezekiel 39:7, after telling Gog he will be destroyed, the Lord says **"So I will make My holy name known in the midst of My people Israel, and I will not** *let them* **profane My holy name anymore."** But Daniel 9:27 tells us that **"in the middle of"** Daniel's seventieth week, the Roman prince **"shall bring an end to sacrifice and offering. And on the wing of abominations shall be one who makes desolate."** There can be no reasonable doubt that this is the time when **"the man of sin," "the son of perdition, who opposes and exalts himself above all that is called God or that is worshiped" "sits as God in the temple of God, showing himself that he is God."** (I Thessalonians 2:3-4) Aside from their blasphemy against and crucifixion of the Lord Jesus, This will clearly be the worst profaning of the Lord's name ever done by His rebellious people. But after Gog is destroyed, the Lord **"will not** *let***"** His people Israel **"profane"** His holy name **"anymore."** So Gog's destruction cannot take place before the middle of Daniel's seventieth week.

We just looked at the first part of Ezekiel 39:7. The rest of that verse is **"Then the nations shall know that I** *am* **the LORD, the Holy One in Israel."** But according to I Thessalonians 2:9-12, **"The coming of the** *lawless one* **is according to the working of Satan, with all power, signs, and lying wonders, and with all unrighteous deception among those who perish, because they did not receive the love of the truth, that they might be** saved. And for this reason God will send them strong delusion, that they should believe the lie, that they all may be condemned who did not believe the truth but had pleasure in unrighteousness." During the time of the Antichrist **"God will send them strong delusion, that they should believe the lie."** But beginning with the destruction of Gog, **"Then the nations shall know"** that Israel's God is the Lord. This has to be after the time they are under a divinely sent **"strong delusion, that they should believe the lie."** So Gog's destruction cannot take place before the time of the Antichrist.

The same argument applies to Ezekiel 39:22, but even more strongly. In this verse the Lord says, **"the house of Israel shall know that I *am* the LORD their God from that day forward"** But in John 5:43 Jesus told the Jews (see verses 5:18-19); **"I have come in My Father's name, and you do not receive Me; if another comes in his own name, him you will receive."** This plainly shows that the Jews will worship the Antichrist, so at that time they will not know that the Lord is **"their God."** Thus we see that Gog's destruction cannot take place before the time of the Antichrist. But when Gog is destroyed, **"the house of Israel shall know that"** He is **"the LORD their God from that day forward."**

During the millennium **"No more shall every man teach his neighbor, and every man his brother, saying, 'Know the Lord,' for they all shall know Me, from the least of them to the greatest of them."** (Jeremiah 31:34) So Gog will be destroyed before the millennium.

Again, in Ezekiel 39:29 the Lord says that after this great deliverance He **"will not hide"** His **"face from them anymore."** But during the tribulation **"they will cry to the Lord, But He will not hear them; He will even hide His face from them at that time, Because they have been evil in their deeds."** (Micah 3:4) This again shows that the deliverance from Gog will take place after the tribulation.

For more information on when Gog will attack, see pages 79, 206, and the chart on page 6.

11. Many hold that **"the king of the North"** who attacks Judah in Daniel 11:40-45 is the king of Russia, but verses 2-35 of this chapter give a highly detailed account of a series of wars between **"the king of the North"** and **"the king of the South."** In this passage, every act of **"the king of the North"** was committed by one of the ancient Seleucids, who reigned out of Antioch in Syria. And every act of **"the king of the South"** was committed by one of the Ptolemies, who reigned out of Alexandria in Egypt.

The area ruled by the Seleucids corresponded closely to the area of the previous Assyrian empire, (see the map on page 230) and included most of present day Syria and Iraq. This absolutely identifies **"the king of the North"** as a king over this region, or **"the Assyrian"** of Isaiah 10.

There is no excuse for changing this to Russia. It is true that in Ezekiel 38:15 and 39:2, Gog, the prince of Rosh (Russia) is said to come from **"the far north."** This is also said of Togarmah in verse 6 of chapter 38, but this term is not the same as **"the north."** The difference, though subtle, is significant.

Further, in Joel 2:20 the army of **"the king of the North"** is destroyed in **"a barren and desolate land,"** between **"the eastern sea"** and **"the western sea."** But Gog's end comes in a different place. For the Lord says, **"It will come to pass in that day *that* I will give Gog a burial place there in Israel, the valley of those who pass by east of the sea; and it will obstruct travelers, because there they will bury Gog and all his multitude. Therefore they will call *it* the Valley of Hamon Gog."** (Ezekiel 39:11) It is important to realize that if these two passages described the same location, it would have to be **"a barren and desolate land"** on Israel's Mediterranean seacoast. The sea mentioned in Ezekiel 39:11 could not be either the Dead Sea or the Sea of Galilee because a spot on the west coast of either of these Seas would not be between **"the eastern sea"** and **"the western sea."** Further, Ezekiel 39:4 says that Gog **"shall fall upon the mountains of Israel."** But Israel's Mediterranean seacoast between **"the eastern sea"** and **"the western sea"** is a fertile plain. So it could not be the **"barren and desolate land"** where Joel 2:20 says **"the king of the North"** will be destroyed.

Finally, there are significant differences between the prophecies about Gog's attack in Ezekiel 38 and 39 and the attack of **"the king of the North"** in Daniel 11.

The most notable of these is that the attack in Daniel 11 ushers in **"a time of trouble, Such as never was since there was a nation, *Even* to that time."** (Daniel 12:1) But the attack in Ezekiel 38 and 39 ushers in a time when **"'I will not hide My face from them anymore; for I shall have poured out My Spirit on the house of Israel,' says the Lord GOD."** (Ezekiel 39:29) All this makes it plain that **"Gog"** and **"the king of the North"** are two different individuals.

12. Many Preterists claim that the church had always taught their doctrine until the early 1800's. No argument of this type is appropriate, for the only acceptable test of a doctrine is scripture. But this one is not even correct.

The earliest Christian commentary on Bible prophecy (of any significant length) which has survived to the present day, was the last twelve chapters of the famous work titled "Against Heresies," by Irenaeus, which is believed to have been published between 186 and 188 A.D. There were earlier Christian works on Bible prophecy, but all of them either have been lost or were only short. Irenaeus wrote:

> "In a still clearer light has John, in the Apocalypse, indicated to the Lord's disciples what shall happen in the last times, and concerning the ten kings who shall then arise, among whom the empire which now rules [the earth] shall be partitioned. He teaches us what the ten horns shall be which were seen by Daniel, telling us that thus it had been said to him: 'And the ten horns which thou sawest are ten kings, who have received no kingdom as yet, but shall receive power as if kings one hour with the beast. These have one mind, and give their strength and power to the beast. These shall make war with the Lamb, and the Lamb shall overcome them, because He is the Lord of lords and the King of kings.'

It is manifest, therefore, that of these [potentates], he who is to come shall slay three, and subject the remainder to his power, and that he shall be himself the eighth among them."[106]

Irenaeus was far from alone in his views. The earliest Christian commentator on Bible prophecy known to modern scholars was Papias, who was reported to have been a personal acquaintance of the apostle John. All of his writings have been lost. But Eusebius complained that it was due to Papias that "many church writers after him held the same opinion, relying on his early date; Irenaeus, for example, and any others who adopted the same views." From this we know that the futuristic views of Irenaeus were also held by Papias, and that, though these ideas were rejected by Eusebius, they were held by "many" of the early church writers.[107]

But the extreme nature of the error in the Preterist claim that the church had always taught their doctrine until the early 1800's can best be seen in a statement by Jerome, who wrote in the fifth century:

> "We should therefore concur with the traditional interpretation of all the commentators of the Christian Church, that at the end of the world, when the Roman Empire is to be destroyed, there shall be ten kings who will partition the Roman world amongst themselves. Then an insignificant eleventh king will arise, who will overcome three of the ten kings... Then after they have been slain, the seven other kings will bow their necks to the victor."[108]

Thus we see that, even as late as the fifth century, futurism was considered "the traditional interpretation of all the commentators of the Christian church."

13. Like the Preterists, many Amillennials also claim that the church had always taught their doctrine before the early 1800's. But this is also

---

106 "Against Heresies", Book 5, chapter 26, paragraph 1, (pp.554-555 in the volume cited in footnote 93 on page 192.)

107 "The Church History," by Eusebius, book 3, chapter 39. Taken from pg. 129 Of the volume cited in footnote 99 on page 195. Used by permission.

108 "Commentary on Daniel," by Jerome, as found in "Jerome's Commentary on Daniel," pg. 77, translated by Gleason L. Archer, Jr., Baker Book House, Grand Rapids, 1958. Used by permission.

incorrect. A writer even earlier than Irenaeus was Justin, who is often called Justin Martyr, because he died as a martyr. He wrote:

> "I and others, who are right-minded Christians on all points, are assured that there will be a resurrection of the dead, and a thousand years in Jerusalem, which will then be built, adorned, and enlarged, [as] the prophets Ezekiel and Isaiah and others declare."[109]
>
> "And further, there was a certain man with us, whose name was John, one of the apostles of Christ, who prophesied, by a revelation that was made to him, that those who believed in our Christ would dwell a thousand years in Jerusalem; and that thereafter the general, and, in short, the eternal resurrection and judgment of all men would likewise take place."[110]

As we have already noticed, Papias was even earlier than Justin. All of his writings have been lost, but Eusebius said concerning him:

> "Papias supplies other stories that reached him by word of mouth, along with some strange parables and unknown teachings of the Savior, as well as other more legendary accounts. Among them, he says that after the resurrection of the dead there will be a thousand-year period when the kingdom of Christ will be established on this earth in material form."[111]

So we see that both Papias and Justin, two of the three earliest Christian writers on Bible prophecy known to modern scholars, explicitly said the coming kingdom would last a thousand years. In addition to these, Jerome said of Papias that "He is said to have published a ***Second coming of Our Lord or Millennium***. Irenæus and Apollinaris and others who say that after the resurrection the Lord

---

[109] "Dialogue With Trypho," by Justin Martyr, chapter LXXX From "Ante-Nicene Fathers," ed. Alexander Roberts, D.D. and James Donaldson, D.D., Edinburgh, 1884, in the American Edition by A. Cleveland Coxe, D.D., Peabody, 1995, vol 1, pg. 239.

[110] Dialogue With Trypho, by Justin Martyr, chapter LXXXI. (pg. 240 in the volume cited in footnote 109).

[111] "The Church History," by Eusebius, book 3, chapter 39. Taken from pg. 129 of the volume cited in footnote 99 on page 195. Used by permission.

will reign in the flesh with the saints, follow him. Tertullian also in his work *On the hope of the faithful*, Victorinus of Petau and Lactantius follow this view." [112] All this is conclusive proof of the falsehood of the claim that the church always taught Amillennialism previous to the early 1800's.

14. Again, many of those who teach Replacement Theology also claim that their doctrine was always taught before the early 1800's. This can actually be made to seem to be correct, for not even one of the early Christian writers whose works were preserved explicitly taught a future blessing of Israel in their homeland, even though that could well be inferred from what they said. But the record shows that this doctrine was indeed taught in ancient times, even though the medieval monks did not see fit to preserve any such documents.

For instance, Eusebius tells us of:

> "Nepos, a bishop in Egypt, who taught that the promises made to the saints in the divine Scriptures should be interpreted in a more Jewish fashion and that there would be a sort of millennium of bodily indulgence on this earth. Thinking to support his peculiar opinion from the Revelation of John, he wrote a book on the subject, ***Refutation of the Allegorizers***. Dionysius answered him in the books, ***On Promises***..." [113]

It is important to read the actual words of Dionysius concerning Nepos. Even though he was opposing Nepos on this doctrine, he said:

> "I have to say, that in many other respects I accept the opinion of Nepos, and love him at once for his faith, and his laboriousness, and his patient study of the scriptures, as also for his great effort in psalmody, by which even now many of the brethren are delighted. I hold the man, too, in great respect still more, inasmuch as he has gone to rest before us." [114]

---

[112] "Lives of Illustrous Men, by Jerome, chapter 18. From "Nicene and Post Nicene Fathers," Second Series, ed. Philip Schaff, D.D., LL.D. and Henry Wace, D.D., Edinburgh, 1884, in the American Edition by A. Cleveland Coxe, D.D., Peabody, 1994, vol 3, pg. 367.

[113] "The Church History," by Eusebius, book 7, chapter 24. Taken from pp. 270-271 of the volume cited in footnote 99 on page 195. Used by permission.

[114] "On the Promises," by Dionysius, part 1, fragment 1. From "Ante-Nicene Fathers," ed. Alexander

Further on, Dionysius commented that "in the Arsinoitic prefecture... this doctrine was current long ago."[115] Thus we learn both that Nepos was highly respected and that his doctrine had been widely accepted "long" before Dionysius wrote this, which is thought to have been between 252 and 257 A.D.

We also know that this was being taught from the opposition this doctrine received. As an example, the so-called Epistle of Barnabas says:

> "Ye ought therefore to understand. And this also I further beg of you, as being one of you, and loving you both individually and collectively more than my own soul, to take heed now to yourselves, and not to be like some, adding largely to your sins, and saying, 'The covenant is both theirs and ours.' But they thus finally lost it, after Moses had already received it."[116]

Thus we know that a future restoration of Israel was indeed taught in the first few centuries of the church, even though no document explicitly teaching it was preserved. This is conclusive proof of the falsehood of the claim that no doctrine contrary to Replacement Theology was ever taught before the early 1800's.

15. Finally, many imagine that a future fulfillment Daniel's seventieth week is a notion "invented" in the early 1800's to justify the doctrine of a future restoration of Israel. But again, this is completely incorrect. The very oldest commentary on scripture that has survived to the present day is a commentary on Daniel by Hippolytus. This is thought to have been written

---

Roberts, D.D. and James Donaldson, D.D., Edinburgh, 1884, American Edition by A. Cleveland Coxe, D.D., Peabody, 1995, vol 6, pg. 81.

115 "On the Promises," by Dionysius, part 1, fragment 2. From "Ante-Nicene Fathers," ed. Alexander Roberts, D.D. and James Donaldson, D.D., Edinburgh, 1884, American Edition by A. Cleveland Coxe, D.D., Peabody, 1995, vol 6, pp. 81-82.

116 "Epistle of Barnabas," chapter IV. From "Ante-Nicene Fathers," ed. Alexander Roberts, D.D. and James Donaldson, D.D., Edinburgh, 1884, American Edition by A. Cleveland Coxe, D.D., Peabody, 1995, vol 1, pg. 138.

between 202 and 211 A.D. Hippolytus clearly taught that this seventieth week remains to be fulfilled, saying:

> "For after sixty-two weeks was fulfilled and after Christ has come and the Gospel has been preached in every place, times having been spun out, the end remains one week *away*, in which Elijah and Enoch shall be present and in its half the abomination of desolation, the Antichrist, shall appear who threatens desolation of the world. After he comes, sacrifice and drink offering, which now in every way is offered by the nations to God, shall be taken away." [117]

Some chapters later he expanded on this, saying:

> "Just as also he spoke to Daniel, "And he shall establish a covenant with many for one week and it will be *that* in the half of the week he shall take away my sacrifice and drink offering," so that the one week may be shown as divided into two, after the two witnesses will have preached for three and a half years, the Antichrist will wage war against the saints the remainder of the week and will desolate all the world so that what was spoken may be fulfilled, 'And they will give the abomination of desolation one thousand two hundred ninety days. Blessed is he who endures to Christ and reaches the one thousand three hundred thirty-five days!'" [118]

And even earlier than Hippolytus, Irenaeus had said:

> "And then he points out the time that his tyranny shall last, during which the saints shall be put to flight, they who offer a pure sacrifice unto God: 'And in the midst of the week,' he says, 'the sacrifice and the libation shall be taken away, and the abomination of desolation [shall be brought] into the temple: even unto the consummation of the time shall the desolation be complete.' Now three years and six months constitute the half-week." [119]

---

[117] "Commentary on Daniel", by Hippolytus, Book 4, chapter 35, paragraph 3. From the translation by T. C. Schmidt. Used by Permission.

[118] "Commentary on Daniel", by Hippolytus, Book 4, chapter 50, paragraph 2. From the translation by T. C. Schmidt. Used by permission.

[119] "Against Heresies", Book V, chapter 25, paragraph 4, (pg.554 in the volume cited in footnote 93 on page 192.)

So this concept was indeed taught by highly respected writers within the church's first two centuries, rather than having been "invented" in the early 1800's.

Note:

> The historical quotations in sections 12 through 15 of this appendix are all of Christian writers from truly ancient times. It is critical to note that none of these are made with any imagination that the antiquity of these authors makes them authoritative. They are quoted solely to disprove the claims that the doctrines in question are relatively new concepts, dating only to the early 1800's.

But the ancient writers quoted here are far from the only Christians that taught these ideas long before the early 1800s. Any student interested in this subject will find much other material, quoted mostly from original sources, in "Dispensationalism Before Darby," by William C Watson, pub. 2015 by Lampion Press, Silverton, OR, USA, ISBN: 978-1-942614-03-6, and in "Ancient Dispensational Truth," by James C. Morris, pub. 2018 by Dispensational Publishing House, Taos, NM, USA, ISBN: 978-1-945774-29-4.

MAPS

About the maps:

Most of our knowledge of ancient borders comes from written descriptions. Various modern scholars have drawn maps based on these descriptions. The general information shown in these maps is reasonably accurate. But the borders shown are often nothing more than guesses. In a few cases such information is available from actual ancient maps. But unfortunately, these are never very accurate.

The information in these maps has been selected from what seemed to be the best maps available. The borders shown in the source maps were adjusted to follow the closest natural borders, such as rivers or mountain ridges. These natural borders were determined from highly accurate computer generated relief maps.[120] These relief maps made it possible to determine natural boundaries with a very high degree of accuracy. The borders determined

---

[120] The maps were generated by from a data set (GTOPO30) published by the United States Coast and Geodesic Service. This data set gives the earth's surface elevation every 30 arc seconds (that averages about every half a mile in the region of the Holy Land.) This information was rendered by the author into maps with a computer program called ArcView.

in this way are thus reasonable assumptions, but they are only assumptions. So the actual borders may vary somewhat from those shown.

As the maps are of Biblical subjects, the nations are shown by their Biblical names, with names from secular history noted.

Comments on the individual maps:

The Lands of Gomer and the Roman Empire *(page 228)*

This map demonstrates that Gog's attack on Israel cannot occur at any time during the reign of the Beast. It shows that the descendants of Biblical Gomer now occupy most of the European portion of the ancient Roman Empire. These lands will be ruled by the Beast, who will be allied to Judah. So Gomer could not attack Israel during his reign. Since Gomer will come with Gog when he attacks Israel, this shows the attack could not take place during that time.

The Land of Magog and Gog's Northern Allies *(page 229)*

This map shows the presumed flight of Meshech and Tubal when the Turks drove them out of their original homeland in what is now Turkey. The Turks were so brutal that most of the population fled before they arrived. No ancient Russian chronicle contains any name resembling Moscow (Russian Muskow) or Tobol in reference to any time earlier than the date (about 1050 A.D.) of this flight. Togarmah, that is, Armenia, was reduced to a fraction of its original size. The other nations almost completely disappeared.

The Lands of the Kings of the North and South With the Assyrian Empire *(page 230)*

This map shows that, aside from sparsely inhabited regions like deserts and high mountains, the kingdom of the ancient King of the North covered the same area as the previous Assyrian Empire, and thus that the prophetic terms "The Assyrian" and "The King of the North" refer to the same future individual. The land of the King of the South is shown for reference.

The Path of the Assyrian *(page 231)*

This map shows the path the Assyrian will follow as he approaches Jerusalem (as described in Isaiah 10:28-32). This path was never followed by any ancient Assyrian invader. The rest of the Assyrian's path is drawn from various other scriptures.

Future Israel and the Lord's Campaigns *(page 232)*

This map shows the millennial boundaries of Israel (as defined in Ezekiel 47:13-20) and the Lord's campaigns when He returns, as traced in the chapter titled "Rescue - The LORD's Campaigns" on pages 132 to 147.

The Lands of Gomer and the Roman Empire

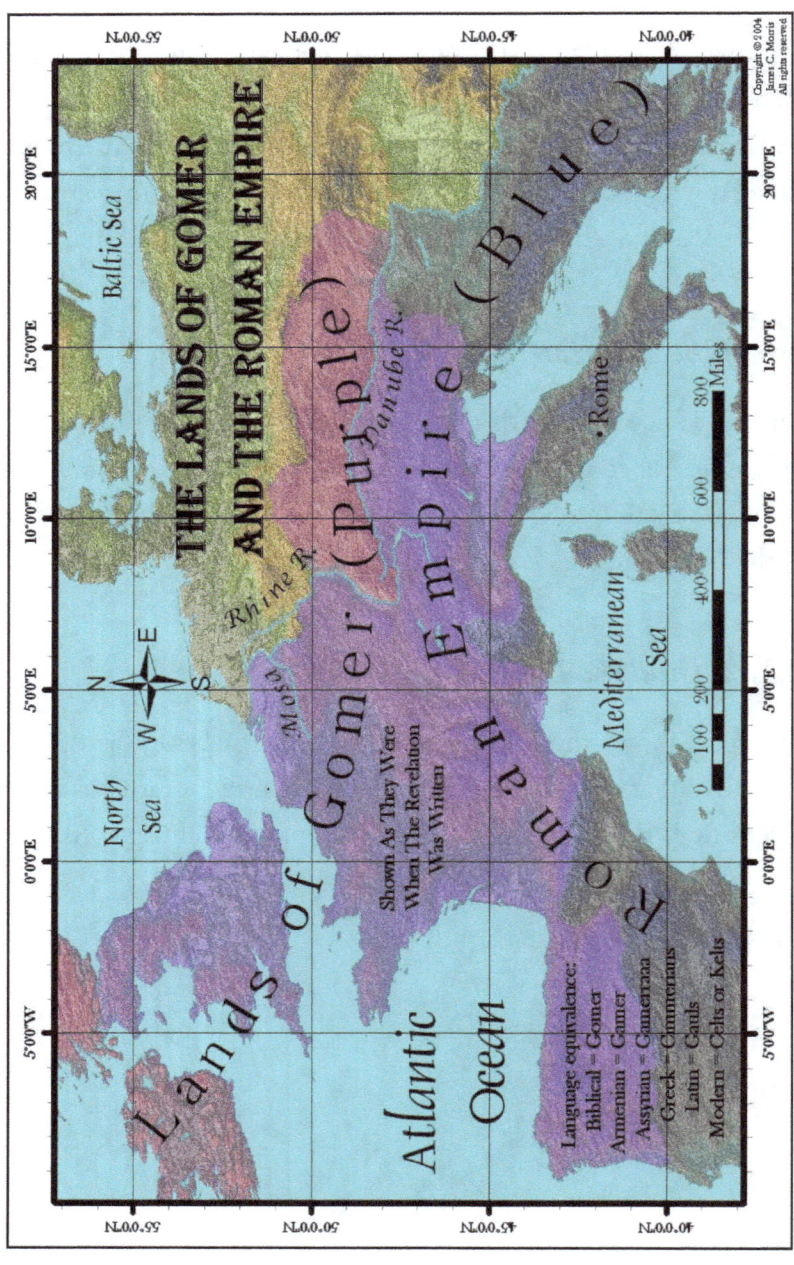

The Land of Magog and Gog's Northern Allies

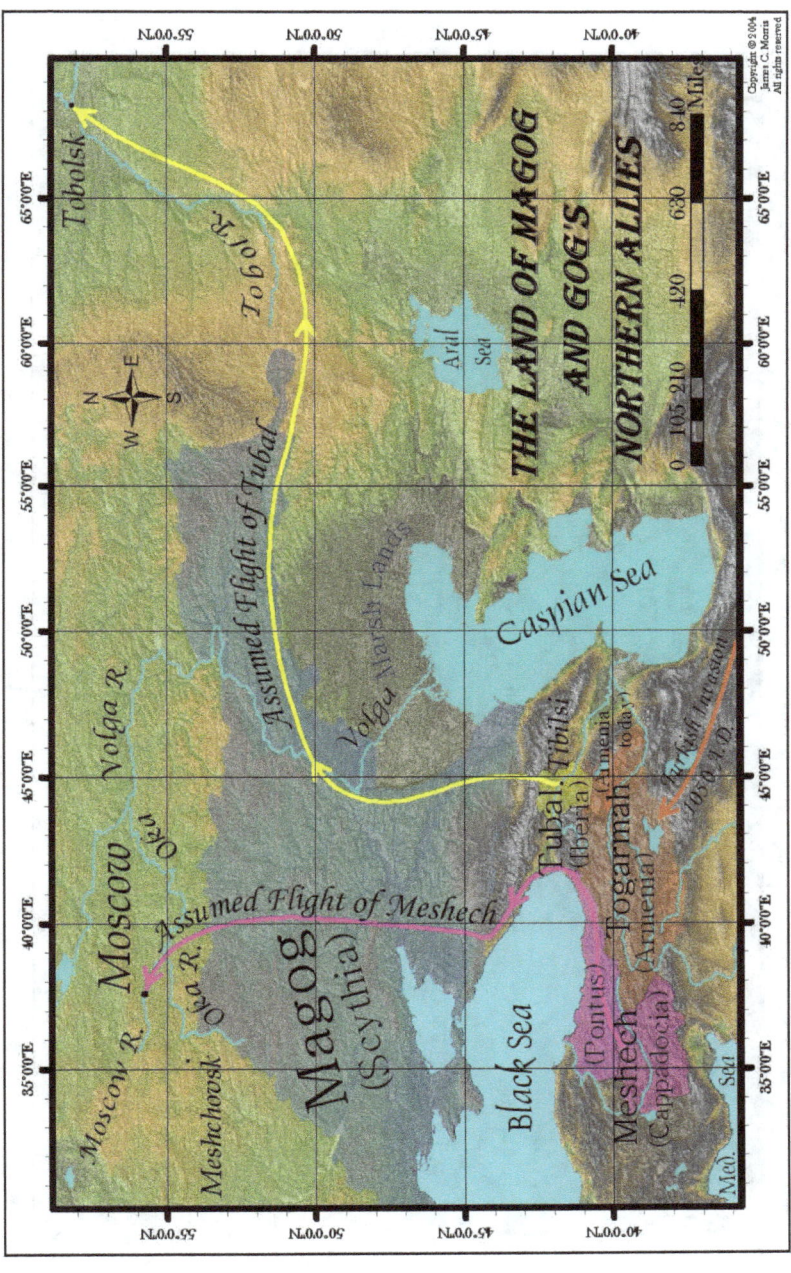

The Lands of the Kings of the North and South
With the Assyrian Empire

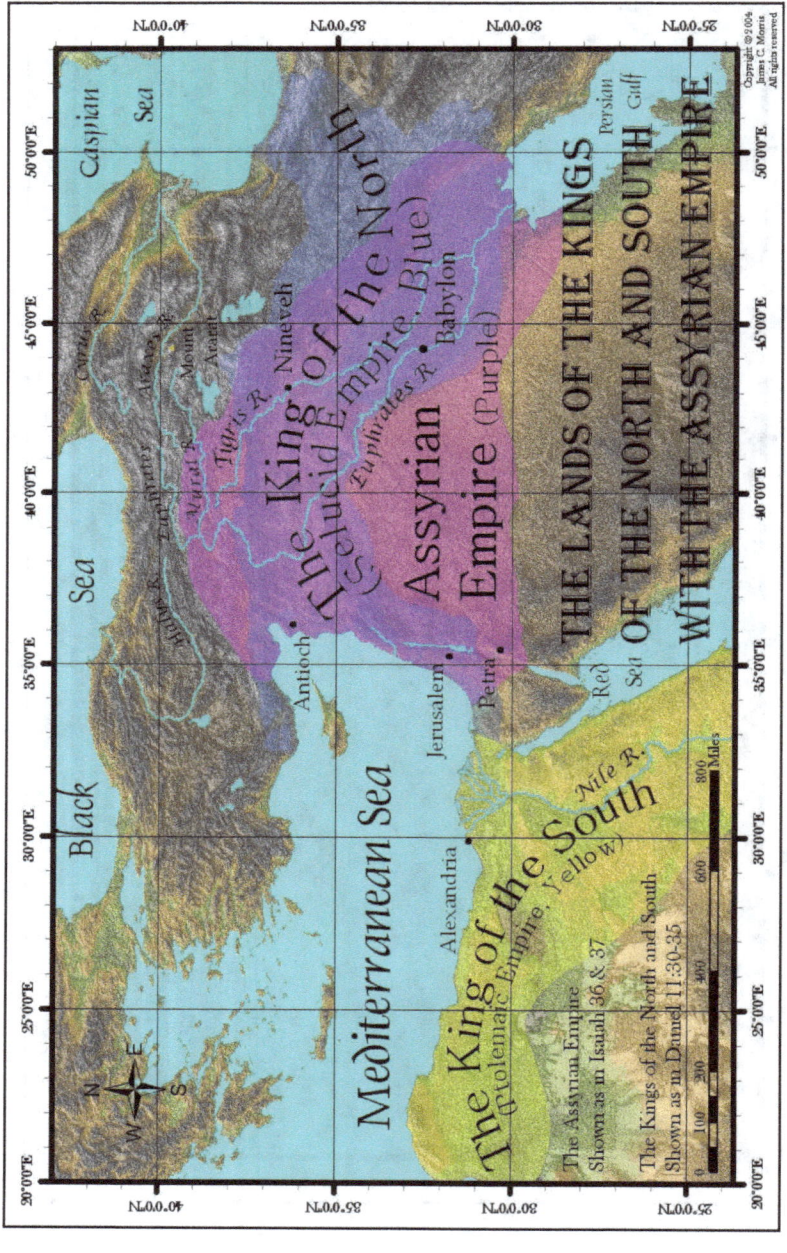

The Path of the Assyrian

Future Israel and the Lord's Campaigns

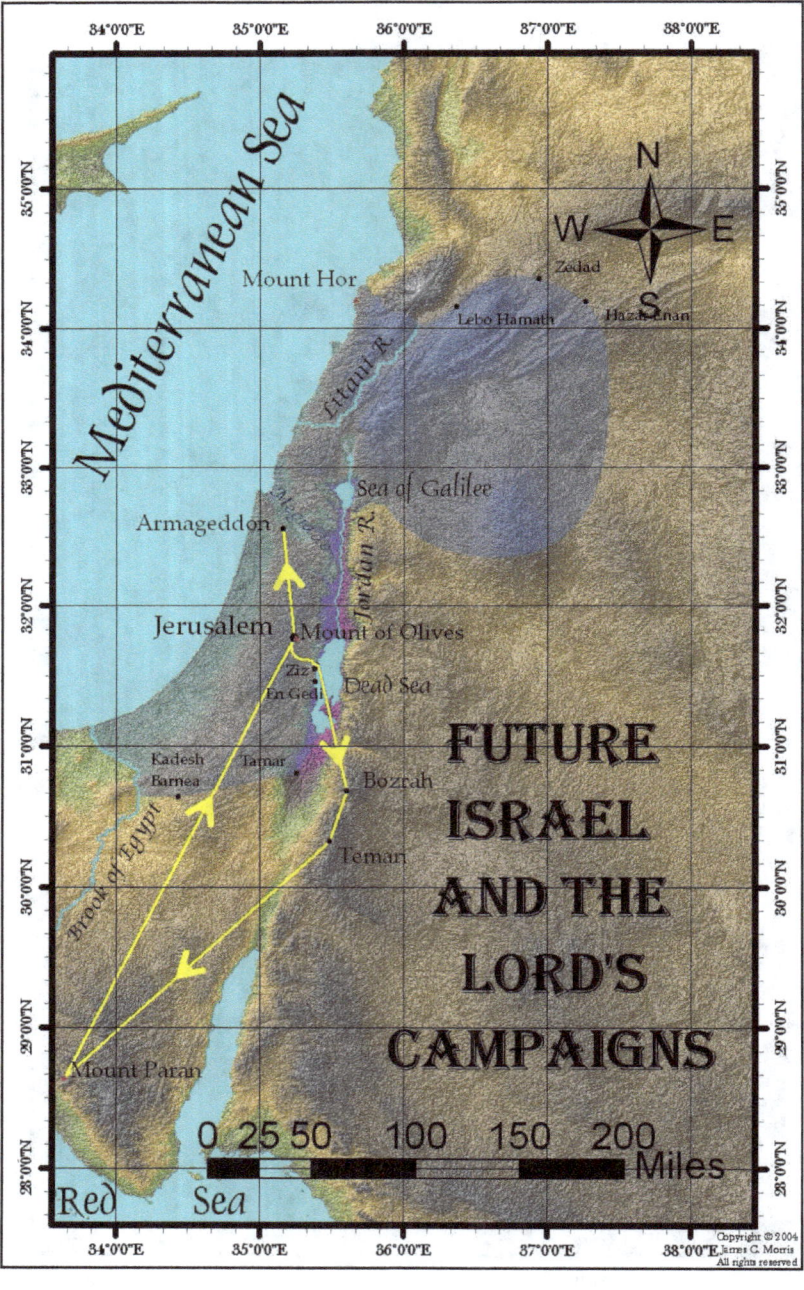

INDEXES

Scriptures Cited

Genesis
- 3:17 ... 169
- 5:22-24 ... 48
- 5:24 ... 103

Exodus
- 3:15 ... 43
- 12:14, 17 ... 164
- 12:24 ... 164
- 20:8-11 ... 10
- 25:23-39 ... 27
- 28:38 ... 165
- 28:43 ... 165
- 29:9 ... 165
- 29:28 ... 166
- 29:38, 42 ... 166
- 29:42 ... 166
- 31:16 ... 164
- 40:15 ... 165

Leviticus
- 6:18 ... 166
- 7:34, 36 ... 166
- 10:15 ... 166
- 23:4-43 ... 164
- 23:42 ... 165
- 24:9 ... 166
- 25:2-4 ... 9
- 25:32-34 ... 165

Numbers
- 14:18 ... 173
- 18:11, 19 ... 166

Deuteronomy
- 6:4 ... 43
- 32:39-43 ... 133, 134

1 Samuel
- 9:16 ... 25
- 10:1 ... 25
- 13:13-14 ... 166
- 13:14 ... 25
- 25:30 ... 25

2 Samuel
- 5:2 ... 25
- 6:5 ... 119
- 6:21 ... 25
- 7:8 ... 25

1 Kings
- 1:35 ... 25
- 14:7 ... 25
- 16:2 ... 25
- 20:5 ... 25

2 Kings
- 2:11-12 ... 48
- 2:11 ... 103
- 18:5-6 ... 51
- 18:17 ... 114
- 18:21 ... 66
- 19:35 ... 53
- 19:35-36 ... 63

1 Chronicles
- 6:3-8 ... 165
- 11:2 ... 25
- 17:7 ... 25

28:4	25
29:22	25

2 Chronicles

10	148
11:22	25
20	136
20:2	136
20:15-17	136
20:16	137
20:20	136
20:22-24	137
20:26	137, 139
26:16-21	166
30:12	51
30:14	138
32:1	51
32:9	114
35:22	78, 145

Ezra

1:5	59

Nehemiah

2:5-6	9

Job 43

Psalms

First book *99*

1-41	99
2:7-9	18
7:1	99
12:1	100
19:13	100
19:13 KJV	100
31:11	99
31:15	99
41:5	99
41:6	99

Second book *99, 107, 133*

42-72	99
42:1-6	107
42:2	108
42:4	108
42:6	108
45:3-5	133
63:1	107, 108

Third book *99, 118, 119*

73-89	99
74:3-8	118
79:1-3	119
83:1-8	120
84:2-3	119

Fourth book *99, 147*

90-106	99
90:3-9	188
90:4	188
93:1	147
95:2	147
96:10	147
96:8	147
97:1	147
99:1	147
100:2	147

Fifth book *99, 152, 153*

107-150	99
109:6-20	99
110:6	153
118:10-12	153
126:1-3	152
133:1-3	152
149:5-9	153

Proverbs
28:26 179
30:6 180

Ecclesiastes
5:1-2 180

Isaiah
2:4 170
4:3-4 150
5-10 53
5:25 .... 53, 54
7:10 .... 66, 208
7:17-20 .... 66, 208
7:18 68
8:7-8 61
9:12 54
9:17 54
9:21 54
10 .... 50, 51, 216
10:4 54
10:6 .... 51, 62
10:7-14 61
10:7 51
10:11 51
10:12 .... 37, 51
10:20 .... 37, 51, 52
10:24-25 .... 54, 68, 113
10:25 .... 56, 206
10:27 113
10:28-32 .... 65, 106, 113-116, 227
10:28 113
10:29 113
10:32 .... 54, 113
10:33-34 125
10:33-34 KJV 125
11:11-14 202
11:11-13 151
11:13-14 154

11:14 124
11:6-9 169
13:9 199
13:19 57
14:24-27 .... 52, 125, 139
14:29-31 .... 52, 125
14:29 53
14:31 125
15:1 124
16:3-4 108
17:12-13 135
19:4 68
19:22-24 158
20:2-6 65
22:3 117
22:5-7 123
22:9-11 130
22:11-14 .... 130, 134
26:20 108
28:10 3
28:14-18 .... 96, 213
28:14-15 .... 64, 209
28:18 .... 64, 104
29:1-4 131
29:4 131
29:5 135
30:31 63
30:33 50
31:8-9 140
31:8 63
34:2 143
34:5-10 142
36-37 50
36:2 114
36:6 66
37:35 .... 51, 53
41:2 59
41:25 .... 65, 114

45:1-3	58
46	59
46:10-11	59
49:22-23	149
49:26	152
51:22-23	152
52:7	147
55:4	25
57:7-9	48
59:19	26
63:1-6	143
64:6	173
65:9	202
65:20-25	170
65:22	202
66	203
66:3-4	49, 102, 210
66:6	144
66:15-20	146, 147, 212
66:15-16	185
66:15	203
66:18-22	185

Jeremiah

3:16	167
4:4	62
4:6, 7, 10, 14	62
4:9	44, 116
4:20	65, 106
6:23	65
6:26	65
7:32	136, 138
10:22	62
16:14-16	147
19:6	136
24:7	151
30:5-7	129
30:6-7	83
30:7	20, 129
30:18	184
31:2	108
31:7-9	148
31:34	79, 215
32:6-33:14	184
32:7-9	184
32:25	184
32:36	184
32:37	184
32:43-44	184
33:4	184
33:7	184
33:12-14	184
46:10	199
47:1-5	126
48:10	153
49:8	141
49:17	135
49:19	135
49:20-22	142
49:35-38	61
50-51	59, 60, 103
50	57
50:1	57, 58
50:3	58
50:4	59
50:8	57
50:9	57, 58
50:20	60
50:25	57
50:40	57
50:41	58
50:44	135
50:45	57
51	57
51:4	57
51:8-9	57
51:8	57

51:9 58
51:24 57
51:26 58
51:35 57
51:48 58
51:54 57

Ezekiel
16:53-55 157
20:33-38 150
20:38 20
25:1-14 124
25:14 154
36 183
36:1-15 183
36:8-12 157
36:8 .... 148, 212
36:10-30 82
36:10 .... 148, 212
36:16-36 183
37:15-28 183
37:16-17 .... 151, 158
37:21-22 .... 151, 202
38-39 .... 22, 68, 160, 211, 217
38:2-6 69
38:2 .... 69, 72
38:4 68
38:6 .... 76, 216
38:8,11,14 213
38:8 .... 68, 78, 158
38:11 .... 78, 213
38:12 68
38:14 .... 78, 213
38:15 .... 68, 76, 216
38:16 .... 68, 78, 158, 183
38:18-22 159
38:19-39:6 22
38:19-22 171
38:23 158

39 206
39:2 .... 76, 216
39:3-5 77
39:4 .... 77, 216
39:7 .... 37, 79, 214
39:9-10 159
39:9 .... 22, 150
39:11 .... 77, 78, 216
39:12-15 150
39:12-14 .... 23, 150
39:12 133
39:21 159
39:22 .... 37, 79, 206, 215
39:23 68
39:28-29 76
39:29 .... 79, 80, 215, 217
40-43 .... 22, 183
40-42 163
42:14 165
43-46 164
43-44 183
43:7 .... 163, 183
43:12 164
43:18 .... 164, 183
44:15 165
44:17-19 165
44:21 165
44:24 164
44:29-30 165
45-46 183
45:17 .... 164, 166
45:21-25 164
46:1-5, 12 164
46:9-11 164
46:13-15 166
46:14, 21, 31, 41 164
47-48 183
47:8-12 .... 168, 169

47:13-20	183, 227
47:15-20	156
47:21-23	156
48:1-29	183
48:1-7	156
48:14	165
48:23-29	156

Daniel

2:38-40	28, 89
2:40	29
2:44	161
4:16, 23, 25, 32	12
5:30-31	28, 89
5:31	58
6:28	58
7:2-3	28
7:3	12
7:7, 17	204
7:7-8	13, 29
7:7	89
7:8	29, 30, 91, 92
7:9-12	161
7:9-10	31
7:11	31, 34, 92
7:15-17	28
7:17	12, 46, 89
7:18	31
7:19-25	204
7:19	29
7:20	29, 30, 92
7:21-22	163
7:21	30, 93
7:22	31
7:23-25	13
7:23	15, 29, 89, 91
7:24-25	14
7:24	29, 30, 32, 33, 88-92, 204
7:25	12, 13, 15, 20, 30, 93
7:26	31
7:27	163
8	59, 60
8:3	58
8:5	56, 111
8:7	28
8:8-9	111
8:8	56
8:9	56, 59-61, 103, 112, 118, 123, 209
8:11-12	97, 112, 118
8:11	118
8:11 Darby	118
8:11 GWN	118
8:11 JPS	118
8:11 Kelly	118
8:11 KJV margin	118
8:11 NIV	118
8:11 NRSV	118
8:12	62, 112
8:13-14	21
8:13	22, 62, 104, 105
8:14	22
8:17	111
8:19	21, 22, 56, 59
8:20-21	28, 89
8:20	58
8:21-22	56, 111
8:23-25	61
8:23-24	112
8:23	56
8:23 KJV	56
8:23 NASB	56
8:23 RSV	56
8:25	63
8:26	22
9:24-27	8
9:24	8, 10, 88, 96

9:25-26	96
9:25	9, 10, 25
9:26	10, 11, 26, 27, 42, 61, 62, 64, 96, 104, 118
9:27	10, 11, 16, 20, 28, 62-65, 76, 96, 98, 104, 106, 118, 207, 209, 213, 214
11	17, 67, 112, 217
11:1-2	29
11:2-35	216
11:2-27	68
11:3	54
11:4	54, 55
11:5-32	30, 54, 55, 111, 204
11:21-32	105
11:21-24	30
11:21	105, 204
11:31	104, 105
11:36-40	42, 110, 207
11:36	44, 110, 111, 117
11:37-39	45
11:37	42-44
11:38	42, 43
11:39	43, 110
11:40-45	17, 30, 54, 55, 207-209, 216
11:40-41	17, 65, 66, 207, 211
11:40	44, 65 68, 111, 112, 204, 207, 208
11:41-45	44, 66, 207, 208
11:41-43	65
11:41	65, 67, 112, 124
11:42-43	68, 127
11:43	127
11:44-45	127
11:44	61, 128
11:45	61, 63, 128
12	17, 20
12:1	16, 17, 76, 128, 217
12:4	197
12:7	11, 12, 17, 21
12:8	21
12:9	197
12:11-12	21
12:11	104, 105
12:12	21

Hosea

2:14	108

Joel

2:11	199
2:20	63, 77, 138, 140, 216, 217
2:28	205
3:1-6	125
3:1-3	122
3:1-2	135, 138, 139, 145
3:2-12	78
3:2	136-139, 145
3:4-6	122
3:9-14	140
3:12-14	140
3:14	138, 153

Amos

1:6-8	121
1:6	126, 213
1:7-8	126
1:8	214
1:9	121, 125, 214
1:10	125
1:11	121, 141, 213
1:12	141
5:18-20	199

Obadiah

1	141
7	141

7 Young	141
10-14	120
10	141
15	141

Micah

1:3-5	134
1:3-4	80
2:12	149, 212
3:4	80, 215
4:3	170
4:9	44, 116
4:11-12	131
5:5-6	52, 156
7:5-6	99

Nahum

1:9	53
1:11	53
1:12	53
2:8	53
3:7	53
3:18	53

Habakkuk

2:8	152
3:3-6	143
3:3	142

Zephaniah

2:4-7	154
2:9	155
3:11-14	82
3:11-12	150

Haggai

2:6	174

Zechariah

4:2-3	102
4:11-14	103
6:12-13	163
6:13	167
8:20-22	168
9:5	127
9:9	133
9:13-15	155
9:13-14	202
10:2	44
10:6	182
10:7	182
11:16-17	116
11:16	44
11:17	44, 46, 117
12:2-3	131, 186
12:5	154
12:6-8	154
12:7	134
12:11-14	80, 150
12:11	78, 145
13:6	80, 150
13:6 Darby	80
13:6 KJV	80, 150
13:6 NCV	80
13:6 NIV	80
13:6 NRSV	80
13:6 Young	80
13:8-9	186
13:8	20, 128
14:1-2	117, 130, 131
14:2-3	186
14:2	20, 119, 130
14:3-4	134
14:3	135
14:4	134, 139
14:5	134
14:16-19	165, 167, 168

Malachi

3:1-3	97, 144

Matthew

2:12-16	18
2:16	106
2:19	19
5:14	31
5:17-18	167
13:11	3
13:24-30	200
13:30	200
13:37-43	200
13:41-43	200
13:47-50	200
13:49	201
16:27-17:2	190
16:28	189, 190
17:1-2	190
22:7	191
23:32-35	93
24	105
24:8	129
24:9-10	98
24:15-21	16, 62
24:15-18	105, 128
24:15	105
24:16	105
24:16-21	17, 77
24:19-22	129
24:21	105
24:22	129
24:29-30	198, 201
24:30	133
24:31	201
24:32-34	189
24:34	189
25	200
25:1-12	199
25:10-12	87, 199
25:11	200
25:31-46	140
25:31-45	109, 161
25:40	109, 161
25:45	109, 161
25:46	161
27:1	36, 205
28:18	175

Mark

9:1-4	190
9:43-48	41
13:12-13	99
13:14-19	63

Luke

4:29	31
9:27-29	190
16:22-24	41
17:27	36, 205
20:26	103
21:5-6	26
21:20-24	26
22:53	93
23:50	205
23:51	36, 205

John

1:1	45
1:14	45
1:29, 36	46, 98, 205
3:16-18	173
3:16	42
3:18-19	42
3:18	173, 174
4:21-24	47, 211
4:48	47
5:18-19	210, 215
5:24	174
5:43	45, 210, 215
7:50-51	36, 205

8:42 45
10:11-15 ....44, 116
14:2-3 82
14:16-17 86
16:7 86
16:8 86
16:13 86
19:39 ....36, 205

Acts
1:9 106
1:12 129
2:17 205
13:39 173

Romans
3:23 173
6:23 173
8:19 169
9:6-9 19
9:21 ....35, 206
11:1 182
11:11-25 182
11:15 169
11:26 .... 82, 151, 182
11:29 182
14:10 174

1 Corinthians
4:5 174
7:37 ....35, 206
15:24-28 176
15:52-52 202

Galatians
2:16 173

1 Thessalonians
2:3-4 214
2:9-12 214

3:13 82
4:16-17 ....86, 201
4:17 189
5:4 197

2 Thessalonians
1:7 189
2:3-4 .... 37, 48, 97, 104
2:3 79
2:4 ....28, 63, 79
2:6-8 ....85, 87
2:8 50
2:9-12 .... 49, 101, 210
2:10-12 87

2 Timothy
3:16-17 180
3:16 3
4:8 199

Titus
2:13 199

Hebrews
1:10-12 175
6:10 174
9:28 199
10:14 164
10:18 164
10:25 197
10:31 174
12:26-27 174

1 Peter
1:10-11 ....50, 198
2:24 173

2 Peter
1:16-18 190
1:19 1
2:4-9 85

2:9	85	12:1	18, 19
3:3-4	188	12:3-4	17
3:5-10	188	12:4	18
3:7	174	12:5-6	19
3:8	187, 188	12:5	18, 106
3:9	188	12:6	11, 20, 21, 108
3:10-12	175	12:9	18, 46, 98, 205
3:13	175, 176	12:12	84

1 John

2:18 .... 44, 197

Jude

14-15 133

Revelation

1:1	187, 197	12:13-15	107, 211
1:3	187	12:13	19, 108
1:9	195	12:14	11, 12, 17, 19, 20
3:10	82-85	12:15	54
4:4	87	12:16	65, 109, 211
5:1	197	13	14, 35
6-9	88, 197	13:1	13, 15, 34, 46, 98, 204
6-8	197	13:3-6	92
6:2	30, 204	13:3	34, 36, 46, 90, 205
10:2, 8	197	13:5	11, 14, 15, 39, 207
10:9	197	13:6	14
10:10	197	13:7	14, 35, 36, 38, 93, 205, 206
11	204	13:8	14, 36, 84, 205
11:1-2	15	13:11	46, 98, 204
11:2	11, 15	13:12-15	14
11:3-8	102	13:12	46, 84, 98, 100
11:3	11, 14	13:13-15	47
11:7-8	15	13:13	47, 98
11:7	35	13:14-15	47, 100
11:8	192	13:14	84
11:10	84, 103	13:15	109
12	18	13:16-17	38, 101
12:1-5	106	13:16	109, 110
12:1-2	17	13:18	39
		14:6	84
		14:9-11	38, 101
		14:13	174
		15:2	39
		16	37, 128, 206
		16:2	39

16:10	39	19:19-21	146
16:12-16	145	19:19	40
16:12	37, 144, 206	19:20	40, 47, 48, 50, 67, 98, 117, 162, 209
16:13-14	40, 145, 207	20:1-8	24
16:13	47, 98, 117	20:1-3	162
16:14	37, 144, 145, 206	20:2	106
17	18, 34	20:3	162
17:1-2	94	20:4-6	162, 203
17:1	95	20:4	40, 162
17:3-18	204	20:7	80, 171
17:3	32, 34, 89	20:8	80, 171
17:4	94	20:9	171
17:5	94, 192	20:10	40, 48, 98, 172
17:6	94	20:11-15	41, 172
17:8	31, 34, 35, 84	20:12	173
17:9	18, 31, 89, 90	21:1-2	175
17:10-11	33	21:1	176
17:10	33, 34, 90 92	21:3-4	176
17:11	33, 34, 93, 218	21:3	176
17:12-14	145, 217	21:4	176
17:12-13	33, 90	21:5-8	177
17:12	14, 34, 39, 89, 191, 206	22:3	169
17:13-14	76	22:7	187
17:13	33	22:10	197
17:14	34, 191	22:12	174
17:16	94	22:18-19	180
17:17	90, 94	22:20	177
17:18	18, 32, 89, 94		
18	95, 192		
18:2-3	95		
18:3	95		
18:4	95		
18:7-8	95		
18:24	95		
19:1-5	95		
19:6-9	95		
19:11-16	132		
19:17-18	145, 146		

Authorities Cited

Abegg	116
Ambrose	70
Appian	33
Barrington Atlas	74
Cook	116
Correspondence of Sargon II	75
Dead Sea Scrolls	116
Dionysius	220, 221
Donaldson	192-195, 219-221
Epistle of Barnabas	221
Eusebius	195, 218-220
Gallagher	114
Hippolytus	195, 221, 222
Irenaeus	192-196, 217-219, 222
Jerome	194, 218-220
Josephus	69, 71, 72, 74, 75, 191
Justin	194, 219
Maier	69, 191, 195
Moses of Khronosis	74
Nikonian Chronicle	72
Olmstead	115
Oriental Institute Prism	4, 115
Papias	218, 219
Ptolemy	55, 71
Roberts	192-195, 219-221
Roman coin	32
Royal Correspondence of the Assyrian Empire	75
Russell	191, 192, 195, 196
Russian Primary Chronicle	72
Septuagint	69
Styme	71
Tacitus	33
Tertullian	220
Vermeule	32
Victornius	193, 194
Waterman	75
Watson	223

Whiston...69, 191
Wieczynski..71
Wise..93, 116, 148
Young..38, 63, 80, 116, 119, 129, 140-142, 157, 169
Ziletti...71

Ancient Words Discussed

Greek Words *36, 85*

   christos..45
   ek 82, 83, 85
   exousia..35, 206
   hapas..36, 205, 206
   ho 83
   holos..84
   hora..83
   hysteron..200
   kairos..12
   oros...31
   pas 36, 205, 206
   peirasmon...84, 85
   peirasmos...84
   proton..200
   protos..69
   tereo...83

Hebrew and Chaldee Words

   berakah..137
   betach..213
   biq'ah..78, 145
   boqer..22
   gay'..78, 138
   kiy 52
   kol 119, 148, 205
   mashiyach..45
   melek...42, 209
   meshomem...104

mow'ed	12
nachal	138
nagiyd	25, 42, 209
rosh	69, 76, 216
shabuwa'	9
shamem	104
shena	91
shomem	104
umimenu	118
yasha'	83
yehudah	212
yeudiy	212
'elohiym	43
'elowahh	43
'emeq	78, 138, 139, 145
'ereb	22
'iddan	12

Latin Words and Titles

consular tribunes	33
consuls	33
decemvirs	33
denarius	32
sestertius	4, 32

Ancient Individuals Mentioned

Abijah	25
Abraham	19, 43
Adam	169
Agrippa	191
Alexander	54-56, 68, 112, 122, 155, 192-195, 209, 219-221
Antiochus Epiphanes	105, 204
Antiochus	191
Ashkenaz	74
Baasha	25
Darius	28, 58, 89
David	25, 80, 119, 130, 131, 134, 150, 154

Domitian	193-196
Elijah	48, 103, 222
Elisha	204
Enoch	48, 103, 222
Ham	74
Herod	19
Hezekiah	25, 50, 51, 66
Isaac	19, 43
Jacob	43, 152
Japheth	74
Jeroboam	25
Joseph	19, 36, 71, 151, 205
Judas	99
Madai	74
Malchus	191
Mary	18, 19
Nebuchadnezzar	12, 28, 89
Noah	74, 84, 85
Ptolemies	55, 68, 111, 204, 216
Ptolemy	55, 71
Rehoboam	148
Riphath	74
Sargon	53, 66, 67, 75
Saul	25, 113, 166, 167
Seleucids	54, 55, 111, 204, 216
Seleucus	55, 56
Sennacherib	50-53, 66, 114-116, 125, 126
Shem	74
Sohemus	191
Solomon	25, 148
Tiglath-Pileser III	53
Tiras	74
Titus	4, 10, 26, 27, 96, 196, 199
T'iras	74
T'orgom	74
Uzziah	134, 166, 167
Vespasian	4, 32, 193, 196
Yapeth	74

Peoples and Nations Mentioned

Amalek	120
American	39, 70, 71, 76, 105, 118, 192-195, 219-221
Ammon	65, 120, 124, 136, 154, 155, 158, 207
Armenia	4, 71, 72, 74-76, 226
Assyria	4, 50-53, 66, 67, 75, 80, 103, 115, 120, 125, 140, 151, 155, 156, 158, 185, 186, 208
Assyrians	53, 57, 75, 80, 158
Australian	76
British	76, 185, 187
Caphtor	126
Cappadocia	71, 72, 74
Celtic peoples	76
Celts	75, 135
Chaldeans	57, 59, 60, 103, 122, 123, 135, 134
Cherethites	154
Cimmerians	75, 185
Cimmerii	75
Commonwealth of Independent States	71, 74
Edom	65, 107, 120, 121, 124-126, 135, 141-143, 154, 207, 213, 214
Edomites	107, 121
Egypt	4, 15, 19, 54, 55, 61, 65-68, 102, 111, 127, 128, 130, 147, 149, 151, 155, 158, 168, 192, 208, 216, 220
Egyptians	158
Elam	60, 61, 103, 123, 151, 158
Ephraim	66, 82, 148, 151, 154, 155, 202, 203, 208
Ethiopia	65, 69, 75, 76, 227
Ethiopians	227
Galatia	75
Galatians	75, 173
Gamer	74, 75
Gamerraaa	75
Gamirra	75
Gauls	75
Gebal	120
Gentiles	15, 26, 68, 133, 147, 185, 212
Georgia	71, 72, 74
Germany	75

Gimiraa 75
Gomer 69, 74, 75, 185, 226, 228
Greece 4, 28, 29, 56, 89, 111, 112, 155, 202
Greek 12, 31, 35, 36, 45, 69-71, 82-85, 112,
            122, 155, 197, 200, 205, 206, 233
Greeks 69, 75, 122
Guriania 75
Hagrites 120
Iberia 74
Iberians 74
Iran 60, 61, 75, 76, 103, 123
Iraq 50, 53, 55, 57, 59-61, 103, 120, 123, 216
Ishmaelites 120
Israel 4, 8, 19, 20, 22, 23, 25, 37, 42-44, 50-52, 58-60, 65,
            68, 76-83, 87, 88, 96, 98, 106-110, 119, 120, 122, 129, 134,
            136, 146-160, 163, 165, 166, 169, 181-187, 203, 206,
            211-217, 220, 221, 226, 227, 232
Jacob 37, 51, 120, 134, 141, 148, 149, 202, 212
Javan 74, 147, 185, 212
Jews 8, 12, 45, 64, 65, 69, 79, 88, 96, 109, 129,
            185, 187, 209, 210, 212, 215
Jordan 120, 124, 213
Judah 8, 25, 37, 42, 44, 45, 49 52, 59, 60, 62, 66 68, 76 83, 88,
            96, 97, 104, 110, 114, 120, 122, 123, 131, 134 138, 141,
            148, 151, 153 155, 157, 160, 181, 184, 186, 187, 202 204,
            207 209, 211 214, 216, 226
Lebanon 120, 122, 125, 126, 214
Libya 69, 75, 76, 127
Libyans 127
Lud 147, 185, 212
Magogites 69
Medes 28, 58, 89
Media 58, 60, 103
Meschera 72
Meshech 69 72, 74, 226
Moab 65, 107, 108, 120, 121, 124, 136, 154, 155, 158, 207
Moabites 107
Mongols 91

Moschi 70 72, 74
Moslem 71, 72, 74
Moslems 72
Nagiu 75
North American 76
Palestine 125
Palestinian 120
Palestinians 121, 214
people of the East 154
Persia 4, 58, 60, 69, 75, 103
Persian 58, 70, 71
Persians 28, 58, 89
Philistia 52, 53, 120, 122, 125
Philistines 52, 66, 121, 122, 126, 154, 214
Pontus 71, 74
Portugal 74
Pul 147, 185, 212
Roman 10, 11, 13, 18, 25, 30-36, 46, 65, 71, 88-91, 93, 95,
                                            96, 109, 204, 209, 210, 226, 228
Romans 10, 27, 96, 191
Ros 59
Russia 55, 56, 64, 69, 70, 72, 75, 76, 112, 209, 216
Russian 4, 56, 70-72, 74, 112, 209, 226
Saudi Arabia 120, 127, 213
Scythians 69, 75, 76
Seleucid empire 54, 55, 76
Spain 74
Syria 54, 55, 111, 120, 136, 216
Tarshish 147, 185, 212
Togarmah 69, 74, 216, 226
Tubal 69, 70, 74, 76, 147, 185, 212, 226
Turkey 71, 72, 75, 226
United States 38, 225
Urartu 75
USSR 70, 71, 74, 88
Yugoslavia 96

Places Mentioned

Aiath	113
Alexandria	55, 68, 71, 111, 216
Anathoth	113
Antioch	54, 55, 111, 216
Ariel	131
Armageddon	78, 117, 140, 144, 145
Ascent of Ziz	136, 141
Ashdod	121, 126, 154
Ashkelon	121, 126, 127, 154
Asia Minor	75
Azal	134
Babylon	12, 57-59, 94, 122, 123, 192
beloved city	171
Black Sea	71, 75
Bozrah	141-143
British Isles	76
Canaan	154
Caspian Sea	71
Caucasus Mountains	71, 74
Dead Sea	77, 116, 137, 141, 142, 216
Dedan	141
eastern sea	63, 138
Ekron	121, 126, 127, 154
En Eglaim	168
En Gedi	136, 137, 168
Euphrates	144
Europe	75, 76, 88
Gallim	113
Gaza	121, 126, 127, 154, 213, 214
Geba	113
Gebim	113
Gibeah	113
glorious land	17, 44, 56, 60, 65, 67, 103, 111, 112, 118, 123, 124, 207, 211
Gomorrah	57, 84, 142, 155
Great Sea	28, 168
Hadad Rimmon	80, 150
Hermon	107, 108, 152

holy place	16, 27, 62, 105
Iberian Peninsula	74
Jerusalem	8, 9, 11, 15, 16, 21, 26, 27, 37, 51, 62, 64, 65, 80, 88, 96, 102, 113, 114, 117-120, 122, 123, 126, 129 131, 134-140, 143, 145, 147, 150, 154, 160, 165, 167-169, 175, 184-187, 191, 192, 195, 196, 209, 210, 212, 219, 227
Judea	16, 17, 26, 52, 56, 60, 62, 64, 66, 67, 105, 107, 109, 110, 112, 114, 124, 127, 128, 186, 187, 208
Kidron valley	136, 138, 139
Kir	123
Lachish	114
Laish	113
land of Benjamin	184
land of Nimrod	52, 156
lower pool	130
Madmenah	113
Mediterranean	77, 216
Megiddo	78, 80, 145, 150
Meshchovsk	70, 74
Michmash	113
Migron	113
Mizar	107, 108
Moschici Mountains	71
Moschii Mountains	71
Moscow	70, 72, 74, 226
Mosul	53, 57
Mount of Olives	134, 139
Mount Olivet	129
Mount Paran	142, 143
Mount Seir	136
Muskova	72
Nineveh	53, 57
Nob	113
Oka River	72
old pool	130
Patmos	193-195
Ramah	113
Red Sea	142

Rome 4, 18, 26-29, 31-35, 56, 64, 89-91, 94-96,
106, 110, 112, 196, 204, 209
Samaria 157
Sidon 122, 125, 126
Sodom 15, 57, 84, 102, 142, 155, 157, 192
steppe 75
Suram Mountains 71
Tarshish 147, 185, 212
Tbilisi 74
Teman 141-143
temple 4, 15, 22, 26 28, 37, 48, 63, 79, 93, 97,
98, 104, 118, 119, 144, 156, 163, 164, 166,
168, 169, 183, 196, 214, 222
the Jordan 107, 108, 122, 135
Tobolsk 70, 74
Tyre 120-122, 125, 126, 214
Vallies of:
    Berachah 137
    decision 140
    Hamon Gog 77, 160, 216
    Jehoshaphat 78, 122, 136, 138, 140, 141
    the son of Hinnom   136
western Europe 75, 76
western sea 63, 77, 138, 216
Wilderness of Jeruel 136
Wilderness of Tekoa 136
Zion 37, 51, 54, 113, 128, 131, 140,
142, 147, 150, 152, 155, 202
Ziz 136, 137, 141

Key Time Periods 7

a time and times and half a time 13, 19, 20, 107, 108
a time, times, and half a time 17
ancient Jewish years 8, 9, 11, 15, 16, 20, 26, 28, 61, 74, 76, 104,
108, 160, 207, 214
first half 11, 12, 15, 20, 96, 207
four hundred and eighty-three years 9

half week............11, 13, 15, 20, 21
half weeks............21
last half............15-18, 20, 21, 124, 160
latter time of the indignation............21, 22, 56, 59
latter time of their kingdom............56, 61, 112
millennium............23, 79, 80, 97, 158, 160, 170, 176, 206, 215, 219, 220
one thousand two hundred and ninety days............21
one thousand two hundred and sixty days............14, 20, 102, 108
one week............8, 10, 11, 28, 61, 76, 96, 209, 222
seven months............23, 159, 160, 133
seven times............9
seven weeks............8, 96
seven year............76, 96, 104, 213
seven years............9, 10, 22, 79, 96, 159, 160
seventieth week............10, 11, 17, 18, 22, 26, 82, 88, 160, 206, 207, 211-214, 221, 222
seventy weeks............7, 8, 10, 25
sixty-nine weeks............9
sixty-two weeks............8, 9, 222
thousand years............8, 23, 24, 40, 80, 81, 162, 171, 172, 187, 188, 203, 219
three and a half years............11, 14, 19, 130, 144, 222
time chart............4, 6
time of the end............65, 110, 112, 182, 197, 204, 207
two thousand three hundred days............21

Key Individuals

The First Key Individual............25

666............39
eighth............31, 33, 34, 93, 194, 218
first beast............14, 46, 47, 100
fourth beast's little horn............28
healed head............34
prince who is to come...............8, 10, 25-27, 61, 62, 64, 96
rising up out of the sea............13, 204
Roman............11, 16, 20, 30, 34, 42, 48, 56, 64, 65, 67, 68, 90, 95, 96, 109, 112, 204-211, 213, 214, 218
the Beast............14-16, 23, 31, 33-35, 38-40, 46-49, 67, 76, 78, 90-95, 98, 100-102, 109, 111, 117, 144-146, 161, 162, 172, 203-207, 209, 217, 226

The Second Key Individual...*42*

    Antichrist....................... 44, 45, 47, 49, 79, 87, 98, 100, 101, 111, 116, 192, 215, 222
    false prophet....................37, 39, 40, 47-49, 67, 98, 144, 146, 162, 172, 207, 209
    lawless one...49, 50, 85, 87, 101, 210, 214
    man of sin 28, 48-50, 63, 79, 85, 104, 214
    second beast 14, 37, 46, 98, 101, 204, 205
    son of perdition 48, 50, 104, 214
    that Wicked 95
    the king..37, 42, 45, 48, 110, 116, 117, 181
    worthless shepherd..44, 46, 116, 117
    out of the earth 37, 46, 49, 98, 204

The Third Key Individual..*50*

    Assyrian 37, 50-57, 60-63, 65-68, 75, 76, 111, 114,
                        124-126, 137-139, 156, 158, 185, 206, 208, 216, 227, 230, 231
    cruel master... 68
    king of the North 17, 44, 53-56, 61, 63, 65, 67, 68, 76, 77,
                        110-112, 122, 124, 125, 127, 207, 227
    male goat's little horn..56, 63
    one who makes desolate 8, 16, 28, 61, 62, 104, 106, 214
    wicked counselor 53
    offspring..52, 125

The Fourth Key Individual...*68*

    king of the South 54, 65, 67, 68, 110, 207, 216, 227

The Fifth Key Individual..*68*

    Gog 22, 24, 37, 55, 63, 68-70, 76-80,
                        158-160, 171, 183, 206, 211, 213-216, 226
    prince of Rosh, Meshech, and Tubal 69

Key Events

    abomination of desolation.. 21, 104, 105, 128, 186, 222
    All commerce linked to the worship of the beast 101
    All Israel brought back to the land 148
    All Israel settled in the land... 156

Armageddon	78, 117, 140, 144, 145
Assyrian conquers Lebanon	125
Assyrian destroys Philistia (the area now called Palestine)	125
Babylon the great destroyed	94
Babylon, "The land of the Chaldeans," joins the attack	122
beast and the false prophet cast into the lake of fire	146
beast is allowed to persecute the saints of the Most High	93
collapse of government throughout Europe	88
daily progress of the Assyrians attack	113, 125
devil cast into the lake of fire	172
dragon pursues the fleeing righteous	105
Edom is destroyed	141, 214
Edom joins the attack	120
Edom, Moab, and the prominent people of Ammon spared	124
Egypt and Assyria restored	158
Elam is among the attackers	123
eleventh king rises out of the ancient Roman empire	91
eleventh king subdues three of the first ten	92
Ephraim and Judah re-united	151
eternal state	176
flight of the righteous	19, 105, 110
flight of the king	116
God returns from destroying Edom	143
great tribulation	16, 17, 63, 105, 128
healing river flows out of the temple	168
Heaven and earth remade	174
Helped on by Antichrist, the beast demands worship as God	100
inhabitants of Tyre help the Edomites	121
invasion and defeat of Gog	22, 158
Israel conquers the Philistines, Edom, Moab, and Ammon	154
Israel repents of their rejection of Jesus as their Messiah	150
Israel wastes the land of Assyria with the sword	155
Jerusalem besieged	131
Jerusalem falls	117
king of the North invades Egypt	127
king of the North invades the Glorious Land	112
king of the North overthrows many countries	124
king of the North returns to Judea	127

king of the North subdues Libya and Ethiopia	127
kingdom of God set up on earth	160
kingdom surrendered to God the Father	175
kings of the South and North attack Judah king	110
Lord comes to His Temple	144
Lord of Lords comes	132
Lord sends Israel against the Grecian kings	155
Lord sends united Israel to war	152
male goat's little horn begins his campaigns	103
Mankind's final rebellion	171
Moab, Ammon, and Elam restored	158
nations are destroyed	140
nations are driven away from Jerusalem	135
nations join in the conquest of Jerusalem	119
nations judged	161
nations worship the LORD	167
new temple is built	163
northern army is destroyed	137
Philistines help the Edomites	121
rapture of the church	82
rebellion crushed	171
rebels purged from among Israel	149
rebuilding of the temple and the resumption of sacrifices	97
resurrection and reign of the righteous	162
return of Judah to her land	81, 97, 148
righteous are helped as they flee	109
righteous flee across the Jordan to Edom and Moab	107
rise of ten kings out of the ancient Roman empire	89
rise of the Antichrist	98
rise of the beast	92
Roman prince makes a seven year treaty with Judah	96
ruins of Jerusalem fortified	130
rulers of Jerusalem attempt to flee, but are captured	117
Satan imprisoned	162
Satan released	170
Sidon joins Tyre and the Philistines in this evil project	122
Sodom and Samaria restored	157
survivors from this battle sent to call all Israel home	146
temple is cast down	118
Temple worship resumed, with animal sacrifices	164
ten kings unite, reviving the Roman empire	90

The nations bring the children of Israel home	149
The king escapes	117
Two witnesses testify in Jerusalem	102
whole world blessed	169
wicked dead judged	172
wilful rejecters of the gospel turned over to "the lie"	101

Prophetic Symbols Discussed

another horn	13, 29, 30
Child was caught up to God and His throne	18, 19, 106
Child who was to rule all nations	18, 106
dragon	17, 18, 23, 39, 40, 46-48, 65, 98, 106, 109, 110, 144, 162, 204, 205, 207, 211
four great beasts	12, 28, 89
fourth beast	12, 13, 15, 29, 32-34, 89, 91, 92
great city which spiritually is called Sodom and Egypt	15, 102, 192
mouth speaking pompous words	13, 30, 92
seven heads	13, 17, 18, 31, 34, 89, 90, 98, 204
ten horns	13, 14, 17, 18, 29, 32, 34, 76, 89-91, 94, 98, 145, 204, 206, 217
three of the first horns were plucked out by the roots	13, 29, 91
twelve stars	17, 106
woman clothed with the sun, with the moon under her feet	17, 106

Inspired Explanations of Symbols

another shall rise after them	13, 29
four kings which arise out of the earth	12, 28, 46, 89
fourth kingdom	13, 29, 89
great city which reigns over the kings of the earth	18, 32, 89, 94
serpent of old	18, 23, 46, 98, 106, 162
seven kings	33, 90, 92
seven mountains	18, 89, 90
speak pompous words against the Most High	13, 30
subdue three kings	13, 29, 91, 92, 204
ten kings who have received no kingdom as yet	14, 33, 76, 89, 90, 145, 206
ten kings Who shall arise from this kingdom	13, 29, 32, 89
where also our Lord was crucified	15, 102, 192

Dispensational Publishing House is striving to become the go-to source for Bible-based materials from the dispensational perspective.

Our goal is to provide high-quality doctrinal and worldview resources that make dispensational theology accessible to people at all levels of understanding.

Visit our blog regularly to read informative articles from both known and new writers.

And please let us know how we can better serve you.

Dispensational Publishing House, Inc.
PO Box 3181
Taos, NM 87571

Call us toll free 844-321-4202

www.DispensationalPublishing.com